A CULTURAL HISTORY OF LAW

VOLUME 5

A Cultural History of Law
General Editor: Gary Watt

Volume 1
A Cultural History of Law in Antiquity
Edited by Julen Etxabe

Volume 2
A Cultural History of Law in the Middle Ages
Edited by Emanuele Conte and Laurent Mayali

Volume 3
A Cultural History of Law in the Early Modern Age
Edited by Peter Goodrich

Volume 4
A Cultural History of Law in the Age of Enlightenment
Edited by Rebecca Probert and John Snape

Volume 5
A Cultural History of Law in the Age of Reform
Edited by Ian Ward

Volume 6
A Cultural History of Law in the Modern Age
Edited by Richard K. Sherwin and Danielle Celermajer

A CULTURAL HISTORY OF LAW
IN THE AGE OF REFORM

Edited by Ian Ward

BLOOMSBURY ACADEMIC
LONDON • NEW YORK • OXFORD • NEW DELHI • SYDNEY

BLOOMSBURY ACADEMIC
Bloomsbury Publishing Plc
50 Bedford Square, London, WC1B 3DP, UK
1385 Broadway, New York, NY 10018, USA
29 Earlsfort Terrace, Dublin 2, Ireland

BLOOMSBURY, BLOOMSBURY ACADEMIC and the Diana logo are
trademarks of Bloomsbury Publishing Plc

First published in Great Britain 2019
Paperback edition published in 2023

Copyright © Bloomsbury Publishing Plc, 2019

Ian Ward has asserted his right under the Copyright, Designs and Patents Act,
1988, to be identified as Editor of this work.

For legal purposes the Acknowledgements on p. vii constitute
an extension of this copyright page.

Cover image © Mary Evans Picture Library / Alamy Stock Photo

All rights reserved. No part of this publication may be reproduced or transmitted in
any form or by any means, electronic or mechanical, including photocopying, recording,
or any information storage or retrieval system, without prior permission in writing
from the publishers.

Bloomsbury Publishing Plc does not have any control over, or responsibility for,
any third-party websites referred to or in this book. All internet addresses given in this book
were correct at the time of going to press. The editor and publisher regret any inconvenience
caused if addresses have changed or sites have ceased to exist, but can accept no
responsibility for any such changes.

A catalogue record for this book is available from the British Library.

A catalog record for this book is available from the Library of Congress.

ISBN:	PB set:	978-1-3503-6891-0
	HB:	978-1-4742-1274-8
	PB:	978-1-3503-6869-9
	ePDF:	978-1-3500-7931-1
	eBook:	978-1-3500-7932-8

Series: The Cultural Histories Series

Typeset by Integra Software Services Pvt. Ltd.
Printed and bound in Great Britain

To find out more about our editors and books visit www.bloomsbury.com
and sign up for our newsletters.

CONTENTS

LIST OF FIGURES	vi
NOTES ON CONTRIBUTORS	ix
SERIES PREFACE	xi

Introduction
Ian Ward — 1

1 Justice: Visual Representations of the Subjects of the Law
   Linda Mulcahy — 19

2 Constitution: Utopia, Limited *or a Limited Utopia?*
   John Snape — 35

3 Codes: Police Uniform and the Image of Law Enforcement
   Jane Tynan — 55

4 Agreements: The Social Contract and Child Labor in Elizabeth Barrett Browning's "The Cry of the Children"
   Nancy E. Johnson — 73

5 Arguments: Jury Lawfinding and Constitutional Review in 1840s New Hampshire
   K Crosby — 91

6 Property and Possession: New Languages of Property
   Kieran Dolin — 111

7 Wrongs: Negligence, Neighborliness, and the Duty of Care in Nineteenth-century Narrative
   Jan-Melissa Schramm — 129

8 The Legal Profession: Dickens, Daumier, and The Man of Law
   Gary Watt — 147

NOTES	165
BIBLIOGRAPHY	170
INDEX	186

LIST OF FIGURES

INTRODUCTION

0.1	The funeral procession of Queen Victoria through London.	2
0.2	The opening of the Great Exhibition by Queen Victoria on 1 May 1851.	4
0.3	A rage uncontrollable. Essayist and historian Thomas Carlyle (1795–1881).	8
0.4	Matthew Arnold (1822–1883) English poet and critic.	17

JUSTICE

1.1	Evelyn Manesta by Criminal Record Office.	26
1.2	"Paddy the Devil."	27
1.3	"Thomas Murphy: The Reluctant Sitter."	27
1.4	Mugshot of Michael Lavery.	28

CONSTITUTION

2.1	Prudent judges of the Utopian Supreme Court. W.H. Denny as Scaphio and John le Hay as Phantis in Act I (Cast photograph, 1893).	38
2.2	King Paramount as Chairman of the Board of Utopia, Limited. Rutland Barrington in Act II (Cast photograph, 1893).	39
2.3	Prudent judges of the Utopian Supreme Court as judges of "The Supreme Court of Judicature of England and Wales." W.H. Denny as Scaphio and John le Hay as Phantis in Act II (Cast photograph, 1893).	40
2.4	The ingenuity of English legal reasoning. Enes Blackmore as Sir Bailey Barre, QC, MP (Act I).	40

CODES

3.1	The Crowd Waiting to See a Policeman's Funeral, photo Paul Martin (1864–1944).	57
3.2	A Peeler or Police Officer, 1845.	60
3.3	Vancouver Police Department's first four officers.	62

LIST OF FIGURES

3.4	Group of Royal Irish Constabulary officers and men armed with carbines circa 1870s.	67
3.5	Police remove a Suffragette demonstrator from Buckingham Palace, 1914.	69

AGREEMENTS

4.1	Sketch of "'an air-door tender in a thin mine in the act of opening an air-door to allow a wagon to pass through'."	76
4.2	Illustration depicting children "hurrying or drawing" a wagon of coal.	77
4.3	Agnes Moffat, 17 years old, explains that "'[i]t is no uncommon thing for women to lose their burthen [load]; and drop off the ladder down the dyke below. (Fig. 15) Margaret McNeil did a few weeks since, and injured both legs'."	78
4.4	"[A]n older girl carrying coals."	79
4.5	"The sketch given in p. 79 (Fig. 4) is intended to represent Ann Ambler and William Dyson ... hurriers ... in the act of being drawn up cross-lapped upon the clatch-iron by a woman."	82

ARGUMENTS

5.1	John P. Hale, head-and-shoulders portrait, facing front.	97
5.2	Portrait of John Jay.	99
5.3	Bird's eye view of Dover, Strafford Co., New Hampshire 1877.	103
5.4	Portrait of William Murray, 1st Earl of Mansfield.	106
5.5	Portrait of Thomas Erskine, 1st Baron Erskine.	107

PROPERTY AND POSSESSION

6.1	Randolph Caldecott, The House that Jack Built.	116
6.2	Vase by Charles Frederick Hancock Set on Ebony Table.	123
6.3	John Everett Millais, "Lucius Mason, as he leaned on the gate that was no longer his own" from *Orley Farm* by Anthony Trollope.	127
6.4	Skinner Prout, On the Plenty, near Melbourne.	128

WRONGS

7.1	Engraving of the "Arrival of the Good Samaritan at the Inn" by Gustave Dore.	132

7.2 Image depicting the sculpture by George James Miller which won the Gold Medal for "Best Historical Sculpture" at the Royal Academy of Arts in 1858. 133

7.3 Image depicting the painting by Philip Richard Morris which won the Gold Medal for "Best Historical Painting" at the Royal Academy of Arts in 1858. 133

LEGAL PROFESSION

8.1 Honoré Daumier, "La Caricature Provisoire." 148

8.2 "Light" by "Phiz" (Hablôt Knight Browne) for *Bleak House* ch.51, "Enlightened" (1853). 150

8.3 Honoré Daumier, "Le grand escalier du Palais de Justice" *c.* 1864; watercolor, detail. 153

8.4 "Magnanimous conduct of Mr.Guppy" by "Phiz" (Hablôt Knight Browne) for *Bleak House* ch. 54, "Esther's Narrative" (1853). 157

8.5 Honoré Daumier, *Les Gens de Justice* Plate 24. 161

NOTES ON CONTRIBUTORS

K Crosby is a Lecturer in Law at Newcastle University. Their research mainly concerns the history of jury trial between the seventeenth and twenty-first centuries, and they have most recently completed a project on the first women trial jurors in England and Wales between 1920 and 1929.

Kieran Dolin is an Associate Professor in English and Cultural Studies at the University of Western Australia. He is the author of *Fiction and the Law: Legal Discourse in Victorian and Modernist Literature* (1999) *and A Critical Introduction to Law and Literature* (2007) and has recently edited a collection of essays on *Law and Literature* for the Cambridge Critical Concepts series.

Nancy E. Johnson is an Associate Dean of the College of Liberal Arts & Sciences and a Professor of English at the State University of New York at New Paltz, where she has taught eighteenth-century British literature and contemporary literary theory. She is the author of *The English Jacobin Novel on Rights, Property and the Law: Critiquing the Contract* (Palgrave, 2004); editor of *Impassioned Jurisprudence: Law, Literature and Emotion, 1760–1848* (Bucknell University Press, 2015); scholarly editor of *The Court Journals and Letters of Frances Burney, 1790–June 1791, Vol. VI* (Oxford University Press, forthcoming); and editor of *Mary Wollstonecraft in Context* (Cambridge University Press, forthcoming). She has also published articles on novels of the 1790s and various intersections of law and literature.

Linda Mulcahy is the Professor of Socio-Legal Studies at the University of Oxford. She has qualifications in law, sociology and architecture and her work has a strong interdisciplinary flavor. Her most recent research has focused on the architecture of courts and the use of images in legal scholarship.

Jan-Melissa Schramm worked as a lawyer before undertaking a PhD on the changing idea of evidence in the long nineteenth century. She is now University Reader in Literature and Law, and Deputy Director of the Centre for Research in the Arts, Social Sciences, and Humanities (CRASSH), at the University of Cambridge. She is the author of *Testimony and Advocacy in Victorian Law, Literature, and Theology* (Cambridge University Press, 2000), *Atonement and Self-Sacrifice in Nineteenth-Century Narrative* (Cambridge University Press, 2012), and *Censorship and the Representation of the Sacred in Nineteenth-Century England* (forthcoming, Oxford University Press, 2018). She has also co-edited two volumes of essays: *Fictions of Knowledge: Fact, Evidence, Doubt* (Macmillan, 2011), and *Sacrifice and the Modern Literature of War* (Oxford University Press, 2018).

John Snape is an Associate Professor of Law at the University of Warwick. His work on Gilbert and Sullivan's *Utopia, Limited* combines his interest in nineteenth-century legal history with a love of the Savoy Operas that goes back to his teenage years.

Jane Tynan is Senior Lecturer in visual culture and design history at Central St Martins, University of the Arts, London. Her research concerns the distinctive images that mark transformations in law and order, military conflict, and insurgency. Publications include *British Army Uniform and the First World War* (Palgrave, 2013) and the forthcoming *Understanding Uniform* (Bloomsbury, 2019). She is series editor for Palgrave Studies in Fashion and the Body.

Ian Ward is Professor of Law at Newcastle University. He is the author of a number of books and essays in the areas of legal history and literary jurisprudence, including *Law and Literature: Possibilities and Perspectives* (Cambridge University Press, 1995), *Law, Text, Terror* (Cambridge University Press, 2009), *Law and the Brontes*, (Palgrave, 2012) and most recently *Sex, Crime and Literature in Victorian England* (Hart, 2014).

Gary Watt is a Professor of Law at the University of Warwick. He is co-founding editor of the journal *Law and Humanities* and General Editor of *A Cultural History of Law* (Bloomsbury). Since 2009, when he was named UK "Law Teacher of the Year," he has regularly led rhetoric workshops for the Royal Shakespeare Company. His recent monographs have explored the rhetoric of Equity (*Equity Stirring*, Hart, 2009), Dress (*Dress, Law and Naked Truth*, Bloomsbury, 2013) and Shakespearean performance (*Shakespeare's Acts of Will*, Bloomsbury Arden Shakespeare, 2016).

SERIES PREFACE

The six volumes in *A Cultural History of Law* present a panorama of law's cultural significance over the span of several centuries, especially as it relates to the place of law in the arts and humanities. Each volume focuses on a distinct time period from antiquity to modernity and in each volume a chapter is devoted to one of eight legally significant themes: "Justice," "Constitution," "Codes," "Agreements," "Arguments," "Property and Possession," "Wrongs," and "The Legal Profession." The collection does not seek to provide encyclopedic coverage, but rather to present cultural case studies that highlight how particular cultural artefacts express and explore the key legal—and inevitably the key political and social—concerns of their time. The authors have picked flowers from their field of expertise—a play, a painting, a mosaic, a book, a film—which bring into close focus the cultural and legal flourishing of the time. The volume editors are internationally distinguished scholars with a passion and deep appreciation for the law and culture of their chosen period. Together with the experts that they have assembled to contribute chapters on the eight themes, they are reliable guides not merely to the facts about each period but to the feel of each period. Every volume has an ethos and a style that immerses the reader in the distinctive quality of its era. The series is indebted to the archivist's concern to discover and catalog historical materials, but what sets it apart is its concern to show how the materials of history are materially meaningful. In this way, our retrospective of more than 2,000 years continues to have relevance for lawyers and for all culturally concerned citizens today.

Sometimes we find that artifacts have lost the cultural meanings that first produced them. Likewise, we sometimes we find that artifacts are culturally meaningful today in ways that they were not at the time of their creation. Take the example of Magna Carta—The Great Charter of King John of England sealed at Runnymede on the Thames in 1215. Today, in the United States in particular, Magna Carta has been hoisted to totemic heights in the cultural imagination. It might therefore seem strange to us that William Shakespeare's play *King John* makes no reference at all to this great artifact. The reason for its omission is that for Shakespeare and his early modern contemporaries, the most dramatic historical event in the reign of King John was his surrender of the crown to the papal legate and his receiving it again as a papal vassal. The modern significance of Magna Carta is largely a post-Enlightenment invention and its principal promoters were the great myth-makers who framed the American Constitution and created the idea of the United States. It is some proof of this that the Magna Carta memorial which stands at Runnymede today was erected by the American Bar Association. The small-scale temple, like the much larger Jefferson Memorial in Washington DC, has become a place of secular pilgrimage; a sanctuary to the values of political freedom and human rights under law.

In 2015, to mark the 800th anniversary of the sealing of Magna Carta, sculptor Hew Locke's "The Jurors" was installed at Runnymede. It comprises twelve bronze chairs, each of which (according to the official narrative) "incorporates symbols and imagery representing concepts of law and key moments in the struggle for freedom, rule of law and equal rights." In this respect, it performs a similar function to the eight bas-relief panels by sculptor John Donnelly Jnr that adorn the great bronze doors of the United States Supreme Court in Washington DC. Shakespeare would have appreciated the performative purpose of these "solemn temples" but he would surely be surprised to see today how much has been made of Magna Carta. The rise of Magna Carta as an artifact of cultural history would certainly have amazed the landed aristocrats who first compelled King John to set his seal to the charter in the culturally Christian, monarchal, and feudal context of the High Middle Ages. The narrative accompanying "The Jurors" alerts us to the license that the sculptor has taken with the history of law. We are told that it is "not a memorial, but rather an artwork that aims to examine the changing and ongoing significance and influences of Magna Carta." It is, in short, a cultural reworking of an artifact that owes its great status to creative cultural appropriation. The actual provisions of Magna Carta that survive in law are impressively few, but the three survivors are perhaps all the more significant for their small number. Much is still made of the survival of the right to trial by jury. Rather less is made, nowadays, of the provisions that preserve the "liberties of the English Church" and the "privileges of the City of London." One of the most important contributions we can make to the appreciation of history is to show where cultures are selective in what they present as fact. The artifacts of history are always presented in the cabinets of culture.

The word "fact" comes, in fact, from the Latin *facere* ("to make") and it can be helpful to think of historical facts as things that are produced by the action of culture and as things which, in turn, produce cultures. Even where a society is collectively in error in its understanding of historical fact, a commonly held mistake inevitably becomes part of the cultural history of that society. The story becomes the history. One of the mistakes we often make, as the shifting status of Magna Carta indicates, is to suppose that the modern commentator can claim a monopoly in the present moment to determine "true" history from "false." Today's official history is only ever the history of the present. The past had its own histories. Cultural history allows an appreciation of the cultural stories that give meaning to societies in time and across time. From a cultural perspective, myths can be more meaningful, and in that cultural sense more "true," than many a cold matter of fact.

Another great and oft-repeated mistake that this book series seeks to remedy is the supposition that law can be meaningfully separated from the culture in which it exists. In *Law as Culture*, Lawrence Rosen observes that law:

> never stands apart from life—some refined essence of professional inquiry or arcane speech. Rather, it forms the conscious attention we give to our relationships. Like art and literature, through law we attempt to order our ties to one another ... However it is displayed, however it is applied, we can no more comprehend the roles of legal institutions without seeing them as part of their culture than we can fully understand each culture without attending to its form of law.[1]

There is an historical aspect to this understanding of law as culture. Pierre Legrand writes, for example, that:

> French law is, first and foremost, a cultural phenomenon, not unlike singing or weaving. The reason why the French have the *chanteurs* they have lies somewhere in their history, their Frenchness, in their identity. Similarly, the reason why the French have the legislative texts or the judicial decisions they have, say, on a matter of sales law, lies somewhere in their history, their Frenchness, in their identity.[2]

There are obvious limits to the mechanistic metaphor by which we talk of cultural history as something manufactured or fabricated. Human hands fashion historical artifacts, but legal artifacts grow out of a culture in a way that makes it hard to know where the artifact starts and the culture ends. It might be better to take the "culture" metaphor seriously and to suggest that laws grow out of a society organically and that the artificial intervention of human hands are like those of the gardener—taming, tending, and ordering wild growth. Thus the cultural history of law becomes something like a horticultural history. This is not such a strange thought when one considers that the English word for the "court" of law is derived from the Latin *hortus* (garden). Malcolm Andrews has suggested that "one could write an illuminating, if oblique, history of a nation's cultural development by examining its changing conception of the garden's scope, design and function."[3] The gardening metaphor may be especially useful in helping us to understand the cultural history of law, given the complex relation between natural justice and artificial laws in human society. Dress is another artificial creation of human craft which, as a cultural outworking of the complex relation between nature and human ordering, serves well as a way to understand the artificial and creative nature of law's contribution to culture. Laws are produced in society in much the same way that gardens, dress, and other products of complex cultural systems are produced in society. When we have completed our journey through the six volumes of this series we may conclude that the chief legislator across the ages has been no Parliament nor any body of the people politically represented, but that the great lawmaker has always been the deep, rich, and creative power of human culture.

Gary Watt, Professor of Law,
University of Warwick, UK

Introduction

IAN WARD

REVOLUTION, REFORM AND REACTION

One person dominates British and Imperial history in the Age of Reform 1820–1920: Alexandrina Victoria, only daughter of the Duke of Kent and Princess Victoria of Saxe-Coburg-Saalfeld, was born on May 24, 1819. Victoria, Regina, and Imperatrix, died on January 22, 1901, having spent her last few hours in apparently calm repose clutching a crucifix and leaning on the withered arm of her nephew Kaiser Wilhelm. We can still see grainy images of her funeral held on a dank and drizzly morning eleven days later, replete with four reigning monarchs riding in attendance, streets full of mourning subjects and lots of damp artillerymen struggling to get the gun-carriage cortege to move in the mud. The pathetic fallacy is prescient. Subsequent generations would be invited to recall a dumpy, rather grim-faced old lady, dressed in mourning weeds, as often as not pictured staring wistfully at a bust of her long-departed Albert. It was, as Arthur Balfour observed in the Commons in the days following the announcement of Victoria's death, "the end of a great epoch." In a sense it was. Funerals present themselves as obvious demarcations in the histories of "ages," especially those named after monarchs. The same might be said of coronations. It had been sixty-three years since a pretty, and tiny, princess had walked along the aisle of Westminster Abbey to be anointed and crowned.

But history is never quite so tidy. Centuries get to be termed "long," or occasionally short, ages rarely map to monarchs or anything else. And their margins are always contestable. Balfour was right only in the most prosaic sense; the Queen was dead. But Victorianism did not end in 1901. Seven months after Victoria's funeral, Edward Elgar's Pomp and Circumstance March No. 1 in D Major was given its first public performance at the Liverpool Orchestral Society. Edwardian just, but in spirit and everything else composed as a paean to Victoria and her Empire. It is mortality which tends to tempt the historian though, not musicality. Roy Jenkins suggests that the Victorian age might have ended on Ascension Day 1898. Gladstone died on Ascension Day 1898. Very different, at least in terms of chronological implication, is the notion that it might be January 30, 1965, the day that Winston Churchill's coffin was carried back down the steps of St Paul's Cathedral. The young Winston was in so many ways the quintessential late Victorian imperialist. So was the old Winston, the author of the quintessential Whig history of the British Empire, *A History of the English Speaking Peoples*. Another possibility is that it finished in 1914; representative in a rather different way of so many deaths. The lights went out on lots of things in 1914.

And if the end of the Victorian epoch was perhaps called rather prematurely, announcing the start is not much easier. During the first thirty-seven years of the nineteenth century, three Hanoverians had sat on the English throne, the "mad" George III, his grotesque son George IV, and William IV, variously known to his less than reverent subjects as the "sailor king," "silly Billy," and "pineapple head"; the "damnedest millstone around the

FIGURE 0.1 The funeral procession of Queen Victoria through London. Source: Photo by SSPL / Getty Images.

necks" of the nation, the Duke of Wellington declared of the lot of them (Hibbert 2001: 10). The Victorians needed Victoria; they had waited long enough. As the "times," as Thomas Carlyle and John Stuart Mill had in their different ways already announced, were anyway changing. Dickens was certainly not inclined to wait. The grandest of all Victorian chronicles was already well underway in its writing. As Victoria sat serenely amidst the recorded chaos of her coronation in June 1838, *Oliver Twist* was mid-way through its serialization in *Bentley's*. *Pickwick Papers* had recently completed its run, and *Nicholas Nickleby* had just begun. For some historians, however, it was not simply a matter of months or indeed a few years. As long ago as 1959 Asa Briggs suggested that the 1790s should be comprehended as a Victorian "prelude" (Briggs 1959: 1, 72). Rather more recently, Gertrude Himmelfarb has suggested that the "early" Victorians were already beginning to depart the scene by the time Victoria had settled into the Royal chambers at Windsor (Himmelfarb 2007: 6–10).

Identifying the Victorian is, then, a slippery business. We are not sure when they arrived, and we are not sure when they left, if indeed they really have. In such a circumstance historians have anyway cast around for alternative epochal signifiers. The nineteenth century has, accordingly, long been termed the "age of improvement" or alternatively the "age of reform." Lawyers tend to assume this means constitutional "reform." But there were, as we shall see, lots of things to be reformed, just as there were lots of things that needed improving. An "age of revolution" is another possibility, particularly if the supposed revolution is of the social or industrial variety. Wherever there is revolution, or indeed reform, there is sure to be reaction. There were at least as many moments of darkness and doubt in the "long" Victorian century as there were moments of lightness and hope. We are going to revisit the nineteenth century in these tones and on these terms; charting the dynamic relation of revolution, reform and reaction, and its consequences, variously social and cultural, political, and legal. In so doing we might come to a closer sense of what the Victorians thought of themselves, as the nineteenth century was also an age of intense introspection. And we might come to a closer sense of what we think of the Victorians.

For while the Victorian age might have ended in 1901, or perhaps 1898 or 1914 or even 1965, the age of Victoriana is very much with us still. It is still to Elgar that the English turn in moments of national celebration. It is still to the novels of Dickens and Eliot and the Brontë sisters that we turn for solace and inspiration and for education too; GCSE English literature modules and high-street bookstores alike full of *Great Expectations* and *Middlemarch* and *Wuthering Heights*. Victoriana sells. We love reading the Victorians, and we love reading about them too. The Victorians make for epic history, and tend to get very long, very Whiggish, books written about them. There is certainly something distinctly Whiggish in Simon Heffer's recent, suitably vast, survey of the "high-minds" of Victorian England. It is these minds which made "modern Britain." There are, of course, more skeptical narratives. The England whose "condition" was disinterred by Raymond Williams in his 1958 study *Culture and Anarchy* was painted in rather more variegated shades, and there have been plenty of subsequent accounts of Victoria and her "age" written from a particular critical, Foucauldian, or postmodern perspective. But whilse all might be skeptical to some degree, all too ultimately fall to the same temptation; the felt need to somehow make sense of the Victorians. The chapters which comprise this collection, though they stretch beyond the narrower chronology of Victorian England and indeed beyond its immediate geographical margins, are a testament to the same aspiration and the same frustrations.

REVOLUTION

The Great Exhibition opened its doors on May 1, 1851. Twenty thousand poured in the first day, including Victoria who arrived resplendent in pink and silver, wearing the Garter ribbon and the Koh-i-noor diamond, a crown with two gold feathers on her head, and a broad smile. It was, she later confirmed, even "more touching" than her coronation, one of the "proudest and happiest" days of her "happy life" (Heffer 2013: 308). Next to her, inevitably, was Prince Albert who, forever trying to find things to do, had energetically accepted the offer of becoming patron and chief evangelist of a project which, he famously announced in a speech at the Mansion House a year earlier, would celebrate the "wonderful period of transition" in which they were all fortunate enough to live (Heffer 2013: 297–298). Queen and Consort would visit repeatedly over the following five months until the Exhibition closed in mid-October. Meanwhile that same morning another 250,000 were reported to be stood outside in Hyde Park waiting for the famed aeronaut Charles Spencer to ascend in his balloon. The Whig historian Buckle meditated on "the bright promise of reward to man's genius" (Briggs 1959: 400). Macaulay was enraptured. "I made my way into the building," he reported, "a most gorgeous sight; vast; graceful; beyond the dream of the Arabian romances. I cannot think that the Caesars ever exhibited a more splendid spectacle. I was quite dazzled, and I felt as I did on entering St Peters" (Plumb 1963: 258).

FIGURE 0.2 The opening of the Great Exhibition by Queen Victoria on 1 May 1851. From Cassell's History of England, Vol. VI. Source: The Print Collector / Getty Images.

Inside the vast "cucumber frame," as Ruskin rather dismissively termed Paxton's Crystal Palace, could be found a veritable array of the wondrous, the mundane and the downright peculiar, everything from early sewing machines to steam turbines and locomotives, a telegraphic link to Edinburgh, the air pumps and microscopes, and "a cricket catapulta, for propelling the ball in the absence of a first-rate bowler" (Heffer 2013: 305). Visitors gawped in admiration and amazement; while trying to avoid being hit by the defecating pigeons that had taken to nesting in the rafters and the sparrow-hawks which were brought in to hunt them down (but which turned out to be messier still). The Great Exhibition is commonly taken to represent the exuberant side of mid-Victorian England, its optimism and its ability to make interesting stuff and to persuade people to buy it. The Exhibition itself made £200,000 from entrance tickets and brochures. From a different perspective, however, the same exuberance assumes a different shape; the "age of progressive improvement," as Palmerston famously termed it, was also an age of revolution (Parry 1993: 168; Best 1979: 255).

More precisely it represented three species of revolution, each of which generated myriad emotional as well as intellectual responses. The first was perhaps the most obvious. All the machines and turbines and air pumps were testimony to the dynamism of an industrial revolution. Victorian England basked in the thought that it was indeed the manufacturing capital of the world. It had the biggest bridges and the biggest ships, and fortunately enough the biggest empire, raw materials aplenty, and lots of cheap labor to exploit in the rapidly expanding cities and towns of the north and midlands of England. The evidence was everywhere. The interested mid-Victorian gentleman could travel the length and breadth of the country during the autumn of 1851 visiting all the smaller imitation exhibitions which duly sprung up in the same cities and towns. They were able to do so as a consequence of perhaps the most remarkable expression of the nineteenth-century industrial revolution: the railway.

Between 1841 and 1846 railway mileage in England increased from 1,700 to 3,000. By 1850 it had doubled to 6,000. Fifteen years later it had doubled again. By the end of the century, track mileage exceeded 18,000. Not everyone loved the railways. Wordsworth spent his declining years penning increasingly acerbic verse berating the railway companies that dared to cross his Lakeland horizon. In *Locksley Hall*, Tennyson expressed an aligned anxiety "In the steamship, in the railway, in the thoughts that shake mankind." The *Sunday Times* assumed the higher moral ground in 1850, regretting the "idle debauchery" which railway travel facilitated, and more particularly, blaming Gladstone's 1844 Railway Act, which had introduced fare regulation on third-class "parliamentary trains." But most were far more inclined to applaud the advance of the railway. If England needed a hero, Peel observed in his *Tamworth Manifesto*, they needed to look no further than George Stephenson. Peel liked railways. In 1845 he cut the first sod for the Trent Valley Railway, praising the "wonder-working" effect of promoting the spread of ideas and goods, such that "it will promote the moral and social welfare of this country." The following year he reaffirmed his government's blanket support for all 519 railway bills currently under parliamentary consideration (Read 1987: 9, 149).

For the more sentient and the more skeptical, like Tennyson and Wordsworth, who did not fancy the railway quite so much, there was moreover an alternative; one which again owed everything to the technological innovation which drove industrial revolution. Instead of visiting the revolution, or indeed travelling along it, they could simply stay and home and read about it. The "age" of industrial revolution was also the "age of the newspaper" and the telegraph. Here again statutory reform was as significant as technological advance; the abolition of newspaper stamp duty in 1855, the abolition of excise duty on paper in 1861, and the 1868 Telegraph Act which liberated the provincial presses. By 1864, the circulation figures for provincial weeklies had reached 2.5 million. May's *British and Irish Press Guide for 1874* listed Newcastle-upon-Tyne as having five dailies and five weeklies. No self-respecting market-town was without at least one weekly: Driffield had three, Trowbridge two. Here again, of course, there were doubters and detractors. Newspaper-reading, Lord Melbourne opined, had become the "vice of the present day" (Mitchell 1997: 22, 25). The revolution in print technology ushered in another new, and altogether less welcome age, that of public opinion. Its "expectation," as Peel put it, was a "great compound of folly, weakness, prejudice, wrong feeling, right feeling, obstinacy and newspaper paragraphs" (Read 1987: 16; Briggs 1959: 194). Much later, in 1891, Oscar Wilde affirmed the same in his essay *Man Under Socialism*: "In old days men had the rack. Now they have the press. That is an improvement certainly. But still it is very bad, and wrong, and demoralising" (Himmelfarb 2007: 306).

There was so much more to read and so many more readers too. In the first year of Victoria's reign it was reported that the Chartist in-house journal *The Northern Star* was shifting 50,000 copies a week. The 1851 census revealed that 31 percent of men and 45 percent of women were illiterate. By 1871 the figures had reduced to 19 percent and 27 percent. The number of children attending school in London had doubled between 1820 and 1834. Later statutory reform of educational provision would contribute still further to the advance of what John Stuart Mill termed "useful learning," which was the "great end" of utilitarian social policy (Newsome 1998: 55). By 1860 there were 610 Mechanics Institutes established across the country, all running evening classes in basic literacy and numeracy skills. The "schoolmaster," Brougham had pronounced in his *Observations on the Education of People* in 1825, was "abroad in the land." There were, inevitably, concerns. Dr. Arnold worried about the comparative lack of training in the classics. The future Cardinal Newman articulated a darker anxiety in regard to the advance of the "intellectual man as the world now conceives him." He was supposed to have "views on all subjects of philosophy, on all matters of the day," views that could only shaped by the prejudices of "periodical literature" (Himmelfarb 2007: 25). Carlyle agreed with the sentiment, if not the peculiarity of the prejudice. It was not just periodicals, as he confirmed in his 1841 *Heroes and Hero-Worship*. The "writers of Newspapers, Pamphlets, Poems, Books" could now be compared to a "real working effective Church." There is "no class comparable for importance to that Priesthood of the Writers of Books" (Carlyle 1986: 242–3, 247). The poignancy of the metaphor was presumably appreciated at Oriel College, where in 1841 Newman was agonizing over drafts of his final *Tract for the Times*.

And if there were too many unlicensed literary priests, there were certainly far too many commercially savvy priestesses. "We are living," the revered critic E.S. Dallas declared in 1860, "in the age of the lady novelist" (Ward 2014: 17). Dallas was referring more precisely to those female novelists who had found a rather sudden, and very lucrative, success as writers of sensation novels. Sensationalism burst onto the cultural scene at the very end of the 1850s, its novels full of sex and crime and beautiful murderous heroines. The critics complained. But the novels sold, like novels had never sold before. It might be supposed that the best-selling novel of the century would be a classic Dickens or a Brontë or a Gaskell. It was not. Far and away the best-selling novel of the century was Ellen Wood's breathless tale of adultery and its inevitable consequence *East Lynne*. The tens of thousands of bored mid-Victorian wives and daughters who bought *East Lynne* were the same tens of thousands of bored mid-Victorian wives and daughters who became devotees of the various still more shocking novels of Mary Elizabeth Braddon, *Lady Audley's Secret*, *Aurora Floyd*, and *The Doctor's Wife*, a shameless rewriting of Flaubert's classic, *Madame Bovary*. Braddon dealt, by her own admission, in "highly-spiced fictions," writing for the "reader whose palette requires strong meat, and is not very particular as to the qualities thereof" (Ward 2014: 63). Horrified critics sought common recourse to pathological metaphors. Devotees of the sensation novel were "addicted" and "diseased." Trollope varied the metaphor slightly in his *Autobiography*, suggesting that sensation novels were consumed "as men eat a pastry after dinner not without some inward conviction that the taste is vain if not vicious" (Trollope 1996: 140). Dean Mansel followed suit. There was "something unspeakably disgusting in this ravenous appetite" for sensationalist "carrion" (Ward 2014: 62).

The rise and rise of the lady writer, and the lady reader, signified another revolution which, in the perception of many Victorians was thoroughly unwelcome, the sexual. The Victorians worried a lot about the "question" of their women. Too much, according to George Eliot, who concluded that there was, in fact, no subject "on which I am more inclined to hold my peace and learn, than on the Woman Question" (Thompson 1996: 12). The received wisdom suggested that the ideal woman was the "angel in the house;" a descriptor sanctified in Coventry Patmore's iconic poem of that name. A less poetic term referred to "separate spheres," which supposed that while women occupied the private, the natural sphere of male activity was the public. It was, as Elizabeth Lynn Linton in her rather misleadingly entitled *Laws Concerning Women* put it, "the very first principle of domestic existence." "Let men enjoy in peace and triumph the intellectual kingdom which is theirs," the ubiquitous Sarah Lewis confirmed in one of her innumerable self-help guides for the troubled Victorian housewife, the "moral world is ours by position, ours by qualification, ours by the very indication of God" (Ward 2014: 6). Needless to say lots and lots of men lined up to express their agreement, including John Ruskin in his influential lecture *Of Queens Gardens*. Man, Ruskin observed, was the "doer," his wife the embodiment of "sweet ordering, arrangement and decision," in the home at least (Ruskin 2004: 158). It was only too apparent than an increasing number of women were not inclined to be especially angelic and were positively fed up with being stuck in the house. It was for these women that Wood and Braddon wrote. Josephine Butler later paid tribute to those women writers who had created for "us" a "literature of our own," and as a consequence allowed nineteenth-century women to break through the "conspiracy of silence" which "enslaved" them (Ward 2014: 17). Particularly fed up, it became apparent, were those whose husbands were abusive or adulterous or both. It was these women who, in their hundreds and then thousands, had pitched up at the newly established Divorce Court which opened its doors for business in 1858.

The revolution in reading was, of course, a rather allusive threat. It was not really questioning women that troubled the right-thinking mid-Victorian gentleman, at least not in the more immediate sense. It was wrong-thinking men asking the wrong questions. A few hundred yards away from the Queen and her Consort and the 20,000 subjects who milled around Hyde Park on May 1, 1851 could be found the five cavalry regiments which the Home Secretary had thought it sensible to deploy. Only three years earlier, the same park had been full of Chartists demanding all kinds of thoroughly unacceptable things. In the end, the incipient revolutionaries of spring 1848 had settled for a decent picnic and a sing-song. But it had all been very concerning; so much so that the royal family had been despatched to Osborne House on the Isle of Wight as a precaution. Hyde Park had developed a reputation as a good place, not merely to gawp at weird inventions or to enjoy picnics, but also to gather lots of people together and demand reform. Or, more accurately, restoration of those liberties won long ago in the meadows of Runnymede. The people, the Chartist *Despatch* observed, had too "long submitted to the delay of their new Magna Carta" (Royle 2000: 74). Invocations of Norman yokes and "ancient" constitutions were invariably present in Chartist petitions, alongside the customary "Six Points" extracted, with a certain interpretive license, from the original "great" Charter; universal suffrage, a ballot, the removal of property qualifications, the payment of MPs, equal constituencies, and annual parliaments. "Here's that we may live to see the restoration of old English times, old English fare, old English holidays, and old English justice," declared the Chartist leader Feargus O'Connor (Thompson 1991: 255).

If the Chartists were lost in the reverie of Runnymede in 1215, others were haunted by a rather more recent dream, or more accurately nightmare, that of Paris in 1790. Nineteenth-century England, in the words of the Whig lawyer Cockburn, remained "soaked in this one event" (Briggs 1959: 129). When nearly eighty years later Queen Victoria expressed her dismay at the provisions of the 1867 Reform Act, Disraeli thought fit to insinuate that if she did not give her assent there might be a "new French Revolution" (Longford 1998: 352). Years later Charles Kingsley was asked why his compatriots seemed to be so obsessed with the possibility of revolution. He simply replied "Look at France, and see!" (Craig 1983: 79) Another reason, perhaps, was because they were always reading about it. Victorian England, Gladstone conceded, was "steeped" in Edmund Burke and his *Reflections on the Revolution in France* (Gardiner 2002: 183, 186–189). "In Mr Burke's writings," Coleridge had opined a few years earlier, "indeed the germ of almost all political truths can be found" (Coleridge 1977: 129). And then there was Carlyle and his *History of the French Revolution* which, as its author conceded, owed so much to the "great" Burke (Frye 1997: 100). Carlyle's own *History* quickly assumed a similar critical authenticity, in the words of an admiring Mill simply the "truest of histories" (Heffer

1996: 173). And a necessary urgency too, as Carlyle reminded readers of his essay on *Chartism* written a couple of years later. "These Chartisms, Radicalisms, Reform Bill, Tithe Bill, and infinite other discrepancy" and "acrid argument and jargon that there is yet to be, are *our* French Revolution" (Caryle 1997: 161). Of course, what terrified was also what entertained. Charles Dickens penned *A Tale of Two Cities* as a "faithful" testament to Carlyle's "wonderful book," with its same "rages uncontrollable" and "sansculottes" dancing dementedly in the streets running with blood (Dickens 2000: x–xi).

Something which both Carlyle and Dickens appreciated was the extent of the desperation which was felt by so many of their compatriots. Carlyle famously referred to a "Swammery," just as despairing as that which rampaged through the streets of Paris in 1790. Dickens wrote about it copiously, nowhere more pointedly, perhaps, than in his narrative of the 1780 Gordon riots, *Barnaby Rudge*. They were not alone in their anxieties. The Radical John Bright likewise referred to a "sunken sixth," a class of "almost

FIGURE 0.3 A rage uncontrollable. Essayist and historian Thomas Carlyle (1795–1881). Photo by Hulton Archive / Getty Images.

helpless poverty and dependence," and resentment (Best 1979: 142). Rather later, in 1868, Henry James expressed a genuine and "sudden horror" when he arrived in London for the first time, the rows and rows of "low black houses," the gin shops on every corner, the "rookeries" and brothels, and the open sewers running along the streets (Best 1979: 27). It is easy with hindsight for historians to look back on the nineteenth century and dismiss the possibility of revolution in nineteenth-century England. It was not so easy for contemporaries.

There again the Victorians were not opposed to all constitutional revolutions. The "great and glorious" revolution of 1688, for example, was a "wonderful" thing, as readers of Macaulay's *History of England*, the first volumes of which had been published in 1848, would have known. Indeed it had served to restore precisely those liberties which might be traced to Magna Carta, and to improve them. The events of 1688 and 1689 were to be appreciated as part of a narrative which could be projected through to the Reform Act of 1832. "To the Whigs of the seventeenth century we owe it that we have a House of Commons," Macaulay had informed his Edinburgh electorate in 1839, "to the Whigs of the nineteenth century we owe it that the House of Commons has been purified" (Firth 1938: 260). The 1832 Act had completed the revolution of 1688 and brought "finality" to a great constitutional process. As it stood in 1848, the "main principles of our government" were set by the reason of a long history. While they "were not, indeed, formally and exactly set forth in a single written instrument" they "were to be found scattered over our ancient and noble statutes; and, what was of far greater moment, they had been engraven on the hearts of Englishmen during four hundred years" (Macaulay 1986: 290). And as a consequence, and most importantly, the "highest eulogy which can be pronounced on the revolution of 1688" is "that it was our last revolution" (Macaulay 1986: 294). Macaulay was not the only Whig to be obsessed with the "great and glorious" revolution. Victoria once remarked of Lord Russell that he was in clear need of a "third subject: because he was interested in nothing except the Constitution of 1688 and himself" (Hibbert 2001: 204). The same mindset, and the same narrative, would define successive generations of Whiggish historians, from Gardiner to Trevelyan to Winston Churchill. But there was one essential flaw in Macaulay's prospective history. The 1832 Act had not brought "finality," for which reason neither the prospect of further reform nor indeed the fear of revolution could ever be properly exorcized from the collective Victorian mind.

REFORM AND REACTION

Mrs. Disraeli had been out shopping on July 23, 1866 and was on her way back home to the rather grand house she shared with her husband at Grosvenor Gate. She got as far as Curzon Street; but no further. Yet again there were lots of people, by estimation as many as 20,000, wandering around Pall Mall and Hyde Park demanding things: chiefly constitutional reform and free beer. It was held under the auspices of the Reform League. Some railings had been accidentally dislodged, but fortunately no one had damaged the famed flower beds. The police, however, panicked and charged in. A melee ensued, during which a police officer was killed. Reports reached Westminster, leading Disraeli to despatch his secretary Montagu Corry to see that all was well, with both his wife and his house. It was. The house was untouched, and as for Mrs. Disraeli, who was now safely returned, Corry added in evidently bemused tones, "I really believe she sympathises with them" (Aldous 2007: 167–168).

Mrs. Disraeli might have been sanguine. Others were not, including the Queen. Disraeli sought to reassure his rather twitchy monarch. Such assemblies, he suggested soothingly, were the "safety valves" of a "free constitution" (Aldous 2007: 168). Victoria was not easily soothed. But Disraeli was right. By 1867, the occasional inebriated picnic aside, the question of constitutional reform had indeed become an essentially "ministerial matter." Disraeli sold the idea to his own party on this precise basis. The 1867 Act was intended to reform governance, not the constitution as such, and it was certainly not enacted in order to democratize anything or anyone. The younger Disraeli had vehemently denounced the treacherous "union of oligarchical wealth and mob poverty" which had conspired to secure the passage of the earlier 1832 Reform Act (Hutcheon 1913: 329, 350). The 1867 Act was to be very different, enacted not to broaden the franchise, but to broaden the electoral base of the Tory party, and irritate Gladstone. It did the latter, but not the former. Disraeli had miscalculated, and a few months later was out of office, which left much explaining to do, not least to his Queen.

Disraeli was, however, right in regard to the differing public mood. Passing the first Reform Act had indeed been a very different experience. The threat of violence had certainly appeared more real. But it had been a "great" Act, and a very good thing, as generations of Whig historians would later confirm; not least because it has been designed to ensure that there would never be the need of another one. The 1832 Act was supposed to represent "finality" to the "great constitutional question," the culmination of an epic process begun back in 1215, and then reinvested most notably in 1688. The Reform Act would reaffirm "revolution principles," securing once again the liberties of Englishmen, particularly the liberties of wealthy and propertied Englishmen. Continuity was central to Whig propaganda in the frenetic months leading up to the enactment of the 1832 Act. That and terror. When the second reform bill arrived in the Lords in later summer 1831, Macaulay, serving as chief government propagandist, raised a familiar and chilling specter: had their Lordships "even seen the ruins of those castles whose terraces and gardens overhang the Loire?" (Cannon 1973: 224) Peel raced off to his country home at Drayton Manor in Staffordshire, and set about fortifying it. The *Despatch* entered joyously into the spirit of the moment, assuring its readers that "Reform or revolution is the cry of every man who deserves the name of Englishman" (Royle 2000: 74). The Duke of Wellington appreciated the affinity, if not the prospective statute. "Beginning reform," the Iron Duke declared, "is beginning revolution," and the "downfall of the Constitution" (Hibbert 1997: 289). He appreciated nevertheless the niceties which attended the same constitution. There was, as Grey repeatedly affirmed, a "public expectation" (Mandler 1990: 71–72, 125–126). Old "Pineapple Head" was not much persuaded. But he assented to the Act nonetheless, *in absentia*.

The 1832 Act broadened the franchise to include all £10 householders in the boroughs, together with 40 shilling freeholders in the counties, copyholders worth £10 and leaseholders worth either £10 or £50 depending on the length of tenure. It also abolished some of the rottenest of the rotten boroughs. The electorate was thus increased by a ratio of approximately 75 percent; impressive enough until it is remembered that 95 percent were still without a vote including, of course, every woman. It was nevertheless a "great" Act, having, as Erskine May recorded in 1861, "conferred immortal honour on the statesmen who had the wisdom to conceive it" by which he meant more closely the coterie of "Grand" Whig peers, and their client MPs, who had steered it through Parliament (Erskine May 1861: 1.357). Not everyone was convinced, not even every Grand Whig. Lord Melbourne wondered if it was "the foolishest thing ever done." Peel, at the other end of the political spectrum, thought it simply "vulgar" (Parry 1993: 112). But enough were, or at least enough were worried enough.

No one saw fit to call the 1867 Act "great," still less glorious; least of all those who had supported the 1832 Act. And not many really saw the need. Walter Bagehot expressed his misgivings with considerable force, most notably in an excoriating preface to the second edition of his *English Constitution* in 1872. The second Reform Act was "mischievous and monstrous," betokening "great changes in our politics," changes more of "pervading spirit" than of "particular details." The 1832 Act had merely enfranchised a generation of "minor English shopkeepers." The 1867 Act had done far more, and its consequences were still unknown. But Bagehot was not hopeful. Peering into the future he could see only "calamity" and the further hideous specter of socialism (Bagehot 2001: 194–8, 201–2). Bagehot's influence was of the more allusive variety; he hoped to shape minds. That of his hero, Lord Palmerston, was more immediate. Palmerston controlled the Whig party in Parliament, and he was implacably opposed. "Power in the Hands of the Masses," "Pam" opined, only "throws the Scum of the Community to the Surface" (Bentley 1996: 161). Palmerston died in office in 1865, at which point further reform at least became a possibility, if hardly one that attracted much enthusiasm in or out of Parliament. Lord Derby, who succeeded to the premiership, was certainly not enthused. It was something of a "leap in the dark," he supposed, but an "extended franchise" might bring "contentment" to the nation (Heffer 2013: 402–403). Carlyle was wholly unconvinced, varying the same metaphor in his disparaging pamphlet on the subject entitled *Shooting Niagara: And After?* It sold 4,000 copies in three weeks. He blamed the "conjuror" Disraeli. So did pretty much everyone else.

The provisions of the 1867 Representation of the People Act, which received reluctant royal assent in August 1867, doubled the electorate, raising it to around 3.5 million, enfranchising all borough householders and lodgers paying £10, reducing the property threshold in counties, and rather more notoriously, investing so-called "fancy franchises" which granted extra votes to those who were graduates, had savings of £50 or who might otherwise be esteemed as "professional" gentlemen. It was estimated that where Russell's failed 1866 bill might have added around 600,000 to the electoral roll, Disraeli's added half as much again. It also continued the process of redistribution, disenfranchising fifty-eight constituencies. The math still looked a bit odd, very odd in places. The Lake District had a representation six times that of the north-east. Manchester, with a population of 350,000 and an electorate of 48,000 had three Members, the same number as the boroughs of Knaresborough, Petersfield, and Andover, with a combined electorate of 2,500. But then the second Reform Act was never intended to be a democratizing measure, any more than was the first. As was the case in 1832, the greater significance of the 1867 Act did not lie in ratios of redistribution, at least not directly. It was a different set of numbers that mattered. The election which followed in 1868 produced a Liberal majority of 112; confirmation, if such was needed, that the "age of equipoise" was passed, along with, or so Lord Stanley predicted, the politics of "indolence and corruption" (Parry 1993: 62, 155–159).

The paradox is, of course, familiar; the 1832 Act promised so much, but in practice did so little; the 1867 Act promised to do little, but in the end did so much more. But one thing it did not do, once again, was bring "finality." There would be a third "reform" Act in 1884. It established a uniform franchise for all householders and lodgers and £10 occupiers. The electorate was further increased by around 80 percent; again impressive enough until it is remembered that 40 percent of all men and 100 percent of all women were still disenfranchised. The supplementary 1885 Redistribution Act provided for uniform constituencies with a minimum threshold of 15,000 voters, and leaving just twenty-three seats, those with over 50,000 voters, with a second MP. Gladstone's Home Secretary Harcourt articulated a familiar disquiet, bemoaning a "frightfully democratic measure which I confess appals me." The Radical Joseph Chamberlain boasted that "government of the people by the people" had "at last been effectively secured" (Parry 1993: 287; Wilson 2002: 479). Harcourt was unduly pessimistic, Chamberlain the converse. It was a kind of democracy. But it was hardly radical. Those who savored a more genuine species of democracy would have to wait, for another half century.

It was not, of course, just the franchise that was reformed. The urge to improve imported a collateral urge to legislate for the reform of all kinds of things. Here again the foundations for the later Victorian regulatory state had been laid well before 1837; most immediately in the shape of a new Poor Law in 1834 and the Municipal Corporations Act in 1835. By the end of the decade there was also a Prisons Act and a first Education Act. Among the myriad reforms of the 1840s could be counted a series of employment statutes, including the 1842 Mines Act, the 1844 Factory Act, and the 1847 Ten Hours Act along with two 1844 enactments intended to better regulate the world of finance, the Bank Charter Act and the Companies Act. The same decade also saw the passage of the 1848 Public Health Act, which was intended to add legal force to the various measures recommended in Edwin Chadwick's report on the *Sanitary Conditions of the Labouring Classes*, including the establishment of a system of local health boards under the broader jurisdiction of a National Health Board. The following two decades were perhaps quieter. But further reforms continued, including the Police Act in 1856, which established county police forces, and the 1866 Sanitary Act, which again addressed a number Chadwick's recommendations on draining things. Another Chimney Sweepers Regulation Act in 1864, vigorously championed by Lord Shaftesbury, revisited the seemingly intractable subject of who might be asked to go up what, when, and why.

By the 1870s, however, Parliament seemed ready for another burst of legislative energy. A first Elementary Education Act appeared on the statute book in 1870. Its purpose, according to its energetic pioneer John Forster, being to further "our industrial prosperity" while securing the "safe working of our constitutional system" (Heffer 2013: 440–441).Others would follow in 1876 and 1893, by which time primary education was state regulated and free. It was, as Ruskin acknowledged in his 1867 essay *Time and Tide*, "the first duty of the state" to "see that every child born therein shall be well housed, clothed, fed and educated" (Heffer 2013: 617). Public Health and Licensing Acts appeared in 1872. The reach of the state into matters religious continued with the 1874 Public Worship Regulation Act, followed twenty years later by the passage of the rather more prosaic Fowler's Act which regularized the governance of parish councils in communities of over 300 persons. A Public Health Act of 1875 sought to regulate food standards, street lighting, markets, and the notification of diseases. The great Factory Act of 1878 consolidated a mass of often conflicting factory, health and safety legislation, while also refining, and re-funding, the operation of an existing factory inspectorate. A little later, the 1888 Local Government Act, which established county councils, addressed a different aspect of local governance. And so it went on. The 1871 Royal Commission on Sanitation reached a blunt conclusion. Increased administrative regulation was "essential," the "essence" indeed of "our national vigour" (Best 1979: 59).

Mid- and later Victorian England, Bagehot concluded in slightly understated terms, evidenced "a sort of leaning towards bureaucracy" (Bagehot 2001: 132–133). Bagehot was approving, if hesitantly. Others were less so, finding the specter of socialism, which Bagehot raised in his 1872 Preface, still more hideous. Albert Venn Dicey was viscerally opposed to the advance of "collectivism," and more particularly still to the shaping of a distinctive branch of administrative law designed, in his perception, to service it (Dicey 1914: lxiv). Administrative law courts, of the kind which could be found in France, hardly much of a recommendation, were a species of prerogative court fundamentally "opposed to those habits of equality before the law which had long been essential characteristics of English institutions" (Dicey 1959: 373, 379–380). The first annual Trades Union Congress had met in 1868, followed in due course by the first employment legislation intended to regulate union activities. The 1871 and 1875 Trade Union Acts legalized peaceful picketing for the first time, while also safeguarding the essential features of collective bargaining. In 1882, W.H. Smith was moved to admit that the country was "drifting into radical socialism very fast indeed" (Bentley 2001: 153). In *Man Versus the State*, published a couple of years later in 1884, Herbert Spencer compared the rise of the Victorian regulatory state to the "tyranny" of "ancient Peru." Spencer was more especially troubled by the Factory Acts and the prevalence of municipal libraries; both of which, he supposed, heralded the "coming slavery" of socialism (Gilmour 1993: 174).

Dicey was not then alone in his opposition to "collectivism" and the idea of the regulatory state; far from it. At the same time he was prepared to accept the case for certain, evidently necessary, reforms in the law. Dicey's juristic mind was shaped by his mentor John Austin, author of the acclaimed positivist treatise *The Province of Jurisprudence Determined*, published in 1832; for which reason, in the matter of legal reform at least, he found himself standing alongside any number of Benthamite disciples. But it was not merely the Benthamites. James Fitzjames Stephen expended much intellectual energy on repelling the "brutilitarians." He spent much of the rest urging the case for the codification of the English criminal law. "It was," he argued in 1872, fresh from having re-written the Indian criminal law, "a new experience to an English lawyer to see how easy these matters are when they are stripped of mystery." The "only thing," he continued, "which prevents English people from seeing that law is really one of the most interesting and instructive studies in the world, is that English lawyers have thrown it into a shape which can only be described as studiously repulsive" (Heffer 2013: 766). It was certainly an impression likely to be shared by the many readers of Charles Dickens; from the chronic procedural dysfunction portrayed in *Bleak House*, to the abused wives and prostitutes found in *Oliver Twist* and *Dombey and Son*, to the myriad egregious lawyers and procedural injustices scattered across the canon. And the picture was little more reassuring in the novels of Thackeray and Eliot and all the sensational novelists. It would have been difficult to put down a Victorian novel without thinking that there was indeed something very wrong with the way that the law worked in nineteenth-century England.

The legal reformer then came in many shapes, some more radical, most less so. Fitzjames Stephen was certainly of the more conservative variety. Mid- and late Victorian England was full of such men, and women, self-proclaimed "conservative" Liberals; supportive of reform if it was designed to make something work better, disinclined to support reform if it was based on nothing more than ideology. Anthony Trollope was another. So, as Asa Briggs famously noted, was Walter Bagehot. And so was Dicey, for whom the necessity of legal reform outweighed any visceral suspicion of the idea. As the century had dawned, Dicey confirmed in his 1914 *Lectures on Public Opinion*, the English common law had been chaotic, resembling nothing other than "the most fanciful dreams of *Alice in Wonderland*" (Dicey 1914: 92). Procedure was a particular failing. So "patent" had its "faults" become by the 1830s that reform was unavoidable. Those who had led the way in legal reform during the 1830s and 1840s, Brougham, Romilly and Peel were all "men of common sense," and "all at bottom individualists" (Dicey 1914: 168–169). In this rather tempered spirit Dicey thus approved a succession of Evidence Acts, Common Law Procedure Acts and, of course, the Judicature Acts. He was positively enthused by the 1857 Matrimonial Causes Act which had established a distinct Divorce Court; a "triumph of individualistic liberalism and common justice" (Dicey 1914: 347).

The 1857 Act addressed an obviously engendered kind of injustice; the "subjection," as John Stuart Mill famously put it, of the married woman. It would be followed by two further statutes intended to address the same. An 1870 Married Women's Property Act represented a first step towards abrogating the ancient common law doctrine of coverture which denied the need for wives to enjoy a distinct legal personality. It was only a small step, introducing the equitable doctrine of separate uses to permit wives to keep their earnings, and to enhance their heritable rights. A second 1884 Married Women's Property Act finally aligned the married woman with the *feme sole*, establishing separate rights to sue as well as be sued, to own, and to buy and sell property. Of course the Matrimonial Property Acts were targeted rather obviously at particular women; those who were married and who had property. But this did not diminish their significance, not least in regard to broader campaigns to address the "question of women," in both their public and their private lives. Aside from the issue of matrimonial property, these broader movements engaged collateral issues such as spousal violence and female education along with most specific campaigns for targeted legal reforms, of which the eventual repeal of the Contagious Diseases Acts in 1886 was perhaps the most striking.

As we have already noted, the precise nature of the "question of women" was not always clear. Clarity, however, came with focus, on the more specific issue of female suffrage; as did a greater sense of injustice and urgency. "What is the good of a constitutional policy," Christabel Pankhurst asked in her *Votes for Women* published in 1911, "to those who have no constitutional weapon?" (Bentley 1996: 335) Suffrage campaigners had agonized about the extent to which their campaign should or should not be lawful for forty years. In 1913 Emily Wilding died under the king's horse at the Epsom Derby, by which time captured suffragettes were being force fed under the provisions of the notorious "Cat and Mouse Acts." Five years later, the 1918 Reform Act enfranchised all adults over the age twenty-one, male and female. Finally, there was "finality," of a kind. It was not, however, the kind that Dicey, who had joined the Men's Anti-Suffrage League, particularly relished. And it was certainly not the kind that would have earned Queen Victoria's approval. The very idea of female "rights" was a "mad, wicked folly," one which neglected every sense of womanly feeling and propriety. The subject, she confided in correspondence, "makes the Queen so furious that she cannot contain herself. God created men and women different—then let them remain each in their own person" (Strachey 1971: 238).

Victoria was often furious, and rarely shy in making her opinions known, and as readers of Lewis Carroll's *Alice* stories knew there was nothing the Queen of Hearts enjoyed more than bossing people around. But there were darker moments of self-doubt too: "I am every day more convinced that we women, if we are to be good women, feminine, amiable, and domestic, are not fitted to reign" (Arnstein 2003: 69). Bossy, opinionated, but also a bit of a ditherer, Victoria tended to vacillate about a lot of things. The place of women in public society was just one. Turning up and opening things was another; at least it was during the years following the death of her beloved Albert in late

1861. For a short while England had understood. Mourning was becoming. But then it became tiresome. When the *Times* ran an April Fools' headline which suggested that the Queen was about to "break her protracted seclusion," Victoria, against all advice, determined to publish a sober contradiction in the same paper; alongside a doctor's note. "The Queen," the letter confirmed, "heartily appreciates the desire of her subjects to see her." But, it continued:

> There are other and higher duties than those of mere representation which are now thrown upon the Queen, alone and unassisted—duties which she cannot neglect without injury to the public service, which weigh increasingly upon her, overwhelming her with work and anxiety. (Strachey 1971: 184)

But she was wrong. There were no higher duties. Eventually after much cajoling, chiefly on the part of her beloved Disraeli, who even went so far as to make her an Empress by virtue of the 1876 Royal Titles Act, Victoria relented. Representation, she came to appreciate, however reluctantly, was everything. No one appreciated this better than Walter Bagehot, who placed the monarch at the apex of "dignified" aspect of the constitution he depicted in his essays which comprised *The English Constitution*. The necessary complement was the "efficient" aspect, the institutions and mechanisms of government represented most obviously in the offices of the Cabinet and the Prime Minister. In a famous passage Bagehot had observed, tongue only partly in cheek, that:

> The use of the Queen, in a dignified capacity, is incalculable. Without her in England, the present English government would fail and pass away. Most people when they read that the Queen walked on the slopes at Windsor—that the Prince of Wales went to the Derby—have imagined that too much thought and prominence were given to little things. But they have been in error; and it is nice to trace how the actions of a retired widow and an unemployed youth become of such importance. (Bagehot 2001: 34)

It was the failing and passing away that Bagehot feared. In time, he would be proved wrong; though also right. He was right insofar as the monarchy has remained an essentially aesthetic element of the constitution, its primary contribution being to open things and to wave a lot. But he was wrong to have worried quite so much. By the time of her death in 1901 Victoria was inordinately popular; Queen of England and lots of other places too, Empress of India, and mother of the nation. It was why, of course, there was such a sense of loss. Monarchs who have reigned for a long time tend to be missed rather more. Longevity enhances the sense of stability, tightening the bond of mutual reassurance which defines the relationship between constitutional sovereign and satisfied subject. It is why, a century on, after six decades of Queen Elizabeth II, no one seriously considers the possibility of an alternative; even if at times the prospect of Charles III is greeted with much the same enthusiasm as that which accompanied Prince Bertie along the nave of Westminster Abbey in spring 1901.

It is also why the sovereign continues to serve as Governor of the Church of England; not because the English are especially God-fearing, or even bother to go to church that much, but because the presence of the Established Church helps to tighten the same essential bond. Interestingly, while she could be chary in regard to performing many of her prerogative responsibilities, such as opening Parliament or dissolving it, Victoria relished the opportunity to appoint senior churchmen. She always liked appointing people to things, ministers to government, colonels to regiments, ladies to bedchambers. She also sensed a higher calling. Her opinion that "obedience to the laws & to the sovereign is obedience to a higher Power" imported a distinctly Jacobean tone as, to an extent, did her collateral supposition, that a "disbelief in God leads to a lack of reverence for those in authority, including parents" (Hibbert 2001: 201). Moreover, Victoria never seemed to question her faith. Unfortunately, as the century progressed it became ever-more apparent that many of her subjects were finding it something of a struggle, especially those who had begun to read their Darwin and their Huxley. A crisis of faith appeared to be a necessary consequence of progress. "Unbelief," as Carlyle termed it, had become "the Victorian disease" (Himmelfarb 2007: 45). The parlous state of the church, and of its churches, had impelled Peel's 1834 Ecclesiastical Commission to address some of the more prosaic concerns, leaky chancels, perceived abuses, declining congregations; in large part successfully. But there were also deeper, more elevated, concerns. In summer 1833, John Henry Newman published the first of a series of *Tracts for the Times*. Another eighty-nine would appear over the following eight years, many questioning the very idea of an Established Church; a "direct disavowal of the sovereignty of God" it might be supposed (Woodward 1962: 512–513).

Of course, many nineteenth-century Englishmen and women followed Charles Dickens's lead, settling for the reassurance of the national faith without paying too much heed to the religious rules of the institutional church. In an obituary notice published in *Fraser's Magazine* in July 1870 it was noted that Dickens "spent no thought on religious doctrines or religious reforms but regarded the Sermon on the Mount as good teaching, had a regard for the village church and churchyard, and quarrelled with nothing but intolerance" (Briggs 1959: 464–465). Literature provided consolation, and reassurance. Trollope's tales of life in the parishes and cloisters of Barsetshire sold in their thousands. But it also allowed for expressions of anguish. While so many thousands of his contemporaries wandered the halls of the Crystal Palace in gaping admiration in summer 1851, Matthew Arnold invited his readers to contemplate:

The Sea of Faith
Was once, too, at the full, and round earth's shore
Lay like the folds of a bright girdle furled,
But now I only hear
Its melancholy long withdrawing roar,
Retreating to the breath
Of the night-wind down the vast edges drear
And naked shingles of the world.
The poem, famously, closes with a final invitation:
And here we are as on a darkling plain
Swept with confused alarms of struggle and flight,
Where ignorant armies clash by night. (Arnold 1986: 136)

It was an invitation which could not be declined. The Victorian age was an age of confusion, of doubt and reaction, precisely because it was an age of progress and indeed reform. But it was also an age of choices too; no matter how distressing.

FIGURE 0.4 Matthew Arnold (1822–1883) English poet and critic. Original Publication: People Disc – HB0331. Source: Photo by Rischgitz / Getty Images.

CHAPTER ONE

Justice

Visual Representations of the Subjects of the Law

LINDA MULCAHY

INTRODUCTION

No history of law and culture in the age of reform would be complete without an exploration of the role that the image played in a criminal justice system largely designed to manage the criminality of a semi-literate population. More specifically, histories of law and visual culture in this era would be seriously lacking without an examination of the function of the photograph in the work of the prisons, the newly professionalized police service and reformed courts. The invention of the photograph in the early nineteenth century quite literally changed the way people saw crime and criminals and the photographic conventions established during this period continue to dominate much contemporary thinking about how criminals are expected to look and be. The photograph invaded the workings of the legal system in ways that had never been achieved by other visual media such as the map, oil painting, or sketch. This medium has been used to create documentary images of the arrested and incarcerated, official and covert images of the courts in action, the ritual and pageantry associated with law, abuses of power in campaigns for legal reform as well as challenging long held views about what constitutes credible evidence. It is not an exaggeration to say that in the 179 years since a photograph was first produced, photography has revolutionized the way we conceptualize and consume law and legal process. Viewed in this way, the mugshot can be seen as emblematic of the new technologies of power that have become possible in the criminal justice system since the nineteenth century.

For a significant period in the age of reform there is no history of law and photography to be told. The photograph was not invented until 1839 following the ground-breaking efforts of Louis Daguerre and Fox Talbot and it was some time before taking a photograph was anything less than a complex process (Edwards 2006). In the decades immediately after its creation cameras continued to be cumbersome and the process of production was

---

The author's thanks go to Ian Ward, Emma Rowden, Katherine Biber, Peter Doyle, Patrizia di Bello for their help with formulating the arguments expressed in this chapter.

so drawn out that the implications of photography for the practice of law were difficult to fully comprehended or explore. Despite these early setbacks, it is significant that as soon as cameras became smaller and lighter, and the process of producing prints faster and more reliable, law was one of the first disciplines to realize the full potential of this new medium. Count Charles Tanneguy Duchatel, the interior minister in charge of the French Police in the mid-nineteenth century argued that Daguerre's invention was so important in assisting the surveillance of criminals that he should be granted a life pension (Lashmar 2013).[1]

The significance of the invention of the photograph has not gone unnoticed by scholars, though it is fair to say that it is art historians rather than lawyers who have written the most regularly cited works on the interface of law and photography. Seminal accounts in the field have commonly focused on the mugshot and have tended to be grounded in a Foucauldian understanding of the emergence of new technologies of power designed to produce docile bodies (Sekula 1986; Tagg 1988, 2009; Edwards 2006; Finn 2009). Viewed from this perspective, mugshots showing compliant prisoners of the state, provide an excellent, if not an ideal, exemplar of the bio-politics of power in modernity. Mugshots in the nineteenth century became part of a sophisticated tracking system which allowed bodies to be observed across time and place. Throughout the world they also prompted the need for, and were closely associated with, another major phenomenon linked to the age of reform: the archive. People arrested by the police or sent to prison in the Victorian era were the first to experience a new form of multiple incarceration by the state which involved physical capture by the police, mechanical capture by the camera, bureaucratic capture by archives and synoptic surveillance in rogues' galleries.[2] The advent of the mugshot allowed the bodies of criminals to be classified, analyzed, and ordered in the absence of the person.

These seminal accounts of law and photography remain compelling but the aim of this chapter is to disrupt them by focusing on the possibility that the "studios" in which mugshots were taken also had the potential to be sites of resistance or counter-capture. In an attempt to explore this alternative history of the relationship between law and photography, the emphasis here is on the *failure* of state surveillance methods to produce docile and disciplined subjects. Rather than restricting the study of mugshots to an analysis of the increasingly subtle ways in which power was wielded over criminal bodies, the approach adopted is to pay attention to the symbiotic relationship between power and resistance that mugshots reveal. This interrelationship of power and resistance was clearly recognized by Foucault (1980, 1988, 1991) but rarely emerges as an important, or well-evidenced phenomena, in existing scholarship. By looking at a variety of ways in which the purpose of the mugshot was subverted, I hope to reveal the ways in which surviving photographs of suspects and criminals circumvent expectations of them by hinting at agency and what Sekula (1986) has called polyphonic testimony.

In the sections that follow I aim to make four key arguments. First, that everyday and mundane acts of resistance have not received the attention they deserve. Secondly, that evidence of resistance is there to be found by those interested in looking for it. Thirdly, that resistance is often more subtle than imagined by scholars interested in power, resistance and agency. Fourthly, that mugshots can also be seen as constituting an artistic and cultural artifact with an afterlife, rather than just a sociological phenomenon of only historical interest. I suggest that these arguments have important implications for the ways in we conceptualize resistance, look for it and use it in discussions of the criminal body.

DOMINANT NARRATIVES OF CAPTURE AND CONTAINMENT

The possibility of producing mugshots of those arrested and incarcerated by the police and prison authorities provided a solution to an identification problem that had emerged in the wake of changing attitudes towards crime. Branding and tattooing of criminals had become unpopular by the Victorian era and contemporary jurists and criminal anthropologists became concerned that repeat offenders were exploiting the anonymity of the new unmarked criminal body. The result was that the task of identifying repeat offenders was rendered problematic for expanding and increasingly professionalized law enforcement agencies. At the same time rapid urbanization made it difficult for the police to commit the characteristics of the increasing number of criminals in a modern city to memory. The burgeoning number of strangers living in close proximity in the new industrial centers was exacerbated by the diminishing value of dress, accent, and appearance to convey social status at a glance. The production of mugshots provided the ideal solution for these identification difficulties and helped to defeat the problems caused by the regular adoption of disguises and aliases by recalcitrant criminals. The mugshot allowed police and prison authorities to develop a new way of controlling risks to the body politic by controlling risky bodies.

The French began to make daguerreotypes[3] of prisoners as early as 1841, though the earliest mugshot still in existence was taken by Belgian officials in 1843 (New Zealand Police Museum 2015).[4] In Britain, the police employed their first professional police photographer in the 1840s (Tagg 1988; Phillips et al. 1997) and the mugshot gained legal recognition with the passing of the Habitual Criminals Act 1869 (Pavlich 2009).[5] This Act required that the British police had to attain photographs of all criminals sentenced to at least one month's imprisonment, together with finger prints and recording of other details such as hair and eye color. Prison Governors were also responsible for distributing this information to those responsible for crime prevention. From 1884, the Criminal Records Office published many of these details in *The Police Gazette* which was circulated daily to all police forces in Great Britain (The National Archives 2013).

Despite the lively interest in photography among the police, procedures varied considerably across police districts. Photographic records of prisoners were not common until the 1860s and the passing of the Habitual Criminal Act (Sekula 1986; Edwards 2006; Lashmar 2013). Variation in styles during the period seem more common than is generally acknowledged, but it is still the case that certain mugshot conventions became associated with criminality.[6] Most notable among these was the full frontal upper body and side view. As Lashmar (2013) reminds us:

> At its simplest, it is a photograph of a person. We can immediately recognise that it is a police photograph, or as they are more colloquially known, a mugshot, as key institutional signs are there: the deadpan expression of the subject, a vertical measurement stick for showing height, the neutral background … but what is consistently signified is the person has been 'arrested' or has been a criminal, a signal we recognise even if we do not recognise the subject. (p. 60)

The irony is that these poses were heavily influenced by the conventions of privately commissioned domestic photographs in the Victorian era,[7] though the mugshot was always destined to be an accusing image. It rested on the suspicion that those apprehended had committed a crime and an assumption that they were likely to re-offend (Lashmar 2013).

This is a change in association which Sekula (1986) has labelled a shift in portraiture conventions from honorific to repressive.

Most readers would no doubt be able to imagine a typical mugshot without needing a visual prompt. A recent exhibition by the Welcome Trust displayed a host of typical sepia-printed head-and-shoulder shots of criminals staring directly into the camera and holding up their hands to show tattoos or missing digits.[8] Photograph albums containing frontal mugshots of untried prisoners dating from 1897 held at the UK National Archives also provide evidence of the conventions we expect of this genre of identification photography. These albums contain hundreds of images of the head and shoulders of suspected and convicted criminals sitting in the same position, wearing identical prison clothes, and even holding their matching jackets in the same way to reveal their hands.[9] Other surviving nineteenth-century archives show mugshots accompanied by other signs of the criminal such as crime numbers[10] or accompanying text detailing their offense and physical characteristics.

Calls for standardization of pose are generally traced back to early proponents of the mugshot who were interested in regularity for very different reasons. Among these, the work of Bertillon, the French police office and biometrics researcher, was prompted by a pragmatic interest in creating sufficiently detailed archives to facilitate the recapture of particular offenders. For him, the minimization of difference in pose facilitated the identification of distinguishing features.[11] Others focused on the use of standardization in revealing typologies of all criminals organized according to certain physical characteristics.[12] In Italy, Lombroso famously used photographs of prisoners to illustrate his theories about the "criminal type" (Rafter 2009) and in England, the statistician Galton (1879) used composite photographs of numerous convicts to identify what was considered to be the biologically determined average offender. The growing popularity of criminal anthropology, psychiatry, phrenology, criminology, and physiognomy were all fueled by the invention of the photograph and served to render the production of the mugshot photograph increasingly legitimate. Mugshots were commonly used in the construction and illustration of seminal research publications which contended that it was possible to read criminality from the face. The result was the emergence of a host of theories linking the propensity to habitually commit crime with physical traits, heredity, and retarded evolution (Finn 2009; Rafter 2009).

The extensive archives of mugshots created by police forces throughout the nineteenth-century system allowed the bodies of criminals captured on film to be analyzed, surveyed, and shared across police forces. In an interesting reversal of panoptical polarity, the involvement of the general public in surveillance also allowed the many to watch the few. In 1854, the Swiss police began circulating photographs of known criminals to the public and the New York police department opened its first "rogues' gallery" to the public in 1864, followed by Germany in 1864, Russia in 1867 and England in 1870 (Nichols 2010). Unlike the consumers of middle-class portraiture who engaged with photography to enjoy the likenesses of loved ones, rogues' galleries transformed the strangers who attended them into emotionally anesthetized and remote spectators of the degradation of others.[13] By actively involving the public in the search for the criminal type, it also rendered spectators complicit in the wider project of constructing and re-constructing criminal identities. As Edwards (2006) has so neatly opined "Some people were authorised to look; others were looked down upon" (p. 22).

Rather than seeing the mugshot as an index of truth or pre-determined criminal personality, contemporary scholars are more prone to see it as part of a new system of signs which associated degeneracy with particular categories of people. Particular emphasis has been placed on the ways in which the mugshot became enmeshed in a class-based binary of normal versus deviant (Sekula 1986; Tagg 1988; Phillips et al. 1997; Finn 2009). Regardless of the many claims of early criminologists to scientific method, photographs of the incarcerated are now seen as a means to socially construct a type which was organically distinct from its bourgeois observers (Sekula 1986); a mirror of what the elite feared might reside within them. It has been convincingly argued that, far from it being a privilege to be pictured as had been the case in the pre-photographic era, the mugshot became the burden of new categories of sitter drawn largely from the poor, the sick, working people, women, and colonized. For Tagg (1988), "[s]ubjected to the scrutinising gaze, forced to emit signs, yet cut off from the command of meaning, such groups were represented as, and wishfully rendered, incapable of speaking, acting or organising for themselves" (p. 11).

Surveillance techniques that were later to become common in England were often tested on colonial subjects (Edge 2004), leading MacSuibhne and Martin (2005) to comment that British colonies often served as laboratories for new technologies of power. The taking of mugshots in prisons was routine in Ireland ten years before it became common practice in England and was even extended to untried prisoners in the 1860s. Others have drawn attention to the fact that early fingerprint techniques, which the English objected to as an invasion of their privacy were pioneered by English colonial powers in India (McDermid 2015). The close association of the mugshot with the disempowered subject is also revealed by the initial reluctance of London's Metropolitan Police to insist on the production of mugshots of the many middle-class suffragettes who chose to draw attention to their cause by going to prison (Mulcahy 2015).

For some, these distinctions were increasingly important to the ideological hegemony of a capitalist project that relied on a hierarchical division of labor (Sekula 1986). In Foucauldian terms, the mugshot created and reflected the production of docile bodies for the industrial age which were watched, categorized, and stigmatized. As Marsh (1999) has argued:

> In postmodern criticism the camera has often been seen as an apparatus of control, one of the surveillance mechanisms of the state, in the service of its institutions and immersed in its technologies of power. The metaphor of the camera as a weapon, as analysed by Susan Sontag in the early 1970s, describes an unbalanced and non-reciprocal relationship between photographer and subject. One is the hunter, the other the prey; one is the agent, the other the victim. (p. 114)

Viewed from this perspective, the police and prison "studio" can be seen as a monological site in which mastery was asserted over the criminal by the state on their terms and subjects were transformed into objects capable of being stored in filing cabinets (Edwards 1990: 64).

THE POSSIBILITY OF RESISTANCE

There is clearly much evidence to suggest that the mugshot is best understood as a new tool of surveillance and identity attribution but it may be that we should be skeptical of the lure of uncritical acceptance of this popular explanation and the singularity of vision it imposes on our understanding. It could be argued that existing accounts of this photographic genre fail to take sufficient account of the complexities of how identity politics is performed, and pays insufficient attention to the ways in which prisoners might have contested a paradigm in which the agents of the state were the primary orchestrators of identity formation. In his critique of theories of panoptic control, Boyne (2000) encourages us to look for counter-narratives which might contribute to the adjustment of the Foucauldian paradigm relied on so heavily in the existing literature.[14] There is a danger that this stance reflects a misreading of Foucault (1980, 1988) who clearly recognized that there is no relation of power without the means of escape or possible flight. For Foucault, power could both constitute subjects as well as disciplining them. In a similar vein, de Certeau (1984) argues that we should be more sensitive to the "tactics" used by the marginalized and how these operate in the gaps of power. This encourages us to look for resistance in the minute, mundane, and obscure practices of the everyday (Cowan 2004). Viewed through this lens, resistance is not seen as being exterior to power but as operating in conjunction with it.

With this alternative project in mind, the challenge to be responded to is Edward's (1990) suggestion that the supposed monological photographic site of the prison or police station is actually capable of being a dialogical site, in which the objects of police photography reclaim subjectivity and are shown to be capable of acquiring autonomy. In a similar vein, Tagg (1988) has acknowledged that it was as a strategy of representation that the mugshot had been most successful and that its significance as a strategy of control has been much exaggerated. Sekula (1986) has also argued that not all the realisms associated with the mugshot will have played into the hands of the police. For him, closer attention to the ambiguous messages conveyed by some mugshots allows us to recognize the possibility of agency and the hint of personal testimony which can prevent the marginalization of subversive narratives in the canon. The problem is that most studies of the mugshot, including those conducted by the authors referred to in this paragraph, have focused on seeking out evidence of docility rather than resistance.

Empirical accounts of opposition are largely absent from seminal accounts of the history of law and photography. Edwards (1990) does allude to debate in nineteenth-century photographic journals about the prevalence of prisoners resisting having their likeness taken. Meier and Wolfensberger (1998) have also argued that considerable attention was paid to the possibility of an individual distorting their appearance while being photographed in 1850s Switzerland. Indeed, such was the concern that this would happen that the federal prosecutor was given special powers to discipline subjects until a "suitable" photograph was obtained. Others have asserted that criminals subjected to the camera would often twist, turn, and change their facial expressions (Brynes 1866; Finn 2009). But detailed case studies of such activity remain scarce. Tagg's (1988) much respected work on *The Burden of Representation* carries a woodcut by Sir Samuel Luke Fildes (1873) on its cover which shows a prisoner resisting arrest, but this is not discussed further in the book and his section on "resistance" is limited to three pages of more abstract debate on the topic.[15] His later book on *The Disciplinary Frame* includes a photograph of a prisoner resisting having his photograph taken, which comes from a book by Byrnes (1866), but Finn (2009: 2) claims that the photograph was probably staged. It would seem that while the possibility of resistance is readily acknowledged, reliable photographic evidence of it is sadly lacking in academic accounts of the subject.

Assessing the incidence of resistance is not without its methodological problems. Many thousands of the photographs taken by the police and prisons in the nineteenth century survive, but it is likely that numerous photographs evidencing resistance would have been destroyed as a failed attempt at producing a mugshot. Likewise, those tasked with the job of compiling albums and rogues' galleries are unlikely to have included photographs which questioned the legitimacy of the exercise. The rarity of overt signs of subversion make those images that have survived of special interest.

EVIDENCE OF RESISTANCE

Some of the most obvious acts of resistance documented in mugshots were carried out as part of a concerted political campaign to resist the authority of the state. By way of example, there is evidence of an aversion on the part of Irish republicans to having their likeness taken in police stations and prisons, especially once it was realized that mugshots would be used to recapture those suspected of terrorist activities. Analysis of records in the National Archives of Ireland demonstrate that Fenian prisoners were generally prepared to comply with the demands made of them by responding to questions from prison authorities and stripping for a physical examination. Some prisoners attempted to use an alias or refused to choose a religion,[16] but such instances appear to have been relatively unusual. Attempts to take mugshots proved much more controversial. From the time the practice was adopted, some political prisoners refused to sit and in the aftermath of the Fenian uprising of 1867 these instance increased to at least 5 percent of the general prison intake (Mac Suibhne and Martin 2005).

In time, Republicans became intensely aware of the power of the photographic record in the construction of histories of political struggle in Ireland (Edge 2004). Baylis (2009) has argued that their success in avoiding having their photographs taken while free meant that Special Branch often had to rely on photographs and descriptions produced by nationalist sympathizers when trying to identify them in the run up to arrest. The fact that these were all that was available meant that photographs taken for another purpose and imbued with a plethora of celebratory and familial representational codes have infiltrated into the official state archive.[17] She concludes that the peculiarity of Ireland's position within the Empire meant that the surveillance paradigm relied on by Tagg and others becomes fractured when looked at in a colonial context.

The refusal of English suffragettes to comply with requests for mugshots provides another valuable case study of the ways in which conventions about the form of the mugshot were capable of being subverted in the interests of an organized political campaign (Mulcahy 2015). The pressure on prison authorities to obtain mugshots of suffragettes increased considerably after the passing of the Prisoners (Temporary Discharge for Ill-Heath) Act 1913. This allowed for the temporary discharge of suffragettes who had been weakened through hunger strikes or force feeding and their readmission once they had physically recovered. Suffragettes such as Evelyn Manesta refused to comply with requests to have an identification photograph taken. Visual archives show Manesta with her hands in her pockets deliberately screwing up her face (see Figure 1.1). Such was the success of their protest that the Metropolitan Police were forced to take a series of rather unsatisfactory clandestine surveillance photographs of suffragettes from a prison van parked in the exercise yard of Holloway prison (Mulcahy, 2015). The unconventional nature of the resulting photographs, which clearly did not comply with established mugshot conventions, remain a permanent testimony of these women's refusal to obey.

Evidence of other, more everyday, instances of resistance by individuals who are not part of a collective political campaign also exists within nineteenth-century archives for those who choose to look for them. The struggles represented in these mugshots is often violent. Fildes image of "The Unwilling Sitter" reproduced in the work of Tagg (1988,

FIGURE 1.1 Evelyn Manesta by Criminal Record Office (original print), 1914. Source: The National Archives, ref. PCOM7/252. Reproduced with the kind permission of the National Archives.

2009), Edwards (1990) and Finn (2009) shows no less than seven policemen holding down a prisoner. Similarly, the photograph of "The Inspector's Model" reproduced in Byrnes (1866) shows four police men using brute force to restrain a resisting prisoner in handcuffs by holding his four limbs in place and forcing back his head.[18] Phillips et al.'s (1997) book on police pictures also includes two images of prisoners having their head held in place while they close their eyes.[19] There is also evidence of similar images from the collection of mugshots held by the Greater Manchester Police. Two examples from this collection are shown at Figures 1.2 and 1.3 below.

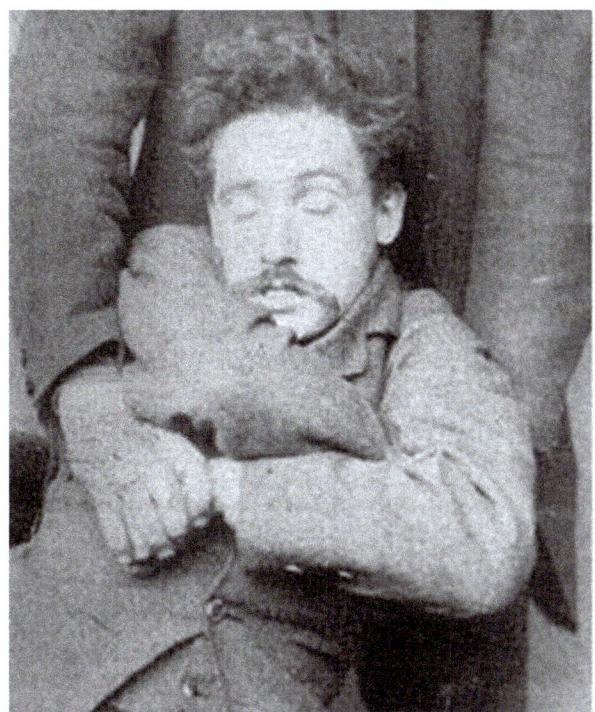

FIGURE 1.2 "Paddy the Devil." Source: Courtesy of Greater Manchester Police Museum & Archives.

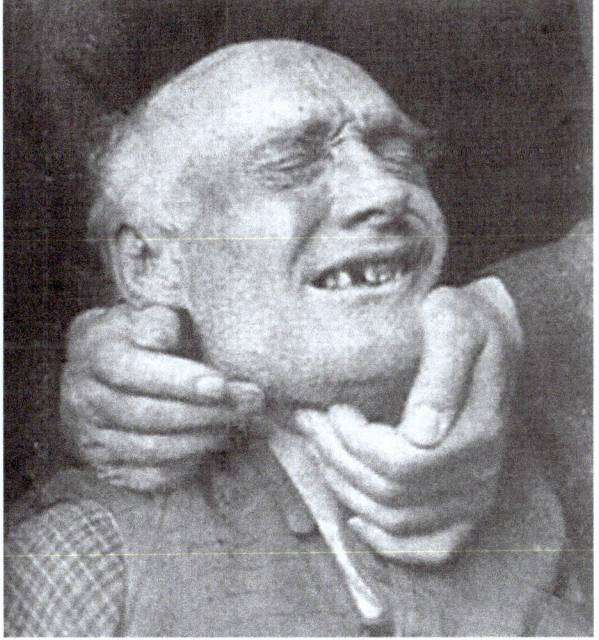

FIGURE 1.3 "Thomas Murphy: The Reluctant Sitter." Source: Courtesy of Greater Manchester Police Museum & Archives.

Even when mugshots have been produced without violence, it does not necessarily mean that free consent on the part of the sitter has been given. A close look at surviving archives makes clear that construction of the non-violent encounter as one in which the photographer "takes" a photograph which the sitter "gives" is deserving of more exploration. Given the power dynamics at play in the prison or police station it can be assumed that many prisoners would have felt compelled to comply with what they were asked to do for fear of retribution. Writing about the practices adopted in the American police force in the final years of the nineteenth century Byrnes (1866: 53–4) makes clear that while resistance was initially common, criminals soon learnt to comply when they realized that the police would obtain a photograph by one means or another, however strong the objections.

These practices do not necessarily mean that prisoners were always docile or compliant and control over the face they "make" for the camera offers us opportunities to challenge the prevalence of docile subjects on the official record. Sitters were surely aware that even producing subtle but visible signs of lack of respect were the opposite of the code or discourse expected in such situations. This allows us to see resistance as more than a mere physical confrontation and to look for agency as being present in much more

FIGURE 1.4 Mugshot of Michael Lavery, reproduced with the kind permission of Tyne and Wear Archives and Museums.

understated forms of deflection and improvised evasion. In their account of everyday resistance Silbey and Ewing (1998) argue that: "[m]uch like courting a new lover, a certain ambiguity of intention is built into the act so as to allow for disavowal or retreat if the situation requires it" (p. 185). These small gestures also serve to reflect the creative resistance of ordinary people attempting to reappropriate visual codes and symbols in the official record anticipated by de Certeau (1984).

Surviving nineteenth-century mugshots regularly attest to the resistance of sitters if re-interpreted in this light. Inspector Byrnes much-cited 1866 exposition of the value of the mugshot contains numerous photographs of prisoners who, while not struggling, have their eyes shut or have chosen to subvert their gaze.[20] Archives commonly contain multiple examples of prisoners exhibiting docility in the guise of looking worn down, resigned, shamed, dazed, frightened, and even surprised, but alongside these images there are those who look belligerent, cocky, proud, angry, frustrated, and contemptuous. The image of Michael Lavery shown at Figure 1.4 does not suggest that he has been wholly captured by the camera. Instead it hints at the distain and contempt of the sitter.[21] In their study of Irish Republicans Suibhne and Martin (2005) reproduce images of prisoners laughing into the camera and Doyle's (2007) collection of police photographs contains several examples of prisoners adopting assertive, dismissive, and even heroic poses. These images disrupt the notion of the hunter and hunted alluded to by Marsh (1991) above. While the body has undoubtedly been captured by agents of the state, these images suggest that the spirit has not and that the success of the hunter is far from being certain.

Attempts to reclaim agency are also evidenced by the activity of the incarcerated once free. While the militant suffragettes discussed above objected vehemently to having their photographs taken in prison, they produced numerous celebratory photographs of former prisoners in prison dress once freed. Models of prison cells and staged postcards of suffragettes in prison were regularly produced for exhibitions and for sale (see, for instance, Atkinson 1996: 37, 69). In contrast to the rather ramshackle photographs of suffragettes taken by the Metropolitan Police, these alternative images were produced to the strict specification of the leaders of the suffragette movement. They portray them willingly wearing copies of the prison clothes they had objected to putting on when imprisoned. The crisp linen version depicted in surviving photographs have been made by members of the movement rather than the prison authorities. The worried and distracted facial expressions of the suffragettes in the clandestine photographs taken when in Holloway are replaced by assertive poses in these celebratory images. In their alternative representations of prison, it is law enforcers who are the absent aggressors while the suffragettes are portrayed as vulnerable, at times even angelic. In this way, these deviant objects of male bourgeois fear transformed themselves into sympathetic and political subjects in the public sphere (Mulcahy 2015).

Budd et al.'s (2010) photographs of twelve wrongly imprisoned men who served between eighteen months and twenty-six years in Dallas prisons for crimes they did not commit fall into the same category. The photographs of these men successfully convicted for rape, kidnapping, robbery, murder, and assault which focus on their resilience rather than their criminality. They show the men as they chose to be seen: smartly dressed and clean with the unconventional props they chose to have with them in the revisionist "mugshots" they choreographed after their release. These props include copies of the Bible, the Koran, a hat, a cigarette, and the legal notes relating to their case rather than the prison garb, measuring sticks, and crime number plates used when mugshots were taken by state authorities. The men appear contemplative and strong, collected in the images they have control over. They rarely smile.

RE-DISCOVERING THE MUGSHOT

Nineteenth-century mugshots were part of a powerful visual code that constructed those captured as deviant and docile. But any debate about the formation of cultural identity is problematic if seen as a stable and fixed concept rooted in the notion of the original (Marsh 1999). Released from the influence of prevailing views about the relationship between crime and bodily characteristics propounded by early commentators, it becomes possible for contemporary audiences to circumvent the burden of Victorian representational codes (Galton 1879). This notion of the rediscovery of the mugshot is both literal and conceptual. Discarded by police forces across the world only to reemerge in second-hand book shops and auctions, albums of mugshots are increasingly being refound by twenty-first century collectors and used for very different purpose to those they were created for. This burgeoning interest in mugshots among collectors, museums, galleries, and the academy[22] attests to a reconceptualization of the meanings attributed to mugshots in which crime is more readily associated with disadvantage and lack of opportunity.

It is striking how frequently present-day writers are moved to empathize with those who stare out at them from nineteenth-century mugshots. Twenty-first-century commentators are more likely to reflect on how mugshots show people at their most desolate, having their weaknesses and fallibility exposed in a public place or to view their obvious disadvantage as the key to their behavior.[23] These reinterpretations of the causes of their capture, and inquisitiveness about the person behind the image, can be seen as a modern-day form of resistance to the constraints of now-unfashionable criminological paradigms. It may be that these interpretative possibilities were always there. In the words of Watts (2005) "photography as a medium of visual communication possesses a deep and lasting power to move, entrance and captivate, even when produced for a purely bureaucratic or investigative purpose with no thought to the reactions of posterity" (p. 9). Such an interpretation raises the possibility of subsequent generations of spectators becoming producers of cultural meaning in the jungle of functionalist rationality (de Certeau 1984).

This recognition of the visual power of mugshots leads on to my final argument which addresses the issue of whether it is possible to further resist their categorization as mundane documentary image by conceiving of them as having aesthetic or even artistic potential. Art historians interested in the mugshot have tended to situate them as an exemplary instance of the documentary or representational photograph in which the photographer attempts to do no more than re-present reality by chronicling and recording events as they happen.[24] This form of photography is seen as standing in direct contrast to artistic or pictorial photography which fulfills the creative vision of the photographer. The fact that the aesthetics of the mugshot have so very rarely been discussed appears to send out a clear message that there is no value in looking for artistic value.

In many ways the lack of attention to beauty in the mugshot makes sense. Most of the photographers responsible for producing these photographs would have been untrained in the photographic arts at a time in which the taking of a photograph was a much more technical and complex process than it is today. It is unlikely that they were given time to reflect on such issues as composition and lighting. By way of example, it was estimated in 1904 that the New York police department took no more than ten minutes to measure a suspected criminal and take a photograph for a mugshot (Scientific American 1904). Moreover, alongside the freelance photographers frequently commissioned to produce mugshots, untrained police officers were often tasked with the job of operating the camera (Baylis 2014; Mulcahy 2015) and it was not unknown in American prisons for another convict to be assigned this job. In Jackson's (1994) words:

> They had no need to learn how to use filters to bring out features in different kinds of skin or make the sky or clouds lighter or darker; they had no need to learn about different photographic emulsions or printing papers; they had no need to learn to change the mood of the lighting to fit the desires or personalities of the sitter. The ultimate consumer of these images was the dossier, and it desired as little variation or art as possible (p. 9).

The *New York Times* was to add in its review of a 2006 exhibition of mug shots held in Chelsea, New York:

> It's hard to imagine worse conditions for taking good pictures: the photographer has little training and less interest, and the subject is unwilling for a variety of reasons, among them being dirty, disheveled, drunk, high, sleep-deprived and/or recently beaten about the head and face. (Kennedy 2006)

It seems unlikely then, that criminals or staff will have had the resources to produce anything other than a perfunctory record in the course of registering a new inmate. But does this mean that mugshots cannot be understood as anything other than mere documentary records? Is it possible that those who produced mugshots were sometimes inadvertent producers of beauty or conscious creators of images that demonstrated a high level of technical skill? Is it possible that looking at mugshots through an aesthetic lens could provide us with another form of counter-capture that allows the canon on the subject to be disrupted?

In line with this possibility there is a growing interest in surveillance photography within the art community. The San Francisco Museum of Modern Art hosted an exhibition on "Police Pictures: The Photograph as Evidence" in 1998[25] and an exhibition of police photographs in Sydney in 2005 was said to have inspired one of Karl Lagerfeld's designer clothes collections.[26] In the press release for a New York exhibition of mugshots spanning the years 1880–1970s in New York, Michaelson (2006) asserted that the collection was a poetic encyclopedia of discarded portraits that were extraordinary visual artifacts,[27] and he was later to suggest that the collection consisted of images that contained some sort of magic. Mugshot images once produced so they could be mounted on an A4 sheet or in a photograph album are frequently enlarged. Some are even restored using techniques only available in the twentieth century to emphasize the core element in the authority of portraiture; the subject's gaze (Jackson 2009: 22). This counter hegemonic turn in understanding mugshots, which subverts the original intention of police authorities, could be understood as a form of what Biber (2013) has called the cultural afterlife of the police photograph. It would seem that the time is ripe for a reassessment of the genre.

The fact that a photograph is taken for the purpose of police surveillance does not mean that it cannot be analyzed by reference to its surface, shading, relationship to other art of the period, lighting, tone, texture, content, technique, and mood. Attempts to understand mugshots as artistic or cultural artifacts are neither impossible, nor unprecedented. Caleb William's (Doyle 2007) discussion of the mugshots of Alice Fisher, an Australian female prisoner from 1919, is a particularly worthy exception to the general tendency among art historians and lawyers to treat mugshots as sociological artifacts. He associates the formal properties of the photograph of Alice, in particular the pose and lighting, to the traditions of Italian renaissance painting and sees it as operating on three different levels: as surface realism, a ghostly manifestation, and as a portrait with literary associations. For him, mugshots are capable of displaying an extra dimensional quality or aura, that Walter Benjamin claimed disappeared from photography at the turn of the nineteenth century as photographers aspired to mechanically reproduce reality. Williams concludes: "Admittedly the archive is more 'record' than 'art', but its power is perhaps as galvanising, mysterious and ambiguous as various forms of art and our reactions to them" (Williams 2007: 226).

It is important to recognize that the amateur or jobbing freelance photographers who were often responsible for producing mugshots were not necessarily incapable of producing an image with artistic qualities. The freelance photographers used will have been experienced in taking a variety of different types of photographs and may well have been blessed with considerable technical and artistic abilities. By way of example, the lithographer Carl Durnheim was one of the first professional photographers in Switzerland to have his work exhibited at the John Paul Getty museum in Los Angeles (Getty 1998), and was later commissioned by the police to take photographs of arrested Swiss itinerants in 1852–1853. Meier and Wolfensberger (1998) claim that Durnheim actually used the commission to test and master new photographic techniques. Elsewhere, the commissioning of freelance photographers has been used to explain variation from the standardized mugshot so extensively discussed in the literature (Nichols 2012).

Interest in mugshots appears to satisfy a twenty-first-century cultural fascination with noir and the underworld. and many of the photographs produced for police records in the nineteenth century were taken in a style that was to become the norm in twentieth-century photography. The self-conscious encounter between photographer and the subject in Victorian mugshots mirrors the sort of images produced by celebrated photographers such as Dorothea Lange and Jacob Riis. It could be argued that the subjects of these photos are potentially no less attractive or compelling than the acclaimed photographs produced for the Farm Security Administration photography program which hang in art galleries across the world or the raw images of marginalized people taken by art photographers such as Diane Arbus. Other images to be found in collections of mugshots satisfy a modern interest in the surreal and would not be out of place in a Eugene Atget cityscape populated by the downbeat and marginalized.[28] Even if there is disagreement about their artistic value, it is undoubtedly the case that rediscovered mugshots have transcended their forensic roots to become cultural objects and collectors' items alongside other forms of vernacular photography (Kennedy 2006). The suggestion that some mugshots may have aesthetic qualities has significant implications for the interface between law and art history. Freed from their regular characterization as an exemplar of documentary style photographs which serve a pragmatic and mundane function, this re-imagining of the mugshot encourages us to take these photographs from the confines of the album, standardized record and filing cabinets and to analyze them on the basis of their individual merit. This leaves us free to see vulnerability where others might have seen moral weakness; spirit rather than the fecklessness; autonomy rather than arrogance.

CONCLUSION

The importance of identifying and recording agency and resistance among those generally characterized as being disempowered has become an important one in the field of socio-legal studies in recent years and has served to challenge the nature of the "law first" approach often adopted by scholars in this sub-discipline (Cowan 2004). In their seminal work *The Common Place of Law,* Silbey and Ewing argue that to overlook small moments of resistance because they are momentary or private, is to reinscribe the relations of power that a person is attempting to oppose and to deny the meaning of that opposition in the context of that person's broader biography. To recognize this activity is not to contend that power is fundamentally challenged or altered in the ways often achieved by collective forms of resistance such as revolutions, rebellions, strikes, boycotts, or class actions. But it does suggest that power is capable of being temporarily stunned or deflected. The apparently futile and fleeting acts described in this essay may also have broader implications. Stories of small acts of resistance can have a radiating effect when told to others and become part of an underground folklore which is capable of forming part of a broader culture of opposition (Silbey and Ewing 1998).

My attempt at a revisionist history of the mugshot seeks to remind scholars of the inter-dependency of power and resistance. Those who struggled or scowled remained incarcerated; their attempts at subverting their categorization did not alter what followed after the photographer's lens had done its work. Their mugshots appeared in rogues' galleries and the archives of law enforcement agencies whatever the sitters did. Despite this their actions allowed them to infiltrate and disrupt the order of the archive; to literally put their objection on the record. The result is that nineteenth-century mugshots continue to capture the imagination of twenty-first-century scholars and curators and to offer the archives the possibility of an afterlife. In an irony that would not have been lost on the suffragettes, some of the images once circulated to the National Portrait Gallery to warn them against admitting militant suffragettes who were likely to damage their art collection are now part of its permanent collection. Genealogy websites and the National Archives at Kew are now acquiring and displaying mugshots so that relatives can identify their criminal forebears and claim them as their own. Other collections of mugshots, once kept in government filing cabinets, are increasingly being liberated by collectors, art galleries, museums and, taking the form of exhibitions, integrated within new art works, and included in glossy coffee-table publications. This display of images, taken without genuine consent and disseminated in ways that were never anticipated when they were produced raises a number of new ethical issues (Dean 2015). But for the purposes of this chapter, what is most important and compelling is that despite their creators' attempts to objectify the criminal, it is a subject's gaze that comes back to haunt us.

CHAPTER TWO

Constitution

Utopia, Limited *or a Limited Utopia?*

JOHN SNAPE*

To Angela Kershaw

SETTING THE SCENE

As you leave Charing Cross Underground station, and head north-eastwards along the Strand, you find yourself in the center of theatrical and legal London. On your left is the Vaudeville Theatre (Mander and Mitchenson 1975: 210) and, to your right, the Savoy Theatre and Savoy Hotel (Mander and Mitchenson 1975: 192; Goodman and Hardcastle 1988: 24–29). *Utopia, Limited* or, *The Flowers of Progress*, an "Original Comic Opera, in Two Acts," by W.S. Gilbert and Sir Arthur Sullivan, was first performed at Richard D'Oyly Carte's Savoy Theatre in October 1893. It was the seventh of Gilbert and Sullivan's joint works to have received its premier there. Beyond the Savoy, you soon reach G.E. Street's Victorian Gothic Royal Courts of Justice, opened officially in December 1882 by H.M. Queen Victoria (Brownlee 1984: 360–363). Stretching down to the Thames and up as far as Holborn are the centuries-old Inns of Court: Inner Temple, Middle Temple, Lincoln's Inn, and Gray's Inn. There must hardly be anywhere that so vividly juxtaposes law and theater.

Not the most popular of the so-called "Savoy Operas," *Utopia, Limited* had a disappointing "initial run" of 245 performances (Wilson and Lloyd 1984: 57; Ayre 1986: 418). The opera tells of untoward consequences when the democratically despotic king of an idyllic South-sea island voluntarily turns over the remodeling of his realm to six English notables, the "Imported Flowers of Progress." *Utopia, Limited* was a sumptuous

---

*Associate Professor, Warwick Law School, University of Warwick. The writer has benefited greatly from discussions with the chapter's dedicatee, Dr. Angela Kershaw, and with John Sears, who each commented on all or part of the first draft. Thanks are also due to Professor Ian Ward, Newcastle Law School, University of Newcastle, for his comments, as well as to Roger Lindley, Audio Visual Services, University of Warwick, for assistance in making usable, for study, a 1989 BBC radio recording of *Utopia, Limited*.

conception, lavishly staged and costumed, with a richly orchestrated score and a large cast. George Bernard Shaw, then the theater critic of the *Saturday Review*, was an early admirer (quoted in Baily 1952: 354–356). Surprisingly, though, while Shaw and others wrote about music, plot, actors, and production, relatively little was said about Gilbert's mordant political and legal satire. Company law—specifically, company law as the basis of a constitution—is the focus of Gilbert's satire. *Utopia, Limited* contains a surprisingly nuanced expression of a certain Victorian attitude to the corporate form, its purposes, and its relationship with government. The opera is a child of the affinity between stage and courtroom suggested by the location of its first production (Mulcahy 2011: 118–119, 174–178). The movie director, Mike Leigh, comments that law is one of "two principal elements of all Savoy Operas" (Leigh 2009: 155) and this seems particularly apposite here.

What commentators originally eschewed, scholars have since supplied. To date, at least five authors have written about the opera's legal and political aspects (Borowitz 1973; Wolfson 1976: ch. 2; Borowitz 1982; Goodman 1983: 185–190; Fischler 1991: 42–43, 60–61, 113–115; Williams 2011: ch. 13). None, however, has carried the legal analysis as far as it might be taken. This chapter will hardly achieve that. It will, however, pursue four main thoughts: how the plot of the opera contains a legal syllogism based on the British constitution, working through an insight of Alan Fischler; how the plot has fun with turning the state "inside-out," by making constitutional law subject to company law; how the plot mocks lawyers and other people who aspire to the office of government; and how it encodes an exhortation to reject "progress" and to embrace instead incremental reform. It is first necessary to outline some features of the British constitution at the time *Utopia, Limited* was first performed.

THE NINETEENTH-CENTURY CONSTITUTION

Throughout the whole period 1820–1920, the British state comprised the United Kingdom of Great Britain and Ireland. Victoria, who had been queen for over five decades by 1893, and her court, still had considerable political capacity, especially regarding higher-level promotion in the army and navy, influence in foreign affairs, and constitutional matters (Searle 2004: 121; Gordon 2015: ch. 13). It was the Cabinet, though, that was "the most important agency of government" (Searle 2004: 121).

This was an imperial state. The "imperial metropolis" in 1893 was London, Ireland being seen as a "colonial dependency" subject to special legislation, to a system of "resident magistrates," to "an armed police force" and a tax system administered from London (Searle 2004: 117). The years 1885–1886 had seen W.E. Gladstone's Government of Ireland Bill, proposing an Irish Parliament, but reserving competence on important tax issues to London (Searle 2004: 118). The reaction was so violent that it split Gladstone's own political party, the Liberals. This "Home Rule" crisis was one matter in which Victoria regarded herself as having an important role (Searle 2004: 121).

Imperial state notwithstanding, Britain had certain democratic features. While, in 1893, votes for women were a distant prospect, a series of "Reform Acts" (1832, 1867 and 1884) had produced what was, in effect, a household suffrage. The Representation of the People Act 1884 had uniformly enfranchized every man aged 21 or above holding a property right in land worth at least £10 per year. This was "16 per cent of the total population, compared with 27 per cent in Republican France … 14 per cent in Denmark and 9 per cent in Norway … " (Tombs 2014: 504n). It meant that, in 1885–1886, the electorate was 5,707,531 (Searle 2004: 133). Gladstone regarded this as a "democracy" (Searle 2004: 129). Most agricultural laborers and coalminers had the right to vote (Searle 2004: 133). In addition, the Local Government Act 1888 had "created fifty county councils for England and another twelve for Wales" in an attempt to mitigate "centralizing tendencies" by "stimulating civic pride and local self-reliance" (Searle 2004: 125). This was truly "the Age of Reform," not revolution. There was not much republicanism about (Searle 2004: 121).

The House of Commons, whose MPs were as yet unpaid (Searle 2004: 130), was the national institution in which votes were cast, by secret ballot (Searle 2004: 135). Turnouts were high at around 80 percent (Searle 2004: 134). By 1893, Governments were increasingly controlling the Commons, using "disciplined majorities ... to carry out the ... programmes around which general elections increasingly depended" (Searle 2004: 122). The House of Lords, unlike now, was overwhelmingly hereditary, aristocratic and landed. The "law lords were the only life peers" (Searle 2004: 129). Even by 1911, only around "one-sixth" of peers "were first-generation peers from non-landed backgrounds" (Searle 2004: 129). In 1893, no one knew how the Lords might adapt to constitutional reform (Searle 2004: 132). Liberals (Unionist and otherwise after 1886) and Conservatives slugged it out bilaterally. But Ireland was the main issue well into the 1890s and Irish nationalist MPs were a vociferous minority (Searle 2004: 144). The Home Rule crisis "was ... responsible for the emergence of a new party system of greater rigidity than anything seen before" (Searle 2004: 145). A.V. Dicey, whose 1885 *Law of the Constitution* had reached its fourth edition by 1893 (Dicey 1908 [1959]), was an opponent of this regimented antagonism (Searle 2004: 146).

CAREFREE LANGUOR AND ANXIOUS PROGRESS

The curtain rises on Act I of *Utopia, Limited* to reveal the palace gardens of King Paramount I.[1] At this stage, Utopia, a South-sea island, is an aimless place, the populace "thoroughly enjoying themselves in lotus-eating fashion" (Bradley 1996: 975).[2] By Act II, matters are transformed. The English have arrived and both a legislative program and a process of cultural transformation are under way.

By Utopia's constitution, the democratically despotic King Paramount is "in theory absolute." In practice, however, he is "nothing of the kind." Instead, King Paramount is "watched day and night" by two Utopian Supreme Court judges, Phantis and Scaphio (see Figure 2.1), "whose duty it is, on his very first lapse from political or social propriety, to denounce him to" Tarara, the Public Exploder, who will despatch him with dynamite (979). "Yes," says Calynx, the Utopian Vice-Chamberlain, "what may be described as a Despotism tempered by Dynamite provides, on the whole, the most satisfactory description of ruler—an autocrat who dares not abuse his autocratic power" (979). But things are about to change. As King Paramount announces to his subjects:

> "My subjects all, it is your wish emphatic
> That all Utopia shall henceforth be modelled
> Upon that glorious country called Great Britain—
> To which some add—but others do not—Ireland." (989)

This, on Fischler's persuasive analysis of Gilbert's comedy, is the major premise of the legal syllogism on which the plot of the opera is based (Fischler 1991: 63). It is the Utopian people's wish to adopt the British Constitution.

FIGURE 2.1 Prudent judges of the Utopian Supreme Court. W.H. Denny as Scaphio and John le Hay as Phantis in Act I (Cast photograph, 1893). Source: Bridgeman Images / British Library.

Thus it is that the "singularly beautiful" (1017) Princess Zara, King Paramount's eldest daughter, having "taken a high degree at Girton" (977), now returns to Utopia along with the Flowers of Progress, six "types of all the causes that have made / That great and glorious country [Great Britain] what it is" (1025). The Flowers of Progress—"a British Lord Chamberlain" (Lord Dramaleigh), an officer of Household Cavalry (Captain Fitzbattleaxe), a Royal Naval officer (Captain Sir Edward Corcoran, KCB), a company promoter (Mr. Goldbury), a Member of Parliament and senior barrister (Sir Bailey Barre, QC, MP), and a County Councilor (Mr. Blushington)—are "experts in various aspects of English life" (Wilson and Lloyd 1984: 57). It is they (Princess Zara tells King Paramount) who, though "now washing their hands after their journey" (1025), "will reorganize your country on a footing that will enable you to defy your persecutors" (1025). Thus, the minor premise of the opera's syllogistical plot is brought into play. It is King Paramount's duty to implement the people's wish to exchange the Utopian constitution for the British one. Chief among King Paramount's persecutors, of course, are the two judges and, as the curtain falls on Act I, they and Tarara prepare to dispatch King Paramount to Posterity (1039).

Act II begins at night in the throne room of the palace. The Flowers of Progress have got to work remodeling Utopia. King Paramount and the Flowers of Progress have incorporated it, plus the Utopian crown, under the provisions of the Joint Stock Companies Act, 1862 (see Figure 2.2). The "corporate entertainments" have started and the palace is to be the setting for a night-time royal Drawing Room and Reception. Captain Fitzbattleaxe, who has fallen in love with Princess Zara (1011), takes stock. Things are shaping up nicely. Scaphio and Phantis, though, are furious. They "come down stage melodramatically—

walking together" (1055). They are "dressed as [English] judges in red and ermine robes and undress wigs" (1055) (see Figure 2.3). Duly incorporated, King Paramount can no longer "conveniently" be blown up (1059). He can only be wound up. So Scaphio, Phantis and Tarara are forced to "devise some plot … to bring the people about … [the King's] ears" (1061), disincorporate him and blow him up. They produce a "capital plan" (1063) and, when King Paramount's subjects crowd into the palace, Scaphio and Phantis act as the people's tribunes. Incorporation has been highly effective but things have become unbearable. War is impossible because, in the face of Utopia's now "irresistible" army and navy, "neighbouring nations have disarmed" (1077). Mr Blushington's "drastic Sanitary laws" have caused "the doctors [to] dwindle, starve and die" (1077) (Wilson and Lloyd 1984: 57). Sir Bailey Barre's remodeled laws "[h]ave quite extinguished crime and litigation," with the result that "[t]he lawyers starve, and all the jails … [have been] let / As model lodgings for the working-classes!" (1077). It is clear that Utopia has travelled from being what Terry Eagleton calls a "carnivalesque" utopia to the other sort, one "in which everything is odourless and antiseptic, intolerably streamlined and sensible" (Eagleton 2015). Everyone is at a loss. Then, Sir Bailey Barre (see Figure 2.4) reminds Princess Zara how all of these innovations can be undone. Recollection blazes for her:

> ZARA. Government by Party! Introduce that great and glorious element—at once the bulwark and foundation of England's greatness—and all will be well! No political measures will endure, because one Party will assuredly undo all that the other Party has done; and while grouse is to be shot, and foxes worried to death, the legislative action of the country will be at a standstill. Then there will be sickness in plenty, endless lawsuits, crowded jails, interminable confusion in the Army and Navy, and, in short, general and unexampled prosperity! (1077–1079)

FIGURE 2.2 King Paramount as Chairman of the Board of Utopia, Limited. Rutland Barrington in Act II (Cast photograph, 1893). Source: Bridgeman Images / British Library.

FIGURE 2.3 Prudent judges of the Utopian Supreme Court as judges of "The Supreme Court of Judicature of England and Wales." W.H. Denny as Scaphio and John le Hay as Phantis in Act II (Cast photograph, 1893). Source: Bridgeman Images / British Library.

FIGURE 2.4 The ingenuity of English legal reasoning. Enes Blackmore as Sir Bailey Barre, QC, MP (Act I). Source: Bridgeman Images / British Library.

King Paramount accordingly announces the dissolution of the company. "[H]enceforward Utopia will no longer be a monarchy (Limited), but, what is a great deal better, a Limited Monarchy!" (1079) (Eagleton 2015). Scaphio and Phantis are thereby "thwarted" and led away (1079) (Fischler 1991: 60–61). English law and English party politics, if not English corporate commerce, has triumphed.

The conclusion of the plot's syllogism, of course, is that it is King Paramount's duty to adopt the British Constitution. This he duly does, with the plot's major premise restated to include government by party. King Paramount must adopt the British Constitution with party government: "Ulahlica! Ulahlica!" (1079), everyone rejoices, in the Utopian tongue.

IDEAL POLITICAL SOCIETIES AND LIMITED LIABILITY COMPANIES

When the opera opened in 1893, the second word of its title appeared in parentheses, which were subsequently dropped: *Utopia (Limited)* became *Utopia, Limited* (Jacobs 1984: 349). Each idiom suggests both the incongruous subjection of the state to the methods of company law and a restricted ideal. Constitutional law expresses the collective legal values. Company law furthers corporate and commercial, and hence individualistic, purposes. So the opera first depicts Utopia's political society as an inversion of what they take to characterize England's, then as an emulation of England's greatest features, and finally, with no further improvements possible, as a resigned collapse into England's actually existing society (1051).

In the late 1860s, the poet and critic Matthew Arnold had summed up the concept of the state as being "the nation, in its collective and corporate character, entrusted with stringent powers for the general advantage, and controlling individual wills in the name of an interest wider than that of individuals" (*Culture and Anarchy* (1869) 56, quoted in Fischler 1991: 12). The state was thus the "correlative" of sovereignty, the "absolute authority" of the combined elements of territory, people, and government (Loughlin 2010: 195). Thoughtful Victorians, including the erudite Gilbert, knew that it was in the law-books that they would find the manifestations of this authority (Loughlin 2010: 192, 195). And legislation, meaning statute law, was only one category of positive law. The others, common law and equity, proceeded deductively by syllogistic reasoning on the facts of individual cases. Legislation, though, was much more wide-ranging. Legislation, unlike judicial syllogisms, was entirely contingent on an unpredictable general will. Moreover, unlike common law or equity, legislation envisaged the potential for the collective pursuit of substantive policy objectives, such as the consolidation of capital in the concept of the limited company.[3] Indeed, much-legislating states might themselves come to assume the qualities of limited companies. Nineteenth and twentieth-century commentators, including Tönnies, Weber, Hayek, and Oakeshott, noted this idea. Oakeshott characterized the legislative state as an "enterprise association," its antithesis as an association of like-minded subjects or "civil association" (Oakeshott 1975: 201–206). Instead of having substantive ends in view, the civil association was a focus of loyalty, its existence represented by parades, ceremonies, and the like. It followed that, once committed to substantive policy ends, a state would relegate the merely ceremonial. Before the arrival of the Flowers of Progress, Gilbert's Utopia is an informal enterprise association, with none of the elements of civil association. Once the Flowers of Progress have got to work, Utopia has become a formal enterprise association, though with a number of civil association characteristics.

The opera's portrayal of the Utopian constitution, as mentioned, follows the pattern of inversion, emulation, and resignation. "Constitution" is used here not in the sense of the constitution of Utopia's *government* but of its *state* (Loughlin 2013: 11–12). So the term describes Utopia's restless political and legal unity, a combination both of what Utopia is and what it might be in the future (Loughlin 2010: ch. 8 (esp. 209–210)).

The inversion stage operates in "topsy-turvy" fashion. Before the Flowers of Progress arrive, the Utopians are the opposite of the British: lazy, corrupt, and credulous. Yet Utopian culture, manners, and traditions are still enough to constitute a state (Loughlin 2013: 12). The curtain rises on "a picturesque and luxuriant tropical landscape" (975). Visions of "Poppydom," "delicate" music, birdsong, rippling streams, and fragrant flowers are all available to the Utopian maidens who are "lying lazily about the stage" (975). How the gloved hands must have raised the opera-glasses as the gentlemen of the Savoy audiences were reminded of the sensuous panoramas of Alma-Tadema or Leighton. Nothing could have been further from late Victorian Manchester or Birmingham.

Gilbert's structure mirrors that of Sir Thomas More's *Utopia* (1516) and, at this inversion stage of the plot, turns More's Utopia on its head to make it satirical. In More's Utopia, there is "a just society," unlike in England (Cotton 2003: 50). More's *Utopia* functions as a critique of England insofar as he presents an ideal state in which all of England's flaws have been resolved. Gilbert's Utopia functions in contrary fashion. In Gilbert's Utopia, it is the realities Gilbert perceives to lie behind the ideals cherished by the English that are presented, satirically, as the foundations of Utopian society. For example, in Gilbert's Utopia, says Calynx, "we have no need to think, because our monarch anticipates all our wants, and our political opinions are formed for us by the journals to which we subscribe" (977). We, in England, have an ideal of freedom of thought and expression. Gilbert's critique is that the papers think for us. Had Gilbert followed More exactly, there would be freedom of the press in Utopia, but in not in England. But things are topsy-turvy and the message is clear: in England, where independence of thought is an important political value, public opinion is, in practice, controlled by the press.

Again, though "nominally a Despot," King Paramount is Scaphio's and Phantis' "helpless tool," since they insist on his complying "with all their wishes," threatening "to denounce" him "for immediate explosion" if he remonstrates with them (1025). Unknown to other characters, Scaphio and Phantis publish a satirical paper, the *Palace Peeper*, the articles in which are written by King Paramount as libels on himself. We, in Britain, have an ideal of a limited monarchy. Gilbert's critique is that, in reality, the monarch has considerable freedom of action (979). But Tarara cannot understand why he has not been called upon "to blow up His Majesty with dynamite" and, as the Utopian constitution requires, reign in King Paramount's stead (979). We, in Britain, have an ideal of constitutional theory and a distinction between public and private realms. Gilbert's critique is that everything is pragmatic, with public and private hopelessly confused (979).

Yet, by the topsy-turvy standards of Utopia, Scaphio and Phantis are skilled judges, as the ungainly waltz-chorus proclaims:

"They're the pride of Utopia—
   Cornucopia
Is each in his mental fertility.
O they never make blunder,

And no wonder,
For they're triumphs of infallibility." (979)[4]

The Utopian constitution is, by its own lights, very effective as Scaphio and Phantis gleefully point out: " [o]ur despot it imbues / With virtues quite delectable," they sing. "He minds his P's and Q's, / And keeps himself respectable" (981).[5]

The emulation stage of the plot also follows More, but this time there is no need for an inversion to get the laughs. The Flowers of Progress visit Utopia just as does Raphael Hythloday in More's original. Hythloday takes English ideas, including printing, to Utopia, and the Flowers of Progress take English ideas, including the limited liability company. The Utopians' "willingness to learn is great" (Cotton 2003: 47). The motif is identical in More and Gilbert. Utopia is both a fantasized resolution and is capable of benefiting from some good things from England, like printing or the limited liability company. After the Flowers of Progress arrive, the Utopians, imitating the English, are energetic, purified, skeptical, rebellious, but also anxious. At the center of their emulation is a theatrical recreation of the Court of St James. This may seem a misplaced satirical target to the eyes of twenty-first-century constitutional lawyers. In the light of what is said above, it would not have appeared so to late-nineteenth-century lawyers (Anson II:1 1935: 156–159). "[T]he court was a major state institution," writes Richard Davenport-Hines, "equivalent to the houses of parliament or the judiciary, and its workings, personnel, group intelligence and moral compass" (Davenport-Hines 2014) are more worthy of analysis than many allow. The royal Drawing Room and Reception in Act II, one of the most lavish elements of the original production, should be seen in this light. To majestic orchestral accompaniment, the Utopian court arrives onstage in the manner of its counterpart at Buckingham Palace: the royal household: "the three princesses" and pages; and Lady Sophy (the Princesses' "English Gouvernante") and ladies-in-waiting (1053),[6] "[C]harmingly scored ... music in gavotte style, though not actually a gavotte" (Dunhill 1929: 207), accompanies the presentation to King Paramount and the three princesses of "the ladies attending the Drawing-Room" (1053).[7] King Paramount, his courtiers and the Flowers of Progress, in an unaccompanied chorus, enunciate Utopia's—and hence Great Britain's—coercive yet magnanimous approach to foreign policy and to international legal norms:

"Let the eagle, not the sparrow,
Be the object of your arrow—
  Fix the tiger with your eye—
  Pass the fawn in pity by.
  Glory then will crown the day—
  Glory, glory, anyway!" (1055)[8]

For Princess Zara, though, even a royal drawing room is has potential for improvement. "Drawing-Rooms are always held in the afternoon" Captain Fitzbattleaxe tells her, disconcertedly noting the timing of the event. "Ah, we've improved upon that," the Princess replies, "we all look so much better by candlelight!" (1053).[9]

Calynx extols England as "the greatest, the most powerful, the wisest country in the world" (977). Emulation leads to England's recreation "with improvements" and idealistic absurdity. In what might be a side-swipe at rarefied late-nineteenth-century academia (Searle 2004: 659), idealism is mocked throughout. The Utopian constitution originally replaced an "ideal Republic" (979). Idealism as a mode of thought is satirized through male romantic attitudes to the female. Scaphio provides an absurd example, anticipating falling in love:

> When *I* love, it will be with the accumulated fervour of sixty-six years! But I have an ideal—a semi-transparent Being, filled with an inorganic pink jelly—and I have never yet seen the woman who approaches within measurable distance of it. All are opaque—opaque—opaque! (983)

Phantis, "topsy-turvily," feels inadequate next to the ideal of English manhood. "Ah! Scaphio, remember ... [Princess Zara] returns from a land where every youth is as a young Greek god, and where such poor beauty as I can boast is seen at every turn" (983). Lawyers are prone to idealized thinking. Scaphio and Phantis are no exception. Lord Dramaleigh idealizes Princess Zara's two younger sisters, the Princesses Nekaya and Kalyba. "May I ask [says that susceptible nobleman]—is this extreme delicacy—this shrinking sensitiveness—a general characteristic of Utopian young ladies?" "Oh no; we are crack specimens" replies Nekaya. "We [rejoins Kalyba] are the pick of the basket" (1065).

In More's *Utopia*, on William Cotton's reading, Hythloday will eventually go back to Utopia and convert it to Christianity (Cotton 2003: 41). More's Utopia has room for improvement. So, when Gilbert's King Paramount resigns himself to government by party and limited monarchy, there is simply no room for improvement. Like Great Britain, Utopia has become the best it can be.

If constitutional law embodies collective legal values, then company law expresses individualistic purposes. Two points seem quite crucial. First, the opera emphasizes that company law facilitates overreaching and inefficient projects. Victorian satire certainly saw limited companies as mini political societies, prone to corruption and waste (Alborn 1998; Taylor 2006). This is a source of amusement in relation to the corporate entertainment that is the royal drawing room and reception: "One or two judicious innovations, I think?" observes Lord Dramaleigh to Mr. Goldbury afterwards. "Admirable" [replies Mr. Goldbury]. "The cup of tea and the plate of mixed biscuits were a cheap and effective inspiration" (1065). Likewise, Mr. Goldbury is unconcerned about the scale and implications of "companification" schemes as, no doubt, were those who had floated Guinness (1886) and "J.&P. Coats, the sewing cotton combine in 1890" (Searle 2004: 92):

> "And soon or late I always call
>   For Stock Exchange quotation—
> No schemes too great and none too small
>   For Companification!" (1031)[10]

Mr. Goldbury recognizes, however, that there are limits to the company promoter's ambition: the nominal sum invested. "You can't embark on trading too tremendous—[he says] / It's strictly fair, and based on common sense— / If you succeed, your profits are stupendous— / And if you fail, pop goes your eighteenpence" (1037).[11] Nonetheless you might be tempted to be ambitious: "Bank, Railway, Loan, or Panama Canal" (1037). (Borowitz 1982).[12]

Secondly, only woe can come to a state that takes on the limited company's characteristics. "Enthusiastically" does King Paramount seize at the possibility of perfecting Utopia:

> "We'll go down to Posterity renowned
>   As the First Sovereign in Christendom

Who registered his Crown and Country under
The Joint Stock Company's Act of Sixty-Two." (1039)[13]

The significance of this is sharply focused when read alongside Martin Loughlin's theory of constitutional law (Loughlin 2010). Public law as constitutional law is the law that undergirds the structure of the state. In theory that law is different from the public law as administrative law that the state posits and which we call "positive law." The latter must serve the former, not the other way round. Company law is positive, not constitutional, law. So, when Utopia is registered under the Joint Stock Companies Act, 1862, the state is literally turned inside-out because a category of positive law is presuming to take the place of the state's constitutional law.

It is clear that *Utopia, Limited*, the structure of which owes much to More's *Utopia*, is antagonistic to the socialistic works on whose heels it immediately followed: Edward Bellamy's *Looking Backward: 2000–1887* (1888) and William Morris' *News from Nowhere* (1890/1891) (Sutton 1975: 113; Levitas 1990 [2011]: ch. 5). When the Flowers of Progress profess the absence of "slummeries in England," just as they avow the intention to abolish hunger there (1051), Gilbert may be glancing at the aspirations of Fabian socialism, at Beatrice and Sidney Webb (though Utopia slightly antedates their rise to prominence), and perhaps also at George Bernard Shaw (Sutton 1975: 113). Ruth Levitas points out that all Utopias have a double structure. Utopia's "double face" is both a "projection into the future of current dilemmas" and a "potential future offering a critical perspective on the present" (Levitas 2013: 130). They are both a critique of the home nation and the projection of an ideal for that nation.

COMPANY PROMOTER, PUBLIC EXPLODER AND THE SPIRIT OF A NATION

The skills of a politician are quite different from those of a commercial man. Politicians have the necessary skills to facilitate, through legislation, the creation of limited companies. However, neither men of commerce, nor even people educated in the spirit of a nation, necessarily have the skills to create a state.

King Paramount, as democratic despot, lacks political prudence (Loughlin 2003: 39–40), not available to him either as the chairman of Utopia, Limited. Utopia's democratic despotism, before the arrival of the Flowers of Progress, is as yet the inverse of Great Britain's parliamentary constitution, if only perilously so (977). "Democratic despotism," as analyzed by Paul Rahe (Rahe 2009: bk. 3, ch. 1), was what Alexis de Tocqueville found in America in 1831: "I see an innumerable crowd of men [wrote Tocqueville], all alike and equal, turned in upon themselves in a restless search for those petty, vulgar pleasures with which they fill their souls" (Tocqueville 2003: 805 (quoted in Rahe 2009: 187)). For Gilbert, no "democrat," it probably seemed that, with the most recent extension to the suffrage in the Reform Act 1884 (Searle 2004: 133–4), Britain was heading the same way (1025).[14] "Democracy's drift" necessitates a user-friendly monarch, so King Paramount has no option but to strengthen Utopia's despotically democratic constitution by portraying himself in burlesque as "King Tuppence, or A Good Deal Less than Half a Sovereign." As Scaphio tells King Paramount:

> During the day thousands tremble at your frown, during the night (from 8 to 11) thousands roar at it. During the day your most arbitrary pronouncements are received by your subjects with abject submission—during the night, they shout with joy at your

most terrible decrees. It's not every monarch who enjoys the privilege of undoing by night all the despotic absurdities he's committed during the day. (999)

Fischler identifies this passage as being important for what it says about Gilbert's comedy enhancing the authority of positive law (Fischler 1991: 54), although a specifically constitutive significance seems more apposite. Gilbert had already warned, in his 1873 play, *The Happy Land*,[15] that there was no virtue to be found in such popular government (Lawrence 1971: 162; Brownlee 1984: 258). Indeed, how could there be, where the rulers' virtue was the virtue of the people? (Sutton 1975: 89–90) "Why do they represent you with such a big nose?" Princess Zara asks her father, critically scrutinizing a cartoon in the *Palace Peeper*. "Eh? Yes [replies King Paramount], it *is* a big one! Why, the fact is that, in the cartoons of a comic paper, the size of your nose always varies inversely as the square of your popularity. It's the rule" (1023). Exactly how perilous the contrast is between Utopia and Great Britain appears from the Utopian's attitude to the senior judiciary before the Flowers of Progress arrive. Utopian democratic despotism places Scaphio and Phantis beyond reproach:

"SCA. We fear no rude rebuff,
    Or newspaper publicity;
PHAN. Our word is quite enough,
    The rest is electricity." (981)

One only needs to think of the *Vanity Fair* cartoons of the British judiciary (Collens 1990) or Gilbert's own verses for the Learned Judge in *Trial by Jury* (1875) to note the contrast between liberal and despotic attitudes. Lady Sophy reproves the infatuated King Paramount about the unaccountable non-enforcement of the law on criminal libel against the *Palace Peeper*. "Well, you are a Despot," says Lady Sophy, "have you taken steps to slay this scribbler?" "Well, no," hesitates the King. "I have *not* gone so far as that. After all, it's the poor devil's living, you know." "It is the poor devil's living that surprises me," replies Lady Sophy (1005).

The Flowers of Progress so far lack the skills of politicians that they almost bring about the dissolution of the Utopian state. Lord Dramaleigh, the Lord Chamberlain, alludes implicitly to the Licensing Act 1737 to explain his rather mundane censorial duties:

"New plays I read with jealous eyes,
    And purify the Stage." (1029)

Gilbert had experience of censorship. In 1873, the Lord Chamberlain had censored *The Happy Land* (Sutton 1975: 89). Perhaps it is better, so Gilbert seems to say, that Lord Dramaleigh's sphere of activity is the scrutiny of presentations at Court rather than the governing of the state (Watson 1952: 229–234). This is not, though, to deny the constitutional significance of the Lord Chamberlain's courtly endeavors. Thomas Dunhill pleasantly recounts how Lord Dramaleigh's idea of refreshments at the Act II Royal Drawing Room and Reception actually resulted in the provision of refreshments at its Buckingham Palace original (Dunhill 1929: 203). Her Majesty's objection to such refreshments, as made in the 1870s, invoked a constitutional argument: "The Queen could not approve under any circumstances tea etc. being provided, thinking that it could … turn a Drawing Room into a party" (quoted in Watson 1952: 231).

Legislators facilitate the creation of limited companies, Gilbert seems to say, because legislators make laws with which all must comply: "Ye wand'rers from a mighty State, / Oh teach us how to legislate" (1033), implore King Paramount and Princess Zara in the Act I Finale. This includes Tarara, sometime functionary, potential future ruler (977). Tarara shows that not all legislative activity is wasted. It probably is a good idea to subject him to the regulatory provisions of the Explosives Act 1875: "Tarara [says King Paramount, in lines ultimately deleted], you deserve some compensation in exchange for the privilege of blowing us up and succeeding to the throne, so we appoint you Perpetual Chief Inspector of Explosives, under 38 and 39 Vic., Cap. 17, s. 62" (1078).

Utopia, though, is fortunate in the wisdom of its judges, Scaphio and Phantis, mouthpieces of non-legislative law. This, no doubt, is because of their syllogistical punctiliousness. They might, however, be confounded when confronted with interpreting legislation. Shockingly, Scaphio and Phantis declare their love for Princess Zara. But Captain Fitzbattleaxe gallantly protects her. He guilefully confronts them with a so-far unknown English statute. "When two gentlemen are in love with the same lady," he explains,

> and until it is settled which gentleman is to blow out the brains of the other, it is provided, by the Rival Admirers' Clauses Consolidation Act, that the lady shall be entrusted to an officer of Household Cavalry as stakeholder, who is bound to hand her over to the survivor (on the Tontine principle) in a good condition of substantial and decorative repair.

"Reasonable wear and tear and damages by fire excepted?" hazards Scaphio, against his own interest. "Exactly" (1017) responds the soldier. It is thus that even syllogistical judicial wisdom has its limits, as Princess Zara and Captain Fitzbattleaxe concur:

> "When sages try to part
>   Two loving hearts in fusion,
>   Their wisdom's a delusion,
>   And learning serves them not!" (1021)

Gilbert's technique is "topsy-turvydom" and the foregoing are fine examples. In Gilbert's "fantastic yet topical world," Jane Stedman tells us, his characters "lead lives ... compounded of the grotesque and the impossibly logical. Cause and effect are dislocated; modifiers annul their nouns; things become their physical, behavioural, or moral opposites" (Stedman 1996: 26).

So delicate, indeed, is the art or science of a legislator that even commercially astute, and highly educated people may lack the skills necessary to legislate. Princess Zara is the willowy, blonde, clever embodiment of the nation, a heroine—as Fischler points out—in the strict sense (Fischler 1991: 132–3. Even Princess Zara, though Girton College has given her "a complete mastery over all the elements that have tended to raise ... [Great Britain] to her present pre-eminent position among civilized nations!" evidently lacks the aptitude for government (977). The same might be said of Mr. Goldbury, although he has no prudence and boasts about the unfeasibly large "loans to foreign thrones" that he has "largely advocated" (1031). So his ambitions know no bounds: "Utopia's much too big for one small head [he declares]— / I'll float it as a Company Limited!" (1035). The problem is that procedures for managing companies are hardly suitable for governing states. Company law, as positive law, is wholly different in character from constitutional law. This does not worry King Paramount. Once installed as chairman, King Paramount is in thrall, not to Scaphio and Phantis, but to the forms of company law: "Gentlemen [he tells the Flowers of

Progress], our daughter holds her first Drawing-Room in half an hour, and we shall have time to make our half-yearly report in the interval" (1049).

Again, as King Paramount informs Captain Fitzbattleaxe, with one eye on companies legislation: "[T]he First Statutory Cabinet Council of Utopia Limited must be conducted with dignity and impressiveness" and he forthwith inquires as to the whereabouts of the other "five [ie excluding Fitzbattleaxe and the King] who signed the Articles of Association" (1049). This illustrates the minimum seven-man association required by the provisions of the Joint Stock Companies Act, 1862. King Paramount's confusion of the distinct principles behind company and constitutional law frustrate Scaphio and Phantis. When they challenge him about the wide-ranging activities of the Flowers of Progress, King Paramount replies that "this is very irregular" and recommends that they "formulate a detailed list of ... grievances in writing, addressed to the Secretary of Utopia Limited," which list "will be laid before the Board, in due course, at their next monthly meeting" (1057). What stupidity. "We have no time for idle forms," (1061) Scaphio says. The revolting populace will be pushing in the boardroom windows even before the apologies for absence have been recorded.

This is why, it could be argued, Fischler somewhat overstates his case when he infers that Gilbert thinks that government would be better conducted along the lines of the government of the City of London. It is true that Gilbert deplores the statutory phenomenon that is what we would call corporate capitalism. But he does not deplore capitalism per se, if it is conducted within the traditional schemes of property and contract. Only there will true commercial and legal principles be found. Gilbert reminds his listeners of the latter, in a reference to the restrictive covenants case of *Maxim Nordenfelt v Nordenfelt* [1893] 1 Ch 630, decided in the Court of Appeal the year before the first performance of *Utopia, Limited*:

> "I'm Captain Corcoran, K.C.B.,
> I'll teach you how we rule the sea,
>   And terrify the simple Gauls;
> And how the Saxon and the Celt
> Their Europe-shaking blows have dealt
> With Maxim gun and Nordenfeldt
>   (Or will, when the occasion calls)." (1033)

Sir Bailey Barre—Princess Zara tells us—is a "complicated gentleman," "the terse embodiment" of "all the arts and faculties" (1027). The Queen's Counsel and parliamentarian is Arithmetician, Logician, Philologist, and more (1027–1029). "To speak on both sides teach your sluggish brains!" (1035), Sir Bailey Barre tells the puzzled Utopians. Gilbert, a veteran litigator, is not mocking Sir Bailey Barre, though the latter is certainly shifty (1029). The essence of common law and equity is the mental agility involved in manipulating them, such agility, and its implications for individual liberty, being a pearl beyond price. Utopia is where lawyers are not to be found.[16]

SPECULATION AND LEGISLATION

In *Utopia, Limited*, the acts of the legislator and of the businessman are incompatible. Legislation is corrupted by business practices and meddlesome regulators. Business practices are corrupted by legislative artifice. Corruption is endemic. These things would be more widely appreciated if people were better educated. People would reject progress and embrace gradual reform.

Corporate business is about formulas and show, legislating is about political prudence and parsimonious explanation. Ignoring the explosive threats of Scaphio, Phantis and Tarara, King Paramount asks Mr. Goldbury a germane question:

> "KING. ... And do I understand you that Great Britain
> Upon this Joint Stock principle is governed?
> MR. GOLD. We haven't come to that, exactly—but
> We're tending rapidly in that direction.
> The date's not distant." (1037–1039)

So, too, was the case with administrative law. Mr. Blushington ("Great Britain's latest toy") (1029) is enamored of the possibilities of the Local Government Act, 1888: "Yes—yes—yes—," he sings, "In towns I make improvements great, / Which go to swell the County Rate— / I dwelling-houses sanitate, / And purify the [music] Halls!" (1031). The level of the county rate was a highly contentious issue in 1893 (Searle 2004: 127n). That the exercise of such powers by such people produces administrative absurdity goes without saying. Scaphio and Phantis might almost be in the pay of Dicey, whose indictment of administrative law had appeared in 1885 (Dicey 1908: ch. 12). "And as if that wasn't enough," Scaphio complains to King Paramount, "the County Councillor has ordered a four-foot wall to be built up right across the proscenium, in case of fire—as in England." "It's so hard on the company," adds Phantis, "who are liable to be roasted alive—and this has to be met by enormously increased salaries—as in England" (1057). The concern over the growth in administration was not shared by F.W. Maitland, the pioneering constitutional law historian, lecturing his Cambridge students in 1888 (Maitland 1908: 505–506, quoted in Loughlin 2010: 442–443n). Such administrative considerations should not preoccupy Scaphio and Phantis, their talents "wasted" as they are on "utility" (981).

Constitutional law and company law perform quite distinct functions. So politics and commerce, the opera emphasizes, are different spheres of activity. The deleted second verse to King Paramount's first song exemplifies Lord Halifax's parallel between governing and sailing:

> "But as it is our Royal whim
> Our Royal sails to set and trim
> To suit whatever wind may blow,
> What buffets contradiction deals,
> And how a thwarted monarch feels,
> We probably shall never know." (988)

That is democratic despotism. The theme is taken up by Captain Corcoran, later in the Act, in a naval metaphor: "Though we're no longer hearts of oak [he sings], / Yet we can steer and we can stoke, / And, thanks to coal, and thanks to coke, / We never run a ship ashore!" (1033).[17] But, if a politician must confront fickle fortune, no such challenge faces Mr. Goldbury. As Princess Zara explains, "[t]o speculators he supplies a grand financial leaven" (1031). And Mr. Goldbury, as the opera has already told us, knows of no practical wisdom: "In ginger-pops and peppermint-drops" he has "freely speculated" (1031). Worryingly, too, companies legislation has given Mr. Goldbury and his like a lawful option as to whether to act with justice:

> "*I* should put it [ie the capital] rather low;
> The good sense of doing so
> Will be evident at once to any debtor.
> > When it's left to you to say
> > What amount you mean to pay,
> Why, the lower you can put it at, the better." (1035)

In other words, the corporate form seems to give the investor the opportunity to choose whether or not to act justly, in affording a legislatively sanctioned choice as to whether and, if so, how much, to repay to creditors. "Marvellous is the power of a Civilization [Captain Fitzbattleaxe tells Princess Zara] which can transmute, by a word, a Limited Income into an Income (*Limited*)" (1045). Indeed, even abject corporate failure can be condoned by the Companies (Winding Up) Act 1890:

> "Do you suppose that signifies perdition?
> > If so you're but a monetary dunce—
> You merely file a Winding-Up Petition,
> > And start another Company at once!" (1037)

Not only that, but limited liability can be exploited in unexpected ways. "You probably know," Scaphio complains to King Paramount, "that we've contracted to supply the entire nation with a complete English outfit. But perhaps you do *not* know that, when we send in our bills, our customers plead liability limited to a declared capital of eighteenpence, and apply to be dealt with under the Winding-up Act—as in England?" (1057). The corporate form is indeed the acme of the corruption of commerce with legislation. As Princess Zara confides to Captain Fitzbattleaxe, in a passage that underlines the fact that, although *Utopia, Limited* might be characterized as an anti-colonialist opera (Williams 2011: ch. 13), such may well not be its principal focus:

> The most beneficent change of all has been effected by Mr. Goldbury, who, discarding the exploded theory that some strange magic lies hidden in the number Seven, has applied the Limited Liability principle to individuals, and every man, woman, and child is now a Company Limited with liability restricted to the amount of his declared Capital! There is not a christened baby in Utopia who has not already issued his little Prospectus! (1045)[18]

However, this does show that the Utopians have become property-oriented and acquisitive as elements of civil association have come to form part of the constitution. The formal possibility of "one-man" companies is, of course, now recognized in companies legislation but it was a technical possibility even in 1893 (see, now, Companies Act 2006, s. 7(1)). A drawback of the corporate form, however, as Scaphio and Phantis point out, is that King Paramount is consequently invulnerable to explosives:

> "PHAN. (*breathless*). He's right—we are helpless! He's no longer a human being—he's a Corporation, and so long as he confines himself to his Articles of Association we can't touch him! What are we to do?
>
> SCA. Do? Raise a Revolution, repeal the Act of Sixty-Two, reconvert him into an individual, and insist on his immediate explosion!" (1061)

Confronting the enraged Scaphio and Phantis, King Paramount (by now the chairman of the board of *Utopia, Limited*, and dressed in the uniform of a British field marshall) (see Figure 2.2), maddens them even further: "You may *wind* up a Limited Company," he tells them, "You cannot conveniently *blow* it up!" (1059).

The fictions of legislators who are also lawyers are enemies to true commercial virtue. That legislative fictions can perform remarkable work is apparent from Mr. Goldbury's corporate and commercial law formularies. Princess Zara introduces him with: "A Company Promoter this, with special education, / Which teaches what Contango means and also Backwardation—" (1031) (Orth 2014). Contango, as betting on a future rise in commodity prices, and backwardation as betting on their future fall (Orth 2014), are indicative of the something-for-nothing immoralities of corporate commerce. Such arcana are indeed remarkable in their effects, as is company law. "Time was when *two* were company [sings Princess Zara]—but now it must be seven" (1031). "A Company Limited? [asks King Paramount] What may that be? / The term, I rather think, is new to me" (1035). Mr. Goldbury is happy to explain, in a song that could almost be a versification of some late Victorian text on company law:

"Some seven men form an Association,
(If possible, all Peers and Baronets)
They start off with a public declaration
To what extent they mean to pay their debts.
That's called their Capital: if they are wary
They will not quote it at a sum immense.
The figure's immaterial—it may vary
From eighteen million down to eighteenpence." (1035)

Barely a month after proceedings had begun in *Broderip v Salomon*, Mr. Goldbury cynically summed up the legal position on the stage of the Savoy Theatre:

"Though a Rothschild you may be
In your own capacity,
As a Company you've come to utter sorrow—
But the Liquidators say,
"Never mind—you needn't pay,"
So you start another Company tomorrow!" (1037)

One wonders whether, when *Broderip v Salomon* [1895] 2 Ch 323 reached the Court of Appeal in May 1895, the problems highlighted in this particular lyric had struck a chord with the judges. They held that a company incorporated "contrary to the true intent and meaning" of the Joint Stock Companies Act 1862, carried on business as trustee for its principal shareholder, who was therefore liable to indemnify the company for the debts that it had incurred in the performance of the trust (French et al. 2011: 123). What is beyond doubt, however, is that by November 1896, the concern had passed and that the House of Lords classically reinstated the principle of separate corporate personality (see *Aron Salomon (Pauper) v A Salomon and Company Ltd* [1897] AC 22).

Corrupt practices are common to the England that the Flowers of Progress have left behind and the Utopia that they have come to remodel. The English tenor starring in the opera written by King Paramount as a satire on himself (999), "Mr Wilkinson," is not really English: "As it happens," says King Paramount, "he's a Utopian, but he calls himself English." "Calls himself English?" queries Princess Zara. "Yes. Bless you," says King Paramount, "they wouldn't listen to any tenor who didn't call himself English" (1023–1025). (If "Italian" is substituted for 'English', as in England, the humor of this becomes apparent.) As to candor in corporate commercial transactions, well, forget it. Mr. Goldbury explains his system:

> "Make the money-spinner spin!
>   For you only stand to win,
> And you'll never with dishonesty be twitted.
>   For nobody can know,
>   To a million or so,
> To what extent your capital's committed!" (1037)

This is destined to remain the case, indeed, at least until the Companies Act 1900, which will require the registration of charges over company assets (French et al. 2011: 123). The Utopians are not, however, dissuaded, despite their reservations about the integrity of corporate capitalism. As King Paramount concludes: "Well, at first sight it strikes us as dishonest, / But if it's good enough for virtuous England— / The first commercial country in the world— / It's good enough for us" (1037).

Better educated—or better trained—people would understand all of these things and think accordingly. Education is not uncritical acceptance. Princess Zara's English education might improve matters therefore. "How good and wise you are," Captain Fitzbattleaxe tells her. "How unerringly your practised brain winnows the wheat from the chaff—the material from the merely incidental!" "My Girton training, Arthur," replies Princess Zara. "At Girton all is wheat, and idle chaff is never heard within its walls!" (1045). (In fact, and despite Princess Zara's "high degree at Girton", it would in reality be many years before the University of Cambridge awarded degrees to women.)

To the truly enlightened, incremental reform is infinitely preferable to progress. The original plan was that Utopia should be "modeled" on Great Britain (989). Again, the idealization of women provides the idealistic image. "Quaff the nectar—cull the roses— [sing the Chorus] / Bashful girls will soon be plenty! / Maid who thus at fifteen poses / Ought to be divine at twenty!" (997). Nonetheless, the Utopians are to be taught "[h]ow to work off their social and political arrears!" (1034). Sing the Utopians in exultation:

> "All hail, astonishing Fact!
>   All hail, Invention new—
> The Joint Stock Company's Act—
>   Of Parliament Sixty-Two!" (1041)

Says Captain Fitzbattleaxe to Princess Zara: "Freed from the trammels imposed upon them by idle Acts of Parliament, all [of the Flowers of Progress] have given their natural talents full play and introduced reforms which, even in England, were never dreamt of!" (1045). This King Paramount and the Flowers of Progress attest to in their Act II ensemble:

> " ... It really is surprising
> What a thorough Anglicizing
> We have brought about—Utopia's quite another land;
>   In her enterprizing movements,
>   She is England—with improvements,
> Which we dutifully offer to our mother-land!" (1051)

These improvements are remarkable: police courts empty; divorce abolished; rich criminals punished more severely than poor ones; socially acceptable peeresses; all buildings look like Belgrave Square; unemployment solved; "poverty ... obsolete and hunger ... abolished" (1051); no "risky" stage-shows; an intellectual peerage (1051); writers and intellectuals in the House of Lords instead of "Brewers and ... Cotton Lords" (1051).

These points are made by parodying a "Cabinet Council" (Anson II:1 1935: 98) as a Christy Minstrels show. This may not correspond to the Court of St James but "it is in accordance with the practice at the Court of St. James's Hall" (1049). By now, the Flowers of Progress are having fun at the expense of the credulous King Paramount: "Then, ladies and gentlemen, places, if you please. His Majesty will take his place in front of the throne, and will be so obliging as to embrace all the *debutantes*," says Lord Dramaleigh. Lady Sophy is *"much shocked."* "What—must I really?" asks the King. "Absolutely indispensable" (1053) replies his Lordship. Resigned, King Paramount's desire to imitate Great Britain gains new significance as the curtain falls:

"By doing so, we shall, in course of time,
　Regenerate completely our entire land—
Great Britain is that monarchy sublime,
　To which some add (but others do not) Ireland" (1079)

The last line may be recognition of contemporary resentment at the coterminous use of "Britain" and "England" (Searle 2004: ch. 1). It hints, too, at the intractable question of Home Rule.

CONCLUSIONS

It would be unwise to expect complete consistency in *Utopia, Limited*. It is a comic opera, not a philosophical tract. Certain lines are simply there for laughs. Nonetheless, as a constitutional satire, with a continuing relevance to the relationship of states and corporate commerce, it certainly coheres.

"With the punning title, Utopia (Limited)," writes Max Sutton, "Gilbert introduced a capitalist contradiction into the stream of socialist thought: his utopia becomes a joint-stock company. At the same time, 'Limited' expresses the usual Gilbertian skepticism concerning human efforts to construct any system of absolute value" (Sutton 1975: 113–114). Quite so. *Utopia, Limited* really does four things. It shows us the impossibility of ideal society. It demonstrates a true understanding of the special nature of constitutional law by making constitutional law subject to company law. It shows us that lawyers, though constitutionally important, do not have any special skills to create a state. It shows us the need to reject progress, to limit Utopianism and embrace gradual reform. It is conservative satire. Leaving things as they are is the precise opposite of "Utopian."

The first British professional revival of *Utopia, Limited* since June 9, 1894, took place at the Savoy Theatre on April 4, 1975, given by the D'Oyly Carte Opera Company. The performance "was so over-subscribed that four further performances were given later in the year at the Royal Festival Hall, London" (Wilson and Lloyd 1984: 203). In 1929, Dunhill had written that, "as a skit upon late Victorian manners and customs [ie the constitution of the late Victorian state] it would have a special interest at a time when the Victorians are being so freely discussed" (Dunhill 1929: 208). Increasingly, *Utopia, Limited* is being revived. The work should be better known among idealistic lawyers. Utopia is always Limited.

CHAPTER THREE

Codes

Police Uniform and the Image of Law Enforcement

JANE TYNAN

Image was central to law enforcement reform in nineteenth-century Britain. Visible codes, such as the uniform, were of particular interest to modernizers. As this chapter outlines, the new uniform embodied values and ideals that assisted the transition from an outdated system to a new form of policing. In Britain, the years between 1829 and 1863 established modern policing in the minds of civil authorities and the public. Most apparent on the streets, however, were the uniforms, the visible codes that were to convey the role of the new force in public life.

This period redefined law enforcement in Britain. Coming from the Latin word *politia*, meaning "civil administration," the term police referred to the whole apparatus that managed crime and punishment. However, by the early nineteenth century, many reformers wanted to see this manifest on the streets in the form of uniformed constables. Visibility was central to the reform agenda. This was in evidence in early experiments in policing, which emerged from the 1750s onwards, at a time when various writings were advocating preventative policing in Britain.

Historians agree that the Bow Street Runners, set up in 1749 in London by the barrister Henry Fielding, was an early instance of modern policing. Before this, law and order was organized around the protection of parishes and businesses: the parish constable supervised the watch, which might have called upon the help of the public. Dating from the Middle Ages, the Night Watch was, by the 1700s, attracting criticism for corruption and inefficiency. For a significant part of the public, the Watch was regarded as a bunch of drunken snorers, more likely to run the other way at the sight of trouble. Their inefficiency prompted the setting up of one of the first publicly funded patrols created to combat crime on London Streets, the Bow Street Runners.

The setting up of the Bow Street Runners was a direct response to concerns about the rise in crime and the lack of effective systems to combat the problems of a growing city. The Runners operated under the authority of the magistrates' office and benefited from a system of rapid communication. Their effectiveness was also down to the reforming zeal of the founders, for whom this was an opportunity to demonstrate their very modern solution to the breakdown of law and order. Such determination drove the Runners all over the country in pursuit of offenders. They were also paid a salary. By 1804, a new horse patrol consisting of two inspectors and fifty-two men uniformed in red vests, blue jackets, and trousers were the first civil police department in England. In a letter to Walter Thornbury in 1862, Charles Dickens recalls the Bow Street runners "standing about the door of the office in Bow Street. They had no other uniform than a blue dress-coat, brass buttons ... and a bright red cloth waistcoat. The waistcoat was indispensable, and the slang name for them was 'redbreasts'" (Dickens 1880: 178). Not entirely convinced of their efficiency, Dickens remembered them as "a very slack institution" whose headquarters in Bow was, according to him, a dubious public house. Despite his dim view, the Runners were clearly a new kind of police, whose qualities would later be valued by reformers: most accounts suggest they were visible, dynamic, and determined.

John Brown, in 1757, described the Runners in his *An Estimate of the Manners and Principles of the Times* as a new kind of "police." Many similar writings followed, describing how law enforcement methods might be overhauled, among them Thomas Gilbert's *A Plan of Police* in 1781 and Patrick Colquhoun's *General View of the National Police System* in 1796. A cluster of publications on policing surfaced in this period, which, according to Francis Dodsworth, sought to legitimize changes that were already occurring in the structure of civil government (Dodsworth 2008). Significant, though, was the emphasis in these debates on imposing regularity and uniformity to those operations. Late eighteenth and early nineteenth-century developments gave rise to the emergence of conspicuous forms of policing as part of a changing criminal justice system (Mladek 2007: 3). Updating what was regarded as the outmoded watch, the "police" idea became part of a whole new discourse about centralizing and rationalizing the work of law enforcement. As Dodsworth observes of the various publications and ensuing public debates, there was a sense that "industriousness, reformation and prevention were bound up together in this discourse" (Dodsworth 2008: 587). The birth of the "police" in the nineteenth century was the spawning of an idea, which then took shape as a professional police force.

This shift in thinking represented the emergence of what the French philosopher Michel Foucault termed the "disciplinary society," which described the reconfiguring of solutions to law and order in the late eighteenth century. The work of Foucault is critical to understanding the role of visibility in the construction of the idea of the "police" in nineteenth-century Britain. Foucault's governmentality thesis is of particular value here; he argues that the body became a significant focus for social control in this period (Foucault 1991; Foucault 2001). For him, modern institutions make the body docile, a process revealed in the making of the modern soldier: "By the late eighteenth century, the soldier has become something that can be made; out of formless clay, an inapt body, the machine required can be constructed" (Foucault 1991: 135). Utilitarians who sought reform, according to Foucault, were eager to seize the power of bodies in an effort to take control of the streets and factories. This was the era of the birth of the modern institution, which routinely subjected bodies to various disciplinary measures, whether in the workhouse, the asylum, or the school.

When Foucault cites the rituals and disciplines of the soldier, it is not the age-old military he had in mind but its modern incarnation, whereby "posture is gradually corrected; a calculated constraint runs slowly through each part of the body" (Foucault 1991: 135). He uncovers what lay behind the drive for reform in a variety of social arenas in the nineteenth century. In the new police, discipline, an internal organizing principle, was to start with the constable, to then be circulated throughout the wider society. Foucault reminds us that power is a function of knowledge; that it gave planners and legislators considerable control over bodies in any urban space. Pro-police reformers were convinced that it was the "duty of the state to know," a phrase that was used to mobilize the setting up of the first census, but also represented new thinking about law enforcement (Reitz 2000: 191). According to John McMullan, forms of policing power that were emerging between 1750 and 1840 sought to comprehend English society panoptically – what he describes as an "arresting eye" (McMullan 1998: 104). This policed society would be characterized by the tireless cataloging of vagrants, the indigent, robbers, deviants, and various people thought to pose a threat to the maintenance of law and order. Foucault's "disciplinary society" was clearly at work in the formulation of ideas and plans for the new police. The state improved its information-gathering powers and amassed data on local occupations, habits, and amusements, which were used strategically to exert power and regain control over what were thought to be the most unmanageable urban spaces.

For Foucault, disciplinary practices were critical to shaping modern institutions; he believed the body took on new meanings in the late eighteenth century (Foucault 1991). In their efforts to gain control over the body politic, officials of all kinds were likely to subject individual bodies to practices of rearrangement, improvement and transformation (Foucault 1991). Nowhere was there a greater desire for control over urban bodies than nineteenth-century London, with its seemingly chaotic markets, brothels, and public houses. Moral panics about public disorder, vice, organized crime, and drunkenness

FIGURE 3.1 The Crowd Waiting to See a Policeman's Funeral, photo Paul Martin (1864–1944). Platinum print. London, England, 1894. Source: Heritage Images / Getty Images.

sparked anxious debates about how best to tackle the problems of the modern city. Despite reformers' claims that they sought to introduce consensual law enforcement techniques, Haia Shpayer-Makov argues that the founders of the English police were intent upon building a potent force "imbued with … distinctly masculine attributes and values" (2012: 141). While plans for law enforcement might have involved a focus on preventative measures, the new police were primarily conceived in physical terms and equated with masculine attributes.

It would be a mistake to interpret the desire for police to possess a strong physical masculinity as mere fashion. It was also motivated, no doubt, by the fear of revolution. In the 1810s, radicals, such as the Luddites, had already exposed government to outbreaks of mass violence. The Peterloo Massacre, in 1819, was key to understanding how large the fear of rebellion had become. With demands for electoral reform and representation strengthening, the massacre was viewed as the savage suppression of popular protest. What Michael Ignatieff calls the "Peterloo era," between 1820 and 1842, saw English rulers quite prepared to launch a sustained attack on radicalism (1978: 174). Arguably, the creating of a modern policing system was a response to social and political upheavals created by the Industrial Revolution. While they could not retain a military presence on the streets, at least not indefinitely, the authorities very clearly felt the need to enforce some kind of policing. It was all about perception; regaining public trust while deterring social disorder by whatever means necessary.

Was the militarism of the new police then covert? According to Francis Dodsworth, the police were able to maintain control through the use of a complex masculinity capable of "passing through" dangerous parts of the city (Dodsworth 2012: 197–198). It was vitally important that they were physically capable of enduring assault and coping with danger. Not only were physically imposing men enlisted to police the streets, but training continually emphasized disciplinary techniques of the body, enhanced by the masculinity of the uniform (Shpayer-Makov 2012: 142). Similar kinds of reforms gave birth to the *Dublin Metropolitan Police* and much of the debate in the 1830s there concerned the poor physical state of the old police, who were often stout or too decrepit for duties (Allen 1977). Once the process of reform was complete, the *Dublin Evening Post* proudly reported that the new police parading for inspection by the Lord Lieutenant in Dublin Castle on January 5, 1838 dressed in top hats and frock coats "altogether presented a very uniform as well as a very efficient appearance" (Allen 1977: 304). A smart new uniform guaranteed a focus on the physical fitness of the police force. Uniform draws attention to the body and a Foucauldian reading might suggest that it makes the body available to a disciplinary gaze. Uniform appearance, whether created through training or neat clothing was valued because it altered the public perception of the police. They were re-molded as a fit, healthy, and efficient organization of men.

Foucault's work highlights the true purpose of public reform projects in this period. Reform of law enforcement involved much attention to its visual manifestation, suggesting that surveillance was critical to new plans for policing cities. By focusing on the visibility of the body in space, and by politicizing the act of seeing, Foucault's distinctive perspective on modernity illustrates how modern institutions sought to gain control over people (Rajchman 1994: 224). Indeed, when an 1856 article of the *London Quarterly Review* described the police as an institution rather than a group of men, it foregrounded discipline and bureaucratic professional organization in the construction of the image of policemen (Reiner 1985: 53). Redefining the criminal justice system involved a new kind of "civil administration," centered on the surveillance and strict control of those who enforced the law. The police in their uniforms were ideally placed to be seen and to see others; their disciplined appearance allowing them to take that discipline to the inhabitants of the cities they patrolled.

POLICE REFORM

There was clearly an appetite for reform of the criminal justice system. As E.E. Wilmot, a London barrister, argued in 1828, the magistrates of England had failed to control the problem of crime because their ancient system of parish constables and watchmen was becoming ineffective (Terrill 1980: 240). Since their establishment, London had seen the effects of the Industrial Revolution, including geographical expansion and a massive rise in population. Troops were often used to keep order and spies tracked down suspected offenders, but despite the desire for a solution to these problems, there was a reluctance to establish a new kind of force. The English were particularly hostile to Continental models of policing, thinking that their use of force might curtail individual liberty and freedom. As far back as the late 1700s, when there were plans to transform Militia Men into a form of police, or civil soldier, debates centered on how they might go about crime prevention without being accused of spying; one of the key objections commonly leveled against the model of policing in France (McCormack 2012). There were also concerns about the intrusion of a centralized bureaucratic system into traditional ways of dealing with law and order.

Sir Robert Peel formed a committee to investigate the state of the police in London, which sat in 1816, 1817 and 1818 to gather information on the organization and administration of policing in the city, and to make recommendations for its improvement. The committee concluded that it was disunited and disorganized, but also agreed that a "more centralized and efficient system of police was too great a threat to their individual liberties" (Terrill 1980: 250–251). Peel would not be deterred. Over a number of years, he went on to invest a great deal of time and energy into the modernizing of police in England. Later in this chapter, I explore the colonial dimension in the creation of modern policing in Britain in more detail, to include consideration of Peel's political experience in Ireland as critical to understanding his motivations.

Peel was convinced that reforming the watch system would be beneficial to the effective governance of London. To that end, he experimented with new forms of law enforcement. In August 1822, Peel hired twenty-seven men as a day patrol until the night watch foot patrol, dismounted and mounted forces came on duty in the evening (Reynolds 1998: 116). His early intervention offers an insight into the value Peel placed in the uniform, "in contrast to the police office constables, the day patrol wore uniforms of blue coats and trousers and red waistcoats," outfits he believed would give the men pride in their work (Reynolds 1998: 116). Attempts to modernize the Watch were chiefly intended to resolve questions about discipline, a concern that led reformers to consider the benefits of uniform clothing. If drunkenness and corruption were undermining the credibility of watchmen, then a uniform was thought to promote a sense of collective discipline among the ranks.

Questions of visibility had long played a part in debates about the role of the Watch and their relationship to the public. In the Clink Liberty, Southwark, as far back as 1813, the watch committee carefully considered the visibility of the watchmen's clothing asking "should the watch wear light coats so that they would be visible or should they wear dark coats so as not to be seen?" The committee debated whether law enforcement would

FIGURE 3.2 A Peeler or Police Officer, 1845. Source: Universal History Archive / Getty Images.

be best deployed through a policy of revelation or concealment. In the 1820s, one of the beadles employed by the Clink Paving Commission was urging the use of dark coats so the watch would be "less liable to be avoided by Depredators who can now escape in consequence of the Patrol being visible at a great Distance" (Reynolds 1998: 120). Questions of visibility would preoccupy police modernizers for some time to come.

Making law enforcement identifiable made the work of the watch transparent, and gave a constable reason to fear that he might be reported to his superiors. This was why better-organized parishes used uniforms to mark the watchmen: "In many parishes, such as St Anne, Soho and St Marylebone, the watchmen had greatcoats marked with their parish and the number of their beat for the same reasons" (Reynolds 1998: 151). Thus, prior to the institution of the "new police" there were measures to improve the discipline and morale of the Watch in ways that anticipated later reforms.

Peel's opportunity came to enact his police reforms when he was appointed to replace Lord Sidmouth at the Home Office in November 1821. His experience as Chief Secretary for Ireland had convinced him that issues of public order were best resolved through a centralized police system. By the time he got to Ireland Peel found the Irish gentry failing to maintain law and order, due to a neglected magistrates system and an army in disarray (Terill 1980 249). Considering the army was being called upon to do most of the policing, nineteenth-century Ireland had serious gaps in the structure of its law enforcement. In a country where a Protestant landed gentry effectively controlled and dominated a Catholic majority of mostly Irish peasantry, policing was largely about quelling rebellion and policing protest. Peel's experience in Ireland transformed his outlook, from a strong belief in traditional structures to a desire for criminal justice reform. Peel came up with a solution for Ireland—and the threat that continued public disorder might pose—which was the creation of a centralized, uniformed police force, first named the *Peace Preservation Force*, then later the *Royal Irish Constabulary*. In Ireland, this disciplined constabulary was under the authority of a stipendiary magistrate; he was salaried, a full-time police official, commanded a special group of constables and was answerable to the Irish government. Peel instituted harsh colonial policing. For him, no doubt, Ireland was a special case: there was little sympathy for the people, neither the gentry who failed to keep control nor the indigenous Irish whom the English considered inferior.

When Peel set his sights on reforming the English police he would have different political challenges. The Irish constabulary had been conceived as a semi-militarized force to police a people who were often hostile to the colonial power, a measure deemed necessary due to the frequent calls being made on the military (Tobias 1972: 214). For his plans to reform the English police, his first step was to appoint a *Select Committee on the Police of the Metropolis in 1822*, to endorse a centralized system. Again they rejected the idea, but he did manage to get smaller reforms through, claiming that the old system had to be dismantled to meet the needs of the sprawling metropolis. On April 15, 1829, Peel argued in the House of Commons that "the chief requisites of an efficient police force were unity of design and responsibility of its agents," neither of which could be guaranteed within what he described as the "present parochial watchhouse system" (cited by Terrill 1980: 253). At this point, following minimal discussion, Peel's first police bill the Act for improving the Police in and near the Metropolis (the Metropolitan Police Act) was passed by Parliament. All police in London now answered to one authority, were under the direction of the Home Secretary, and each recruit was entitled to weekly pay and a new uniform.

The new police were to be a civil force structured along military lines. "Unity of design" was a phrase that suggested the desire for a unified and integrated system, but also evokes images of strict uniformity. Threats to liberty were still a concern, which found its first leaders fearful of criticism, and determined to create a force that appeared to be above reproach (Tobias 1972). Historians associate the setting up of the Metropolitan

FIGURE 3.3 Vancouver Police Department's first four officers, L-R: Jackson T. Abray, Chief John Stewart, V.W. Haywood, and Deputy Chief John McLaren. This photo was taken when the fledgling department received their first uniforms, which they had ordered from Seattle. They are standing in front of a temporary City Hall, erected shortly after the original building had been destroyed in the Great Fire of 1886. Source: Vancouver Police Museum.

Police with the inception of modern policing, widely thought to be the first centralized, uniformed, professional force (Monkkonen 1992). The first Commissioners, Charles Rowan, a Napoleonic War veteran, and Richard Mayne, an Anglo-Irish barrister, oversaw the transition from the night watch to the Metropolitan police in London; the emphasis in their planning was prevention rather than punishment after the crime (Reynolds 1998). They were sure that this was best achieved through hierarchy, the beat system, and the adoption of uniforms. All three were designed to heighten surveillance and thus the preventative powers of constables.

UNIFORMS FOR NEW CONSTABLES

Police reforms were part of a larger move towards institutional power in this period when a range of institutions adopted uniforms to promote an image of collective discipline. Daniel Roche argues that for the military, this disciplined appearance is "to shape the physique and the bearing of a combative individual ... whose obedience transforms individual strength into collective power" (Roche 1994: 229). The uniform was thought to reinforce wider social hierarchies, a systematic approach that fitted with the large projects of modernity that rationalized institutional practices. Uniforms were modern, the result of mass-production techniques and new patterns of consumption in the nineteenth century. Uniforms also had the capacity to reform and recreate the body. For Jennifer Craik, uniform practices and techniques enforce specific kinds of social identities formed around a masculine ideal (Craik 2005). Standardized institutional dress might have expressed control and discipline in the army and police but it was also valued for workers and inmates. The increased use of uniforms in nineteenth-century Britain reflects the move from a privatized body to a publicly owned one.

This was the driving impulse to uniform the police, but it was also when military uniforms took on a functional appearance. In the Napoleonic wars, British soldiers wore uniforms that were extravagant and decorative, but army modernization following the Crimean War, saw a review of uniforms. By the nineteenth century, army clothing had become integral to warfare, and was improving military discipline and morale. The Crimean War brought army clothing to the forefront of military debates, making it a turning point for the design of British army uniform. Thereafter, the new khaki service dress gave military planners enhanced techniques to standardize and discipline recruits. The functional military uniform, which by the late nineteenth century was made in drab colors and without decoration, was designed for the increased dangers of the industrialized battlefield. What, then, does that reveal about changes in police uniform in the same period? Bright colors and elaborate costumes reflected a fading military culture that had valued honor. Modern utility uniforms, however, signaled more instrumental uses of dress in warfare: as a form of protection, to act as effective camouflage devices, and to make combatants mobile in the field of battle (Tynan 2013: 8). Changes in police uniform followed the same pattern of modernization, reform, and discipline changing the appearance of the British army at the time. Adopting uniforms, or indeed the drive to improve the appearance of workers, soldiers, or police reflected a whole discourse of efficiency centered on the control of people's habits and activities.

Principles at work in the making of the new police officer were bound up with ideas about manly qualities, such as physical strength and stamina (Shpayer-Makov 2002: 27). This was particularly entrenched for an institution created by men for men; the police force, like the army, was an ideal place to "become" a man. Shpayer-Makov argues that the "appearance of the policeman embodied features that were highly attractive to young men," who might aspire to be a figure that demanded respect on the street (2002: 25). The new police were imbued with paradoxical qualities: conceived as peaceful and impartial, but with an overt physicality that suggested they sought to be equal to potential criminals in terms of strength and force. Physicality was central to internal disciplinary practices: height regulations and physical training were given priority. James Winter notes that Mayne, in particular, had a strong understanding of the power of image (Winter 1993: 57). He, like many reformers, felt the key to improving the criminal justice system was to get ordinary Londoners on side. They realized that only the cooperation of the citizenry could guarantee law and order. However, it was also clear that shows of force did not sit comfortably with the principle of consent.

The first *London Metropolitan Police* were hardly a militia: they wore three-quarter-length royal blue coats, white trousers, and top hats. They might have been structured along military lines but, perhaps to subdue concerns about threats to liberty, they were fashioned as a civil force. Uniforms were critical to underline the preventative role of the new police, particularly their visibility. The physical presence of the arm of the law served as a warning for would-be offenders but their visibility also meant that the new constables could not be accused of being spies (Reynolds 1998: 151). If tempted to behave badly, their uniforms would give them away on the streets. Police uniforms were carefully designed so that constables would not be mistaken for military police, enhanced by the fact that they were unarmed. LMP constables carried a truncheon, handcuffs, and an oil lamp. The only distinguishing marks were the brass buttons on their suits that bore the word "police" (Lyman 1964: 152). A uniform that gave off an image of efficiency also signified impartiality, and the restraint of the police constable. The top hat represented authority, while the tailed jacket symbolized servitude; the new uniform of the *London Metropolitan Police* embodied public service, but also taught people to fear the force of the law that lay beneath the friendly image.

Keeping the peace was the first priority for the LMP, who were concerned with prevention, rather than waiting for crimes or civil disorder to occur. In addition, the new police officers were answerable to the law, just like everybody else. Members of the LMP were to avoid the use of force, where possible, and remain impassive when insults were thrown at them. A strict code of sobriety found constables suspended if caught drunk while in uniform; a bit difficult since they were required to wear their uniforms in public whether on or off duty (Winter 1993: 55). Peel placed special importance on their appearance, which he viewed as a reflection of their efficiency and respectability. He wrote to his wife in October 1829 saying that "I have been again busy all the morning about my Police. I think it is going very well, the men look smart, and a strong contrast to the old watchmen" (cited in Lyman 1964: 153). News of the success of the "new police" traveled, which found New York first uniforming its police in 1853, explicitly imitating London, with the cities of Savannah, Philadelphia, Baltimore, San Francisco, Chicago, Washington, and Boston following in the same decade (Monkkonen 1982: 577). James Gerard, who made his recommendations for creating the New York police based on Peel's idea for London, sincerely believed that "the sight of a uniform would strike a deterrent fear into the hearts of would be criminals" (Monkkonen 1982: 582). Uniform signaled patriarchal state power and the reach it had into the personal lives of New Yorkers.

Peel could not transpose his solution for Ireland, a colonial armed force, to London but he did manage to retain the emphasis on a disciplined police force, a constabulary that embodied the image of efficiency. The force was impartial but could summon physical power and menace if required. It is clear that the first uniforms of the LMP were not particularly militant or commanding, in contrast to the physical appearance of the Irish constabulary. However, further changes to the LMP uniform in 1863 saw the "stovepipe" hat replaced by the custodian helmet, which was by then worn by police constables and sergeants. Dark blue trousers and a military-style tunic replaced the white trousers and swallow-tailed jackets. Consistent with changes in British military uniform, this moved the LMP image further towards a utilitarian, functional, design. However, it does not account for the adoption of the custodian helmet, a traditional design modeled on the Prussian military helmet, the *Pickelhaube*, from the 1860s. Not particularly functional, the custodian helmet appeared to be deployed to give policemen added height. Some police forces adopted the spike and most had a badge on the helmet. It was clear the LMP was becoming more like the disciplined police force first imagined by Peel, but the desire to hang on to features that enhanced the stature and physical power of the body, such as the helmet, revealed an organization that equated policing with masculinity.

It is perhaps significant that women have never worn the custodian helmet. LMP uniform design changes at this time balanced the new image of physical masculinity with old ideas of gentlemanliness. The mix made for a persuasive image: monochrome uniforms gave the late Victorian police a military bearing, not unlike the militia forces in Ireland. However, the helmet was perhaps reminiscent of gentlemanly soldiering, giving men stature, and evoking traditional notions of imperial power. It created a powerful image, one which combined masculine physicality with patriarchal authority. Right through the nineteenth century, the police, whether old or new, maintained a distinctly masculine image.

The Metropolitan Police did not have its first female police officer until 1919. Sofia Stanley also designed the first police uniform for female officers. Before this, women did work for the police, but were not an integral part of the force. During the First World War they were used as police matrons to supervise women and children in court, essentially acting as a support to male police officers. Considered useful to deal with prostitutes, women bridged the divide between the street and the authorities. Many had feminist sympathies, and were driven by a desire to protect women from men, which often included the threat police posed to women on the street. For many, a woman working for the police was a scandal, a matter that raised widespread concern about their physical ability to deal with difficult prisoners (Levine 1994: 36). As discussed, manly qualities such as physical strength and stamina were emphasized in discourses about policing in the 1800s. Most police forces had a height requirement with the Metropolitan Police not abolishing theirs until the 1990s. An institution created by men for men reproduced the idea that physicality was central to the maintenance of law and order. Yet this existed alongside a belief that the cooperation of the public would restore credibility to the police. Thus it can be concluded that while women's bodies were deemed sufficiently vulnerable to prompt objections to their entry to the police force in Britain, their active and necessary role in wartime anticipated later modernizing features of policing in Britain. At first, women could observe and gather evidence, but once a crime was being committed they had to call in the men. Paradoxically, it was the necessity of war that ensured that they were finally given full status in the organization (Levine 1994). It was not until 1923 that they were allowed to carry handcuffs and make arrests. Women created a role that eventually redefined the police in the twentieth century, characterized by a move away from the military model to styles of community policing.

The focus on a certain version of physical masculinity made it difficult to promote the idea of the detective, however important they were to police operations. Uniforms made police accountable to the public, but how could they apprehend hardened criminals without some form of cover? The whole project to create the new police was predicated upon a show of power and authority, a visible and identifiable constabulary that built relationships with civilians. Thus, reservations about covert policing prevented the setting up of a detective department until 1842. Considered at first to be devious, due in part to his lack of uniform, the idea of a police detective had long caused concern not least among the middle classes. There were concerns about entrapment, as Shpayer-Makov observes, "the systematic concealment of the identity of law enforcers facilitated a much wider scope for devious activity" (2011: 189). There were also worries about intrusion into the inner sanctum of the middle-class family home. It took a long time for the detective to be trusted. Inspector Bucket of Dickens's *Bleak House* (1852–1853) was the first appearance in an English novel of a police detective who followed clues forensically with a view to solving a murder mystery (Watt 2009: 55), but Bucket was ambiguously fearsome and friendly. It was not until some decades later that popular culture had constructed a more popular figure, both of the police and the private detective. Conan Doyle's Sherlock Holmes is an exemplar, as was Wilkie Collins's Sergeant Cuff; both men evincing a peculiar intellectual power to reinforce their physical authority.

THE COLONIAL DIMENSION

One of the questions police historians disagree on is whether modern policing arose from local needs or law and order strategies developed in the colonies. Most notable is a debate in the late 1980s between John Styles and Mike Brogden in the *British Journal of Criminology*. Brogden argued persuasively that colonial policing was the prototype for the "new" police in England: they were formed to police social deviance, they had a focus on preventative policing, and they tended to recruit ex-military (Brogden 1987). According to Brogden, when this kind of policing was adopted at home, it was driven by similar impulses that sought to legitimize external governance in the colonial process, often achieved through what he calls "images of law" penetrating everyday life (Brogden 1987: 10). While John Styles agrees that the new police were conceived as a disciplined, integrated unit with semi-military associations, he was more inclined to emphasize their complex, local evolution. For Styles, the colonial dimension was not particularly significant to understanding the emergence of policing in England (Styles 1987). Styles may not be convinced that the new police were a force of imposition designed to control "alien" forces at home, but for Brogden, the colonial dimension holds the key to understanding how the new police were in this period an example of the reconstruction of legal discourse in imperial terms (Brogden 1987: 10).

For both Styles and Brogden, Ireland was where the early experiments in modern British policing took place. Stanley Palmer highlights the different paths England and Ireland took in establishing their modern police forces: whereas "Irish police *replaced* local civil authorities, in England the police *strengthened* them" (Palmer 1988). According to Palmer, however, the colonial dimension challenges accounts that emphasize consent in the emergence of modern policing in Britain. Colonial police were often enlisted to manage and suppress protest. Thus, the relationship between police and civilians was often difficult. In addition, colonial police were more likely to be armed and trained along military lines, which is why Georgina Sinclair argues that colonial policing was *Irish* in origin, the original role of the Irish constabulary being as "an imposer of force on the people" (Sinclair 2008: 173). Both Sinclair and Palmer highlight the harsh realities of colonial policing, but also hint at an alternative interpretation of the origins and development of modern police forces. What is critical, though, to making the link between uniform and colonial policing is, as Brogden suggests, the way in which external governance was legitimized by the insertion of "images of law" in everyday life at home and abroad.

In the colonies, the scope to test policing methods presented opportunities for both experimentation and abuse. In Ireland, as elsewhere, policing was installed for social control and to impose colonial authority. The Irish constabulary became, according to Sinclair, the "practical prototype" for coercive policing of indigenous populations (Sinclair 2008: 175). Colonial police were alert to political as well as social conflict and were trained to develop strategies to meet either, or often both. Part of the problem for

FIGURE 3.4 Group of Royal Irish Constabulary officers and men armed with carbines circa 1870s. Source: Police Museum, Belfast.

the British, as Palmer suggests, was the inability to distinguish crime from protest. Once the Irish constabulary model had been perfected, it was exported. Indeed, nineteenth-century Indian and African police forces had looked to the Irish model for inspiration. In Ireland the constabulary was military in character, something even Robert Peel was prepared to admit, when he used the term "gendarmerie" in 1814 to outline his plans for the *Peace Preservation Force* (Tobias 1972: 216). Irish policing *was* different: men were often summoned for special duty outside their area, they were armed, patrolled in pairs, were organized in larger units than England and, like soldiers, were housed in barracks (Tobias 1972: 216). They wore a monochrome dark uniform with military styling adopted to fit their "semi-military" role. In addition, the Irish constabulary used military weaponry, such as carbines with sword bayonets, revolvers, shotguns, and repeater rifles (Sinclair 2008: 175). Most importantly, though, government rather than local authorities controlled the Irish constabulary. Discipline shaped the colonial police model, for which the Irish constabulary was a prototype.

For instance, when Sir Charles James Napier established a 2,400-man native police force in Sinde province "well armed and well-drilled" under English officers, a model later adopted in the Punjab and Madras, officers from the Irish constabulary assisted with the setting up. By 1861 the Irish model was centralized throughout the sub-continent under the *Indian Police Act* (Jeffries 1952: 32). Frontier policing was designed to be armed, hostile to the indigenous population and prepared to use force. So important was the Irish model that the RIC depot in Dublin provided a course that from 1907 onwards was compulsory for the imperial police service. The favored colonial model reveals much about British aims at home and abroad, the pattern merely representing the *symbolic* separation of army and police.

The London police model was copied widely, but there is much evidence to suggest that the prototypes were created in Ireland and then India. While it is true that the London model was admired and copied by many cities throughout the world, including Sydney, New York, Boston, Cape Town, Mumbai, and Calcutta, its origins lay in colonial policing (Palmer 1988: 86). The "Irish" model was a semi-military, armed constabulary that came into existence during the Napoleonic Wars when internal disorder in Ireland threatened to result in French invasion. Peel created an armed police force, centrally controlled and under military discipline. Establishing police forces became a critical part of British rule in various parts of the world in the nineteenth century, including India and New Zealand. Significant to their impact on the creation of modern police forces was the management and careful containment of force. The Irish constabulary may have been heavily armed, in contrast with the unarmed LMP, but some aspects of a military-style police force were retained. Policing London was not primarily a physical activity, the emphasis on traditionally masculine characteristics and shows of force do not quite fit with the idea of a peaceful, impartial approach to policing. However, the symbolic separation of army and police, a colonial practice, came in useful when searching for methods to control and suppress what were thought to be "alien" forces at home.

So why was uniform important to the functioning of colonial police? Uniformity promotes ideas of order, stability, discipline, but critically, the right to seize authority. In the colonial context, though, the police uniform had a special significance, to identify the wearers as police and, as Charles Jeffries explains, "to distinguish them clearly from military and other persons who normally appear in uniform when on duty in a Colony" (Jeffries 1952: 49). Image plays a large part in sustaining that sense of power and authority (Watt 2013). David Anderson and David Killingray observe that the colonial policeman was the most "visible symbol of colonial rule," who blended military and civilian roles (1991: 2). In the 1880s, the RIC uniform was military in fashion, resembled the Rifle Brigade, and was supplied through the War Office (Hawkins 1991: 28). Thus, the image of the colonial policeman in Ireland was military, and its control an official matter. In 1891, Sir John Swinburne raised in the House of Commons "the great difficulty of identifying Royal Irish Constabulary constables by reason of their uniforms and helmets which conceal their features, and the repeated refusal of the Government to place numbers on the uniforms of this Force" (Hansard February 12, 1891). The force lacked accountability, but used visible codes to project power, and was controlled by government, all of which suggests a military-style force and one that exerted considerable power. Indeed, the uniform served to conceal the individual constable behind an image of official power.

If colonial policing was the prototype for modern police, such as the LMP, then it effectively exported militarism into a civilian organization. In the military, the body is a resource with much attention directed to its enhancement, training, and re-molding. Colonial policing adopted military disciplines and rituals, which then shaped the image of the modern police force. The question is why English rulers eventually agreed to the institution of a style of semi-military colonial policing at home? This style of policing utilized many of the symbols of imperial power and strength. Did these "images of law" perhaps lend the new system credibility? Did they embody a show of colonial power in the agents of the criminal justice system? Caroline Reitz argues that this "new concept of English criminal justice is one that worked its way back to the metropolitan center from the colonial periphery" in order to restore credibility to that system (Reitz 2000: 193). For Reitz, reformers succeeded in representing both liberty and authority as part of the same, through an appeal to get colonies such as Ireland or India under control. What was agreed to be a necessity abroad found its way back to the imperial center in London.

Thus, before it was brought home to England it had to be tamed and "stripped of its harsh Irish features" (Palmer 1988: 520). What was effectively keeping the lid on revolution in Ireland, and elsewhere, was transposed to England to strengthen failing law enforcement strategies. Its visual impact, the roots of which were found in frontier policing, became a key component of the power of this modern police force.

If ideas about the raced body had been prominent in discourses on military recruitment, they inevitably became part of the culture of police recruitment. Specific ethnic groups were taken from one colony to police another, such as Indians in Mauritius, Chinese and Indians in Malaya, and Sikhs in Hong Kong (Anderson and Killingray 1991: 7). Some of these patterns of policing were informed by ideas of the "martial races," that is, the belief that certain races have distinct military aptitudes. When these methods returned home they were transformed, but many of the features, such as strangers policing other strangers, can be attributed to colonial policing methods. Symbols of power and physicality were useful to energize a new system of policing. What were once symbols of colonial authority, acted as a reassurance of power and prestige, lending much-needed credibility to the new force. A colonial model of policing was merely the *symbolic* separation of army and police, achieved through the careful crafting of an image. This strategy was thought to be effective enough to satisfy legislators who longed for law and order reform in England. It effectively exported militarism into a civilian organization, but retained an image of discipline and restraint. Most of all, the ideal model was a constabulary that appeared efficient and impartial, but could summon physical power if the situation demanded it.

FIGURE 3.5 Police remove a Suffragette demonstrator from Buckingham Palace, 1914. Source: Museum of London.

THE CANADIAN MOUNTED POLICE

Of all nineteenth-century police forces, the Canadian Mounted Police are probably the most romanticized, but their formation had much in common with experiments in colonial policing elsewhere. The Canadian Pacific Railway was completed in 1883, and brought social and economic changes to the region. White settlers and a money economy replaced the traditional system used by the Plains Indians, which was based on the buffalo. Conceived as a transitional institution raised to quell uprisings, the North West Mounted Police (NWMP) were both an arm of government and agents of colonialism. Wearing a uniform unsuited to the climate or terrain, their strong image was designed to help the police to fulfill their colonial role. *The Times* noted that scarlet had been selected "in order that no misconception may exist in the minds of either Yankee ruffians or Indian warriors as to the nationality of the force, and it is indeed a glorious livery to fight in if fighting has to be done" (cited in Atkin 1973: 40). A scarlet coat, the traditional costume of the British army, projected an image of power, but also sent a signal to enemies that they were trained to use force. Bright colors on the battlefield were a matter of honor, but once technological warfare made visibility a risk, British soldiers were inclined to use camouflage colors. It was unusual, and perhaps foolhardy, for either soldiers or police to wear bright colors while fulfilling duties in unknown or dangerous territory. In Mountie literature, these policemen were represented as heroic, traditionally masculine with an Anglo-Saxon superiority to give their colonial role legitimacy while avoiding overtones of "over-civilization" (Dawson 1997). While the image of the policeman was changing in the United States and Europe, the Mountie remained the archetype of the romantic hero. He was part of a frontier corps, fulfilling what Keith Walden observes was "the eternal human desire to reconcile tradition with change" (Walden 1982: 85). Order, the central motif by which Mounties were perceived, was reflected in their scrupulous appearance.

The original uniforms of the NWMP betray a traditional military role: conceived in line with Sir John A. MacDonald's original intention that it should be a small force that would be both soldier and police, with the specific purpose of establishing a federal presence in the North-West territories. This was part of a grand design for a new Canada. Their approach to uniform color stood in direct contrast to colonial police forces elsewhere. The work that the NWMP was doing and the image they projected did reflect a semi-military model, but not the version adopted in Ireland or India. The North West of Canada was vast and under-populated, their quest was dangerous and the land unknowable, all of which inspired ideas of adventure. The result of Canada's first period of nation-building under MacDonald, the Mounted Police represented then "a radical departure from the British pattern of law enforcement" (MacLeod 1976: 5). Everything about the "Mounties," including their appearance, went against models of policing in use in other parts of the world at the time. Often accused of being a dandy, the Mountie projected an image that made him appear "democratic yet exclusive, egalitarian yet elitist" (Walden 1982: 35). Modernizing tendencies were not in evidence, but the particular mix of military and policing functions demonstrates how frontier policing often demanded a formidable image.

MacDonald viewed the Mounties as a temporary organization, which was to be phased out once it passed through the frontier stage of their campaign. In the summer of 1874 the NWMP moved west; the famed "Long March" (MacLeod 1976: 23) made all the more romantic and exciting due to the inhospitable territories of the North-West. As the planner of the expedition described in *Ten Years in Winnipeg*, "to a stranger it would have appeared an astonishing cavalcade" (cited in MacLeod 1976: 24). Perhaps much of the romance and excitement attributed to these uniforms derives from their proximity to violence. Their appearance became a significant part of the myth of the Mounted Police, but to what extent did colonial violence give their uniforms an erotic charge? Historically, uniforms are often considered beautiful because they are linked to a notable campaign or they tell a unique story. The romance of the Mountie derived from his cavalier attitude in the face of danger, and was reflected in his loud uniform; a strong signifier of the violence involved in establishing colonial authority.

These policemen were performing duties normally carried out by the military in the North-West Territories. Further, they looked like soldiers from the Napoleonic era, complete with the military spectacle of redcoats and weaponry. Their show of prestige, a traditional military form of display, reflected the duties they performed and the power they exerted. Their power was considerable. The Mounted Police could apprehend, act as magistrates and pass judgment on criminals (MacLeod 1976: 5). They commanded public support and cooperation in law enforcement through these shows of military spectacle. Frontier police were essentially military, hostile to the indigenous population and prepared to use force. Colonial models of policing were copied, as were the semi-military uniforms, which were often dark, monochrome, and functional. However, the NWMP adopted a very different strategy, their image was heroic and spectacular, a traditional military tactic to intimidate foes. While they may have adopted a warrior aesthetic, the NWMP were similarly constructed through the desire for a semi-military force. Planners and legislators saw the value of the *symbolic* separation of army and police but were perhaps prepared to appropriate the symbols of colonial power and authority to lend credibility to their attempts to modernize policing. For the NWMP, image emphasized spectacle rather than surveillance.

CONCLUSION

The introduction of police in the nineteenth century solved many problems. Cheaper than a military force, they caused less resentment among the public and were more responsive to civil authorities. This was due to a careful balancing act, whereby an image of authority was also capable of conveying humility and embodying the idea of public service. Visible codes were thus instrumental to the smooth operation of the criminal justice system. As I have shown, the uniform, in particular, was an ideal focus for reform, whereby certain values were encoded on the bodies of new recruits in the transition to a new form of policing. In the newly industrialized cities of the nineteenth century, there was a desire for increased surveillance, which meant a more "policed society."

Plans for the London police were not conceived in innocence. The extremes of colonial policing were well within the experience of planners, such as Peel. If establishing police forces became a critical part of British rule in the nineteenth century, was not the modernizing of police forces at home a project to control and contain "alien" forces that threatened to upset the natural order? What worked in the most inhospitable circumstances on the frontier of Empire eventually became a solution to political problems at home. New police embodied the contradictions that characterized the relationship between the margins and the center of Empire. Those who introduced modern policing, first in London, then elsewhere, managed to conceal their true goals. Even more surprising is that this was achieved by making the agents of law enforcement more visible than ever.

CHAPTER FOUR

Agreements

The Social Contract and Child Labor in Elizabeth Barrett Browning's "The Cry of the Children"

NANCY E. JOHNSON

In the transition from the Enlightenment to the Age of Reform in Great Britain, the agreement between governors and those they govern underwent a significant transformation. The paradigm of the social contract that had dominated the political theory of the eighteenth century gave way to the ideals of utilitarianism that would drive many of the social transformations of the nineteenth century. In an effort to achieve the greatest good for the greatest number, protective legislation increased dramatically. But this shift in the conceptualization of agreement between a government and its citizenry was not without controversy. Thomas Carlyle famously called utilitarianism "Pig Philosophy," and John Ruskin claimed that utilitarians would "if they had their way" turn "themselves and their race into vegetables" (Ruskin [1843]1903: 29; Carlyle [1850]1898: 315).[1] In jurisprudence, one of the consequences of the rise of utilitarianism was the displacement of natural law by legal positivism. Jeremy Bentham considered natural law a "phantom;" only positive law had substance ([1928] 1977: 17). John Austin approached the law scientifically, arguing that "[t]he existence of law is one thing; its merit or demerit is another" ([1879] 2002: 157). Both Bentham and Austin considered the law a system separate from that of morality.

Such movements in juridical thought and structure—and the controversies surrounding them—often reveal themselves in cultural sites that are outside the formal confines of the legal system. Moreover, because the law is constituted of narrative, it is often literature that exposes contradictions or fissures in juridical thought. Thus to consider what happens to the concept of "agreement" in the Age of Reform, I will examine a specific moment of the law's entry into cultural discourse that exposed the failures of utilitarianism and legal positivism through narrative and reasserted the promise of the social contract and natural law through literature. The historical moment on which I will focus is the early 1840s when a royal commission was charged with investigating the conditions of child laborers in the mines and manufactories of Great Britain. One of the consequences of the investigation was an act of positive law: the passage of the Mines and Collieries Act of 1842 that restricted the ages of children working underground in the mines. Another consequence was a fervent public reaction to the report, which at more than 2,000 pages, still proved to generate widespread public interest. The investigators' reports were constructed primarily of narratives, and it was the stories taken from witness depositions that captured the attention of the public and drew them into juridical concerns. The literary response I will examine is Elizabeth Barrett Browning's poem "The Cry of the Children" (1843), an impassioned critique of child labor that she wrote in reaction to the commissioners' reports.

The movement of law into public discourse points to a juridical crisis caused by the law's inability to address adequately what is perceived to be not just a legal but a moral crisis. It is Barrett Browning's poem that will clarify both the problem and the inadequacy of the response. Barrett Browning argues in her poem that it was the casting aside of natural law in favor of positive law that not only allowed the abuse of children in British mines and manufactories but also rendered the law ineffective in addressing the problem. In positive law, children are dependents and thus not full subjects. In natural law, they are endowed with a subjectivity that elicits protection and provision, based on their dependency, yet also entitles them to the most important natural right, that of self-preservation. Whereas positive law in conjunction with the goals of utilitarianism has led to the sacrifice of children, the promises of natural law could protect and provide for them. Barrett Browning's efforts to elucidate child labor as a juridical problem with moral implications in her poem "The Cry of the Children" is an example of what Richard Weisberg has termed "poethics": jurisprudence in a work of literature that fills an ethical void (1992: 3–5). Through the act of writing a poem, Barrett Browning attempts to alter the direction of the public discourse on child labor, and strives to force legislators and the public to reckon with the natural law that has been displaced by positive law.

The importance of Barrett Browning's poem to a cultural history of law is its disclosure of a significant failure of utilitarianism just as it has taken hold of English jurisprudence and replaced the social contract. In the late seventeenth and eighteenth centuries, political theorists John Locke, James Tyrell, and Algernon Sidney, among others, embraced the paradigm of the contract as the organizing principle of a community and characterized our agreement to the contract as consent. Their theories elevated the law as it replaced the monarch as the site of legitimate political power. Locke argued that we leave our state of nature, which is a state of *"perfect Freedom"* and *"also of Equality,"* and agree to enter into a society for the safety, peace and comfort society brings ([1689] 1988: 269). However, when we enter into this compact, we reserve certain natural rights, the most predominate of which is the self-preservation that protects us from slavery and despotism.

A reaction against contractarian thought also emerged in the eighteenth century and informed the legal thought of the nineteenth. David Hume dismissed the importance of an originating contract and argued that most governments emerge out of "force and violence" rather than consent ([1748] 1994: 169). Bentham rejected the idea of an originating compact outright and considered it a mere "fiction" and a "chimera." For Bentham, the agreement of the social contract is replaced by "two sovereign masters, *pain* and *pleasure*" and by the concept of utility: "that property in any object, whereby it tends to produce benefit, advantage, pleasure, good, or happiness … or … to prevent the happening of mischief, pain, evil, or unhappiness." The concept of utility as a measure of government is *"the greatest happiness of the greatest number"*; and *"that is the measure of right and wrong,"* argues Bentham ([1776] 2008: 393).

A return to the social contract, natural law and natural rights occurred during the revolutionary decades of the 1780s and 90s by supporters of the American and French Revolutions, such as the Richard Price, William Godwin, and Mary Wollstonecraft. Yet because these concepts, especially natural law and natural rights, were associated with the excesses of the French Revolution, utilitarianism took hold as the rational alternative. John Stuart Mill, picked up the cause of utilitarianism mid-century, reaffirmed the agreement to promote the greatest happiness of the greatest number, and endeavored to reconcile utilitarianism with other moral systems, arguing that "[t]he principle of utility either has, or there is no reason why it might not have, all the sanctions which belong to any other system of morals" ([1861] 2002: 28).

Despite the efforts of legal and political theorists to arrive at a rational and effective system of governance, it was evident by the 1840s that the agreements of utilitarianism and legal positivism had failed the most vulnerable part of the population: the children. The children had been sacrificed in the goal to promote the greatest happiness for the greatest number. Together, the reports of the Children's Employment Commission of 1842[2] and Barrett Browning's poem "The Cry of the Children" put child labor into the public sphere and under public scrutiny to reveal this very flaw. Because of the failure of positive law to protect and provide for children, the Royal Commission and Barrett Browning took the problem into their own hands; the commission reports provided the evidentiary material of abuse, and Barrett Browning provided the evaluation and judgment. Together they found that when the measure of right and wrong is the greatest happiness for the greatest number, children are maimed and killed and those who survive lose their faith; they die a spiritual death. Ultimately, when Barrett Browning dons the mantel of the poet–prophet and casts herself as judge, she reasserts natural law, natural rights, and the promises of the social contract.

REPORT OF THE ROYAL COMMISSION ON CHILDREN'S EMPLOYMENT: MINES

Lord Anthony Ashley Cooper, 7th Earl of Shaftesbury, MP, and social reformer who had promoted legislation to curtail child labor in factories, was the driving force behind the formation of a commission in October of 1840 that was charged with investigating the condition of child labor in British mines. The initial commission focused on "children," defined as less than thirteen years of age; in February of 1841, the inquiry was expanded to include "young persons," that is, adolescents. Appointed by the Queen were four commissioners: Thomas Tooke, economist; Thomas Southwood Smith, physician and reformer; Leonard Horner and Robert John Saunders, both factory inspectors; and twenty sub-commissioners whose duty it was to go out to the mines in their districts and interview the child laborers. The precise mission of the sub-commissioners was to "collect information as to the ages at which they [child laborers] are employed, the number of hours they are engaged in work, the time allowed each day for meals, and as to the actual state, condition, and treatment of such Children, and as to the effects of such Employment, both with regard to their morals and their bodily health" (*First Report* 1842: iii). The sub-commissioners' method of inquiry for employers was a set of queries and a tabular form to be filled out by employers; for workers, the sub-commissioners engaged in direct interviews that were collected as depositions. When the *First Report of the Commissioners* was released on April 21, 1842, it caused public outrage and calls for reform. Oz Frankel notes that private publishers took advantage of the piqued public interest, reprinted the report, and "circulated more than ten thousand copies." He also suggests that the *First Report* was "probably the most widely read document of its kind" (2006: 25).

Although the mining industry employed fewer children than the textile industry, by 1842, according to Carolyn Tuttle, children and youth constituted 19–40 percent of the labor force in mining. In coalmines, they made up one third of the work force underground, usually employed in hewing (cutting coal), ventilation and haulage (1999: 142, 144, 149). On the ventilation systems, which involved opening and closing the doors to the mine, children started as early as six years old. Girls often worked on the surface of the mine as "wailers" and "screeners"; they separated the coal from other debris. Older girls, aged fifteen to eighteen, worked at "cobbing" and "bucking," breaking stones into smaller pieces (Tuttle 1999: 156, 161–162). Children were valuable for their small size, which meant they could crawl into tight spaces to extract and haul coal (Tuttle 1999: 169–170). See Figures 4.1 and 4.2.

While some children were employed directly by the mining company, others were "hired" by their parents, who also worked in the mines, as a means of increasing the family income (Tuttle 1999: 150–151). Sara Horrell and Jane Humphries note that the labor of children had long been a part of the family income and even reformers in the nineteenth century were concerned that too many restrictions on child labor would bring hardship to the poorest families (1999: 77–79). Horrell and Humphries also observe that visibility was one of the most significant differences between child labor in the cottage industries, which largely pre-dated the nineteenth century, and in the factories of industrialized Britain. The labor of children in the nineteenth century entered a distinct public sphere where it could be observed and critiqued, although children in mines were often hidden from public view.

In their *First Report*, the commissioners cite visibility as an important difference between their inquiry and those of earlier commissions which investigated working conditions in

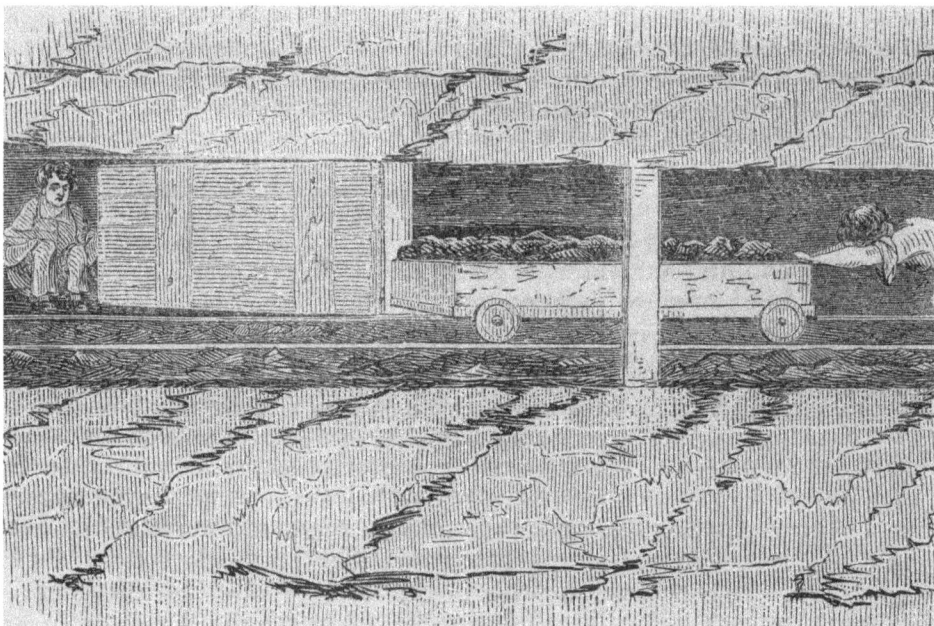

FIGURE 4.1 Sketch of "'an air-door tender in a thin mine in the act of opening an air-door to allow a wagon to pass through'." (*First Report* 1842, Fig. 5, 81). Source: Courtesy of State Library of New South Wales.

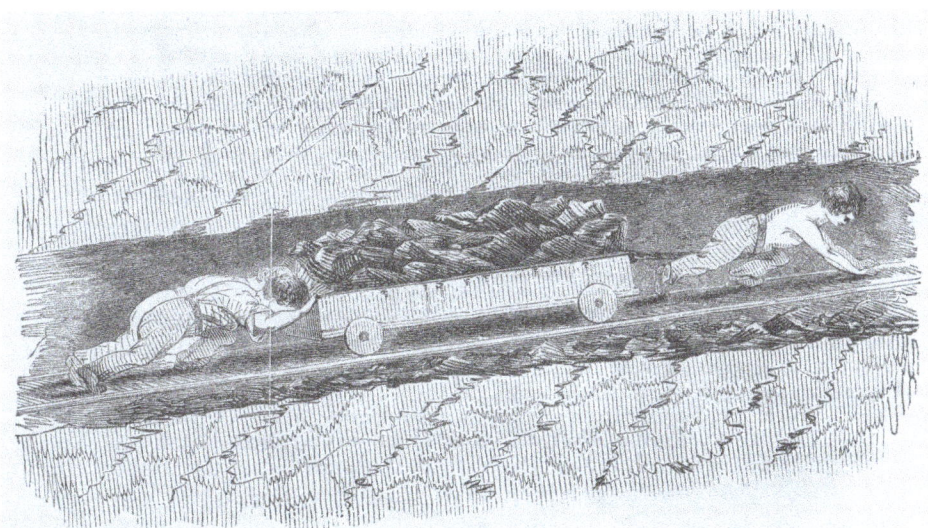

FIGURE 4.2 This illustration depicts children "hurrying or drawing" a wagon of coal. The sub-commissioners note that "the boy in front goes on his hands and feet: in that manner the whole weight of his body is in fact supported by the chain attached to the wagon and his feet, and consequently his power of drawing is greater than it would be if he crawled on his knees." The sub-commissioners also observe that "[t]hese boys, by constantly pushing against the wagons, occasionally rub off the hair from the crowns of their heads so much as to make them almost bald" (*First Report* 1842, Fig. 6, 82). Source: Courtesy of State Library of New South Wales.

factories. Whereas factories were most often in the midst of cities, mines were "wholly removed from ordinary view," their sites were "inaccessible excepting to the employers and the employed," and "the operations ... [had] little in common with ordinary labour" (*First Report*, 4). Hence, one of the goals of the royal commission, traveling to local mines, interviewing child laborers, and publishing reports, was to make the plight of child laborers visible. Child labor in mines may be "notorious," the commissioners observed, but the specifics of the employers' responses and the workers' depositions would force the public to see the situation in its entirety, such that they could not ignore the plight of child laborers (*First Report* 4). Furthermore, in casting light on the working conditions of children in the mines, the commissioners also exposed the inadequacy of the state's response to child labor. While the commissioners note that their mission was only to collect information, not to recommend particular legislation as a remedy, their inquiry revealed the lack of legislation governing child labor in the mines, especially in light of developments in protecting children in factories. The Factory Act of 1833 prohibited children under nine years of age from working in the factories and limited their working hours to nine per day (Humphries 2010: 175).

Although the commissioners deny any role in promoting legislation, the legal implications of their findings were evident, and their work resulted in the passage of the Mines and Collieries Act of 1842 (5 & 6 Victoria, c.99) that restricted those who could work underground, and allowed for routine inspections. According to Peter Kirby, the Mines and Collieries Act of 1842, which had been introduced to Parliament by Lord Ashley, was "the first major legislative effort to regulate the employment of children in British mining" (Kirby 2013: 151). The sub-commissioners' method of inquiry—in particular, taking depositions from witnesses—and the remarkable detail of their reportage were important steps toward bringing issues of legislation into the public sphere. But it was the ubiquitous presence of narrative in the First Report that was most effective in garnering public interest. The witness statements are collected in appendixes to the report, and they are interspersed throughout the report as evidence where needed. In fact they take up the bulk of the report, and the stories the witnesses tell are, in short, captivating.

One of the most effective uses of narrative occurs in the section titled "Sex: Employment of Girls and Women in Coal Mines." Helen Reid, sixteen years old, and working as a coal bearer describes her employment (see also, Figure 4.3 below):

> I have wrought five years in the mines in this part; my employment is carrying coal. Am frequently worked from four in the morning until six at night … Two years since the pit closed upon 13 of us, and we were two days without food or light; nearly one day we were up to our chins in water. At last we got to an old shaft to which we picked our way, and were heard by people watching above. Two months ago I was filling the

FIGURE 4.3 Agnes Moffat, 17 years old, explains that "'[i]t is no uncommon thing for women to lose their burthen [load]; and drop off the ladder down the dyke below. (Fig. 15) Margaret McNeil did a few weeks since, and injured both legs'" (*First Report* 1842: 93). Source: Courtesy of State Library of New South Wales.

tubs at the pit bottom, when the gig clicked too early, and the hook caught me by my pit-clothes—the people did not hear my shrieks—my hand had fast grappled the chain, and the great height of the shaft caused me to lose my courage, and I swooned. The banksman could scarcely remove my hand—the deadly grasp saved my life. (*First Report*, 29)

Margaret Harper, a thirteen-year old putter reports (see also Figure 4.3 below):

I work in Hard-hill Mine. We hurry the carts on the railroads by pushing behind; I frequently draw with ropes and chains as the horses do; it is dirty slavish work, and the water quite covers our ankles. I knock my head against the roofs, as they are not so high as I am, and they cause me to stoop, which makes my back ache. (*First Report*, 29)

Elise Thompson, a forty-year old coal bearer tells her story (see also, Figure 4.4 below):

I wrought all my life, till a stone, 14 months ago, so crushed my leg and right foot, below ground, that I could na'gang [not go]. If women did not work below, the children would not go down so soon; and it would be better for them, as they would get more strength and a little learning. Can say, to my own cost, that the bairns are much

FIGURE 4.4 "[A]n older girl carrying coals" (*First Report* 1842, Fig. 14, 93). Source: Courtesy of State Library of New South Wales.

neglected when both parents work below; for neighbors, if they keep the children, they require as much as women sometimes earn, and neglect them. The oppression of the coal bearing is such as to injure women in after-life; and few exist whose legs are not injured, or haunches, before they are thirty years of age. (*First Report*, 29–30)

While the narratives of girls and women focused on working conditions, narratives by sub-commissioners, managers, stewards, and male colliers in this same section of the report often focused on sexual availability. One of the sub-commissioners investigating the southern part of West Riding, Yorkshire writes:

I visited the Hunshelf Colliery on the 18th of January ... When I arrived at the board or workings of the pit I found at one of the side-boards down a narrow passage a girl of fourteen years of age, in boy's clothes, picking down the coal with the regular pick used by the men ... In two other pits in the Huddersfield Union I have seen the same sight. In one near New Mills, the chain, passing high up between the legs of two of these girls, had worn large holes in their trousers; and any sight more disgustingly indecent or revolting can scarcely be imagined than these girls at work—no brothel can beat it (*First Report* 24).

Matthew Lindley, a collier, says that he can "give proof" that girls in the mines are "worse than the men in point of morals, and use far more indecent language"; George Armitage expresses concern that "the wives who come from pits know nothing of sewing or any household duty"; John Simpkin admits: "I have worked a great deal where girls were employed in pits. I have had children by them myself, and have frequently had connection with them in the pits" (*First Report* 31–32). The outrage in the sub-commissioner's passage and the sexual concerns of managers and miners alike caused direct action. The Mines and Collieries Act prohibited the employment of girls and women underground.

Two major results of the Royal Commission's inquiry and report were an act of legislation to regulate child labor in the mines, and the movement of the issue into the public sphere through the vehicle of narrative. Legislation is a culminating act, a resolution to a conflict, and the Mines and Collieries Act was passed to address the deplorable working conditions of children and youth in British mines. However, thanks to the accessibility of the commissioners' report, its largely narrative form and its circulation, the public was able to continue the discussion beyond the passage of legislation and weigh in on justice. Richard Hengist Horne, one of the sub-commissioners, did so with his article published in the *Illuminated Magazine* a year after the royal commission's *First Report*. His goal was to counter attempts to repeal the Mines and Collieries Act and, further, to remind the public that the problems of child labor in the coalmines have not been solved by the legislation. Horne had been sent by the royal commission to conduct inquiries into child labor in trade and manufactures in Wolverhampton and surrounding districts. His narratives in the *Second Report of the Commissioners: Trade and Manufactures* are among the most riveting as he brings his literary talents (he was a poet, playwright, and critic) to his reports on the dire condition of children who were lacking in the most basic education and health care. Barrett Browning will twice quote from his narratives in her poem.

Horne's article in the *Illuminated Magazine* opens with a call to natural law. "It is an unalterable decree of nature," he begins, "that man, to maintain a healthful condition of body or mind, must *work*; but there is no decree in nature that man should be a slave." The most grievous violation of natural law is the "abject condition in which a father and a mother shall forget the common ties of nature, and sell their children to the worst slavery, even during their tender years" (Horne 1843: 45). But Horne quickly shifts to evidentiary material, making his case that the Mines and Collieries Act should stand and even that additional legislation is necessary. He quotes liberally from the commission's reports, especially from the witnesses' depositions, and he reproduces many of the sketches that so effectively illustrate the confinement and animal-like labor of women and children. He quotes Margaret Hipps, a seventeen-year-old putter from Stoney Rigg Colliery, Stirlingshire, as she describes her work:

> My employment, after reaching the wall-face, is to fill a bagie, or a slype with 2 ½ to 3 cwt. of coal. I then hook it on to my chain, and drag it through the seam which is 26 to 28 inches high, till I get to the main road—a good distance, probably 200 to 400 yards. The pavement I drag over is wet, and I am obliged at all times to crawl on hands and feet, with my bagie hung to the chain and ropes. It is sad sweating and sore fatiguing work, and frequently maims the women. (Horne 1843: 46)

Children and youth took the place of horses in smaller mines, and were thus treated as such. Horne uses this testimony to counter petitions signed by women to repeal the Mines and Colliers Act, which caused them to lose their jobs. Surely if they are reminded of their working conditions, through a witness's story, Horne reasons, they will rethink their objection to the legislation that restricts labor for female colliers.

Aware of the power of narrative to move an audience, Horne goes beyond the witness testimonies and uses other forms of stories. To provide evidence of the physical conditions of a mine, Horne quotes from William Daniell and Richard Ayton's *Voyage round Great Britain* (1814–1825), in which the authors describe a descent into a mine. While he puts this description forward as a form of scientific evidence, it is in fact an engaging narrative that reads like a novel (see also, Figure 4.5).

> We fixed ourselves in the basket, standing, with our hands grasping the chain; the word was given, and down through a duct about six feet in diameter, and wooded all round. I kept my eyes fixed on the aperture above, which contracted as I fell, till at a vast depth I was obliged to look down, as my head grew dizzy, and small pieces of coal and drops of water struck with unpleasant force against my face ... At length, after a descent of 576 feet, I heard the voices of men below me ....
>
> I could here distinguish nothing but a single candle, with the obscure form of a man by it—all around was pitch dark, not a ray of light reaching the bottom from the mouth of the shaft. Before we proceeded to explore the mine, we were commanded to remain quiet a little in order to collect ourselves; and, while we were thus striving to be composed, my nerves were momentarily shocked by a combination and succession of strange noises, among which the loud clank of the chain, as the empty basket dashed to the ground, was particularly offensive. I never saw the object, and had no notice of its approach, till its infernal crash always came to make me jump out of myself. (Horne 1843: 47)

By the end of his article, after an indictment of apprenticeships as another form of slavery, Horne invokes Dickens and his character Smike, a destitute child in the novel *Nicholas Nickleby*. The misery of the children in the mines and factories, Horne argues, rivals anything Dickens's imagination might construct.

While narrative was the vehicle that Horne and the sub-commissioners used to bring the plight of child labor to the public, Elizabeth Barrett Browning turned to poetry and thereby took the debate to a new height. Prose may have overtaken poetry in popularity by the

FIGURE 4.5 "The sketch given in p. 79 (Fig. 4) is intended to represent Ann Ambler and William Dyson ... hurriers ... in the act of being drawn up cross-lapped upon the clatch-iron by a woman" (*First Report* 79–80). Source: Courtesy of State Library of New South Wales.

mid-nineteenth century; however, poetry remained at the top of the literary hierarchy, and if natural law was to be the subject, poetry was required. In "The Cry of the Children," Barrett Browning exposes the ineffectiveness of the legislation that, according to historian Peter Kirby, was difficult to enforce and proved to be a form of "permissive legislation: only operable where it served a particular interest" (1999: 116). It is precisely this utilitarian feature of the legislation that Barrett Browning targets in her poem. For Barrett Browning, the utilitarianism and legal positivism that had dominated juridical thought since the latter part of the eighteenth century, and stirred many of the reform movements in the nineteenth century, were insufficient for addressing child labor. In a juridical argument, she conjures the social contract of the eighteenth century, and casts the treatment of children laboring in the British coalmines as a violation of the social contract and the ethical obligations of that contract. She does not debate the specifics of the Mines and Collieries Act; rather, she makes the discussion one of natural law and thereby fills the ethical void left by utilitarianism and legal positivism. In the domain of natural law, the exploitation of children is the breaking of a covenant with the children of Great Britain.

"THE CRY OF THE CHILDREN"

Barrett Browning's "The Cry of the Children" was first published in *Blackwood's Magazine* in August of 1843, just over a year after the publication of the reports of the Royal Commission on Children's Employment in Mines and Factories in May of 1842, and two months after Richard Hengist Horne's report appeared in *The Illuminated Magazine* in May of 1843. Both texts inform her poem (Hudson and Kelley 1989: 154–156).[3] "The Cry of the Children" is rhetorical and sentimental, of regular stanzaic structure (each stanza is constituted of three quatrains) but of irregular meter.[4] In a letter to her friend Hugh Stuart Boyd in mid-September of 1843, Barrett Browning acknowledges and apologizes for the "whole crime of versification" and explains that "[t]he first stanza came into my head in a hurricane" (Hudson and Kelley 1989: 330–333). Her emotional outrage is indeed palpable in the poem, reaching a crescendo in the children's curse in the final stanza. Despite the formal deficiencies, "The Cry of the Children" was generally well received when initially published in *Blackwood's Magazine* in August of 1843 and when later included in Barrett Browning's collection *Poems* (1844).[5]

"The Cry of the Children" is a public poem that is in dialogue with multiple texts. It invokes Euripides' *Medea* (c. 431 BCE);[6] it looks back to William Blake's "Chimney Sweeper" poems in *Songs of Innocence and of Experience* (1789, 1794); it engages with the reports on the employment of children in mines and manufactures; and it resonates with biblical gravitas. This intertextuality locates the poem in the public exchange of ideas about child labor laws in the early nineteenth century and in the debates surrounding the passage of the Mines and Collieries Act of 1842. The poem also serves as a platform from which Barrett Browning fulfills her role as a prophetic poet, a concept that Barrett Browning inherited most immediately from the Romantic poets, notably Blake and Shelley, and she elaborates on most fully in *Aurora Leigh* (1856) (Stone 1995: 137, 145–146). The protagonist Aurora, who is a poet coming of age, advises other poets:

Never flinch,
But still, unscrupulously epic, catch
Upon the burning lava of a song
The full-veined, heaving, double-breasted Age:
That, when the next shall come, the men of that
May touch the impress with reverent hand, and say
"Behold,—behold the paps we all have sucked!
This bosom seems to beat still, or at least
It sets ours beating: this is living art,
Which thus presents and thus records true life." (lines 214–222)

The poet has a responsibility to create "living art" that "records true life" in the present age and will inform future ages. In "The Cry of the Children," Barrett Browning does just this. She positions herself as a prophetic poet so that she might give voice to the children working in the coalmines and to bring natural law to bear on the treatment of children. The witness testimonies recorded in the child employment reports forced the situation of child labor to a crisis; public discourse began to pulsate with outrage and concern; and therefore the poet was obliged to step into the fray to "catch / Upon the burning lava of a song / The full-veined, heaving, double-breasted Age."

"The Cry of the Children" opens with an epigraph from Euripides' *Medea*: "Alas, alas, why do you gaze at me with your eyes, my children" (lines 439–445). This epigraph, which gives agency to children—they look directly at the woman who threatens their lives—provides Barrett Browning with an opportunity to allow children to speak and to force her readers to listen. She ascribes subjectivity to children who in positive law have no discrete legal identity. Given the context of this line in *Medea*, the epigraph infuses Barrett Browning's poem with urgent emotion and the specter of violence and death. Medea speaks this line as she contemplates killing her children to prevent anyone else from securing revenge on her by killing them first. While it appears in a soliloquy, the line is a rupture in the control that Medea maintains over her revenge on her unfaithful husband. When her children gaze at her, she loses her will and determination, "I despair of what I do. / See my strength / and resolve vanish in the children's / lively faces. It can't be done. / Farewell to my schemes" ([c. 431 BCE] 2006: 1018–1022). Medea will eventually restore her resolve and kill her children; however, this moment when the children become full subjects and gaze at their potential killer is a crucial one for the children. It is a chance for them to bring about a change of heart and alter their fates.

By using this epigraph, Barrett Browning forces her readers to face an egregious violation of natural law: a mother killing her children because she is caught up in a web of revenge. The revulsion spawned by the unnaturalness of this act, particularly when it is invoked in a sentimental poem, prepares the reader to be outraged when encountering another act that goes against natural law: the horrors of child labor. Yet the epigraph also engenders a moment of reprieve. When the children gaze at Medea, her will to slaughter and ultimately sacrifice them wavers.[7] The children provide their mother with a moment of grace, and while she ultimately rejects it, Barrett Browning suggests that we might embrace it. We might truly listen to the children and seize this opportunity of forgiveness and redemption. Hence the "gaze" in Medea becomes the more forceful "cry" in Barrett Browning's poem, so that we might not miss this chance to restore our humanity and our sense of justice. We might honor our agreement to protect our children and acknowledge their natural right to self-preservation.

The opening line of "The Cry of the Children," "Do ye hear the children weeping, O my brothers," invokes in the reader's mind the opening stanza of William Blake's "The Chimney-Sweeper" in *Songs of Innocence*; a poem that profiles a child laborer in a similarly confining and oppressive condition.

> When my mother died I was very young,
> And my father sold me while yet my tongue,
> Could scarcely cry weep weep weep weep.
> So your chimneys I sweep & in soot I sleep. ([1789] 2008: lines 1–4)

Chimney sweeps were indeed "sold" into the trade by parents, as documented by the report from the Parliamentary Committee on Employment of Boys in Sweeping Chimneys (London, 1817). The prospect of parents selling their children into the labor of chimney sweeping is akin to fathers hiring their children in the mines. The chimney sweepers were young—sometimes as young as four—and, like child colliers, valuable because of their small size, which enabled them to squeeze into narrow chimneys. The repetition of the cry "weep, weep," reinforced by the end rhyme of "young" and "tongue," also replicates the sound of a sweeping broom. The end rhyme of "weep" and "sleep," combined with the sound of the broom, constitutes the first reference to death that hovers over the poem.

Barrett Browning transforms the figure of "little Tom Dacre, who cried when his head / That curled like a lamb's back, was shaved," in Blake's poem into "Little Alice" in "The Cry of the Children," but the child is already dead. Tom Dacre's "white hair" becomes Alice's misshapen grave that looks like "a snowball, in the rime" (line 40). Blake condemns the church, represented by the Angel, who comes to Tom Dacre in a dream and tells him that "if he'd be a good boy, / He'd have God for his father & never want joy" (lines 19–20). Barrett Browning is more subtle and careful in her critique of the church; however, little Alice lies "lulled and stilled in / The shroud, by the kirk-chime" and the children agree that "'It is good when it happens ... That we die before our time!'" (lines 49–52).

Barrett Browning's transformation of Tom into Alice calls attention to girls who are exploited in child labor, which is in keeping with the bias of the Commissioners' reports. As Kirby notes, the sub-commissioners considered the employment of young females as "'demoralizing'," and for their interviews they "zealously sought out female workers" (Kirby 2013: 149). It was easier to elicit sympathy for female child laborers than male in part because boys were preparing for adult working lives in the mines. Moreover, in converting Tom into Alice, Barrett Browning also moves the figure of the exploited child from the Christ-like image of Tom as a lamb to a more secular—and thus more common—profile of a child laborer. Yet Barrett Browning still uses the image of Christ as the sacrificial lamb of God (John 1:29) when she likens all of the children in her poem to lambs, who "cannot run or leap" because they are too weary.

Barrett Browning aligns herself more completely with Blake's "The Chimney Sweeper" in *Songs of Experience* where Blake's critique of the church is combined with that of the state. The speaker here has followed the laws of the church and the result is that he is closer to death and unhappy. The Angel's promise has come to naught, and we are reminded of the state of little Alice.

> Because I was happy upon the heath,
> And smil'd among the winters snow:
> They clothed me in the clothes of death,
> And taught me to sing the notes of woe. ([1794] 2008: lines 5–8)

In reference to his parents, the speaker explains

> And because I am happy, & dance & sing,
> They think they have done me no injury:
> And are gone to praise God & his Priest & King,
> Who make up a heaven of our misery. (lines 9–12)

Clearly delineated, and indicted, here are God's Priest and his King. Blake's critique includes the church but moves beyond it and directs itself towards the state. Culpability for the sacrifice of children in the chimneys of London can be found in both civil and natural law, as is the case for children laboring in the coalmines.

Barrett Browning takes a significant step beyond Blake when she establishes her context as the social contract. While the investigation was a royal commission, Barrett Browning does not point an accusing finger at the Queen or even exclusively at Parliament. "O my brothers," the invocation of "The Cry of the Children," identifies the audience of the poem, and thus those she holds responsible, as "the brotherhood." By doing so, she implicates not only the owners and managers of the coalmines, but also the politicians, the clergy, the factory inspectors and anyone of authority who has allowed the abuses of children to continue. Strategically, Barrett Browning also creates an intimacy at the outset between the speaker and the audience when the speaker addresses the audience as "*my* brothers" (my italics); the speaker is either a member of the brotherhood or a sister to it, a fellow member of the social contract. This intimacy captures the audience's attention and requires them to listen. In addition, it obliges everyone in the social contract, including the speaker, to resolve the problem, to end the exploitation of children in the coalmines.

In light of the failure of legislators to solve the problems of child labor through positive law, Barrett Browning turns to natural law for a remedy; she also turns to natural law because the violation has been to the natural rights of children. Her assumption is that children, while not full subjects under positive law, are so in natural law. Barrett Browning was not a jurist; however, she works in the tradition of English natural law theory, which looks back to the jurisprudence of the Dutch philosopher Hugo Grotius. For Grotius, natural law is "What God has shown to be His will" and that will is revealed "in the very design of the Creator," that is, in nature ([1603] 2006: 19, 20). From Grotius to Thomas Hobbes and John Locke, self-preservation became a constant in natural law theory and a natural right that one did not cede when entering into a civil society, a social contract. Divine will found in nature and the natural right to self-preservation are the cornerstones of the natural law theory on which Barrett Browning bases her poem. When Barrett Browning speaks as prophetic poet, she becomes the voice of natural law.

In the frame of natural law, biblical judgment dominates "The Cry of the Children." The poem opens with a rhetorical, sermon-like cadence that is pleading and accusatory:

> Do ye hear the children weeping, O my brothers,
> Ere the sorrow comes with years?
> They are leaning their young heads against their mothers,
> And *that* cannot stop their tears. (lines 1–4)

The rhetorical question assumes that the audience has indeed heard the cries but has done little about it; the sentimental image that follows is a consequence. The rhythm of the stanza quickly shifts to that of a nursery rhyme, with the use of anaphora (repetition) and parallelism, and we are reminded that the social contract is out of sync with nature.

> The young lambs are bleating in the meadows,
> The young birds are chirping in the nest,
> The young fawns are playing with the shadows,
> The young flowers are blowing toward the west—(lines 5–8)

While lambs are bleating, birds are chirping, fawns are playing and flowers blowing, British children are working in coalmines. Moreover, the end rhymes amplify the disjunction. The "meadows" are in "shadows," and birds are in a "nest" that is facing "west," an unnatural direction as birds typically nest facing the east. These seeds of darkness in an otherwise sentimental rhyme, prepare us for the second stanza where we have a passage that mirrors this nursery rhyme, but its focus is on age and mortality.

> The old tree is leafless in the forest,
> The old year is ending in the frost,
> The old wound, if stricken, is the sorest,
> The old hope is hardest to be lost. (lines 17–20)

When Barrett Browning introduces the juxtaposition of "the old," we are returned to the sermon of stanza one and the repetitions here are more reminiscent of those in a liturgical service or the Bible than in a nursery rhyme. The return to the sermon marks one of the most important shifts in the poem: that of the speaker from a peer of the brotherhood to an omniscient judge who stands apart from and above the brotherhood. This omniscient judge is a representative of natural law who is reminding the brotherhood of the natural right to self-preservation—a right one preserves when entering into a social contract. Thus when the children are depicted with "pale and sunken faces" (line 25) and "the man's hoary anguish, draws and presses / Down the cheeks of infancy," (lines 27–28), we see them being pushed toward death unnaturally, and we are forced to grapple with this violation of a natural right. Even the children are aware of the injustice as they admit to being in a state of bewilderment over the nearness of death when "the graves are for the old" (line 36) and the "grave-rest" should be "very far to seek" (line 32).

The children know death, and they equate it with the coalmines. In the scene when the children take us to the graveside of little Alice, "who died last year" (line 39), they conflate the language of death with that of mining. The children explain: "We looked into the pit prepared to take her. / Was no room for any work in the close clay!" (lines 41–42). Like the chimneys that resemble coffins in Blake's poems, the coalmines are graves for these children. They speak as experienced colliers when they remind readers that they are in the pits because they can work in small spaces, and they do so with a sarcasm that indicates their loss of innocence and premature aging. They seek "Death in life, as best to have" (line 54), our speaker / judge tells us, and they are "binding up their hearts ... / With a cerement from the grave" (lines 55–56). When the speaker gives an imperative to "Go out, children, from the mine and from the city, / Sing out, children, as the little thrushes do," they resist and assert their own imperative: "Leave us quiet in the dark of the coal-shadows, / From your pleasures fair and fine!" (lines 63–64).

Barrett Browning gives voice to the children, to their cry, and it is here that she engages most directly with the Royal Commission's reports.[8] Their narratives allow her to enter into the stories and give them poetic form. By infusing the passion of poetry into the commission's narratives, she strives to be more effective in representing the emotions of the children and raising the sentiments of the public. Crucial to that endeavor is placing the stories in the context of natural law, which is what the commissioners did not do. When the children are told to "Sing out ... as the little thrushes do" and "Pluck your handfuls of the meadow-cowslips pretty," the speaker notes that the children respond with confusion and ask "'Are your cowslips of the meadows / Like our weeds anear the mine?'" (lines 61–62). The 1843 publication of the poem in *Blackwood's Edinburgh Magazine* offers a footnote pointing to the commissioners' report: "A commissioner mentions the fact of weeds being thus confounded with the idea of flowers" (Barrett Browning 1843: 261). The sub-commissioner is Richard Hengist Horne.[9] Barrett Browning's representation of the children's confusion of weeds and flowers takes us beyond the mere sadness of children not allowed time to play and unfamiliar with nature. In Barrett Browning's rendition, the children are Christ-like lambs who "cannot run or leap" because they are too weary from work. We have not honored the natural rights of these children.

In another instance of engagement with the commissioners' reports, Barrett Browning again identifies more serious consequences of the commissioners' findings than the commissioners do. When praying, the children admit that

> "Two words, indeed, of praying we remember,
> And at midnight's hour of harm,
> 'Our Father,' looking upward in the chamber,
> We say softly for a charm." (lines 113–116)

An 1843 footnote explains: "The report of the commissioners represents instances of children—whose religious devotion is confined to the repetition of the two first words of the Lord's Prayer" (Barrett Browning 1843: 262). (Again, the sub-commissioner here is Horne.) The children's lack of knowledge of the Lord's Prayer is, for the commissioners, an example of a transgression of civil law in not providing education for the children. But for Barrett Browning this neglect is moral and spiritual. In another passage reminiscent of Blake, the speaker says to her audience "Now tell the poor young children, O my brothers, / To look up to Him and pray; / So the blessed One who blesseth all the others, / Will bless them another day" (lines 101–04). But the children respond that with all the noise in the mines, with "the rushing of the iron wheels," it is unlikely that "God, with angels singing round him, / Hears our weeping any more" (lines 106, 111–112). More harshly, they accuse God of not listening to their cries: "'But, no!' say the children, weeping faster, / 'He is speechless as a stone'" (lines 125–126). They also find God guilty of creating in his own image the very "master / Who commands us to work on" (lines 127–128). In other words, the children have lost their faith, "grief has made us unbelieving" (line 131), they admit, and thus the speaker turns to the brotherhood and asks, rhetorically,

> Do you hear the children weeping and disproving,
> O my brothers, what ye preach?
> For God's possible is taught by His world's loving,
> And the children doubt of each. (lines 133–136)

The children's crisis of faith is the most dire result of their abuse; their spiritual death mirrors their physical death.

The "rushing of the iron wheels" that drowns the children's cries, such that even God cannot hear them, is part of a "wheel motif" that populates the poem. This motif is one of the most effective properties of the poem, as it offers cohesion in the absence of a consistent meter that would otherwise provide unity. "'For, all day, the wheels are droning, turning,—'" (line 77) the children explain, and they continue

> "Their wind comes in our faces,—
> Till our hearts turn,—our heads, with pulses burning,
> And the walls turn in their places.
> Turns the sky in the high window blank and reeling,
> Turns the long light that drops adown the wall,
> Turn the black flies that crawl along the ceiling,
> All are turning, all the day, and we with all." (lines 77–88)

The use of anaphora in this passage recalls the opening stanzas where the repetition evoked both nursery rhymes and Christian liturgy. We are forced, then, to juxtapose the repetition of the wheel movement, the turning upon turning upon turning that is so maddening, with the comforts of childhood and liturgical verse. Those comforts have been withheld.

When the omniscient speaker reappears in the following stanza, reclaims performative language and utters an order to "Let them hear each other breathing," "Let them touch each other's hands," the speaker asserts the position of judge:

> Let them feel that this cold metallic motion
> Is not all the life God fashions or reveals.
> Let them prove their living souls against the notion
> That they live in you, or under you, O wheels!—(lines 93–96)

In these lines spoken by her omniscient speaker/judge, Barrett Browning situates natural law as a counterpoint to utilitarianism and legal positivism. Utilitarianism manifested in culture is the coalmine that employs children. Positive law regulates the coalmining industry, but it does so timidly and in the interests of the industry, which means that it allows for the continued exploitation of children and youth. Poetry for Barrett Browning is a purer source of truth than the law. In *Aurora Leigh*, Barrett Browning declares that poets are "'the only truth-tellers now left to God'," and indeed she uses her position as poet to speak the truth of natural law and hold utilitarianism and legal positivism accountable (Henry 2011: 547).[10]

At the end of Elizabeth Barrett Browning's poem "The Cry of the Children," the children who labor in the coalmines of Great Britain place a curse on their employers.

> "How long," they say, "how long, O cruel nation,
> Will you stand, to move the world, on a child's heart,—
> Stifle down with a mailed heel its palpitation,
> And tread onward to your throne amid the mart?
> Our blood splashes upward, O gold-heaper,
> And your purple shews your path!
> But the child's sob in the silence curses deeper
> Than the strong man in his wrath." (lines 153–160)

In this passage, the children are empowered with biblical righteousness; God is on their side and thus their Old Testament-like curse is justified and sanctioned by Providence.[11] In addition, they act with the authority of natural law. The "'cruel nation'," absorbed by the systems of positive law that infuse politics ("'your throne'") and govern the marketplace ("'the mart'"), has broken the promises of natural law to protect children, to ensure freedom from slavery, and to honor the most fundamental natural right: self-preservation. Thus the children's tyrants (the "'gold-heaper[s]'")—that is, the owners and managers of the coalmines, and the politicians and clergy who enable them—have earned the curse of the children on whose hearts they have tread.

CONCLUSION

The Age of Reform saw an attempted transition from government as a social contract that honors natural rights to a government guided by the agreement to pursue the utilitarian ideal of greatest happiness for the greatest number. The crisis of child labor revealed a significant defect in this reforming ideal. Children were not considered to be within "the greatest number" and were therefore apt to be sacrificed to "the greatest happiness" of those who were. Acknowledging this problem, government stepped in to investigate by means of a royal commission. However, it took literature—poetry in particular—to elucidate the nuances of the social issue and offer a solution: a return to natural law and a restatement of the social contract. Barrett Browning's poem epitomizes this elevated effort of reform and well deserves its place in the cultural history of law. Just before the children issue their curse at the end of the poem, Barrett Browning draws a portrait of the child laborers that depicts them in dark tones as victims of the failed social contract, every bit as pathetic as slaves and martyrs:

> They know the grief of man, without its wisdom.
> They sink in man's despair, without its calm;
> Are slaves, without the liberty in Christdom,
> Are martyrs, by the pang without the palm. (lines 141–144)

Worse off than martyrs, the children may be lacking even the comfort of faith, of an understanding of the divine, and the message of forgiveness in "the palm," a symbol of victory in "Christdom." Still, however despondent the end of the poem, the epigraph from *Medea* provides an opportunity for grace. If Medea had listened to her children, she might not have slaughtered them; Barrett Browning's poetic plea is that if her peers and fellow parties to the social contract will only listen to the cries of the children in coalmines, they might save the children's lives and souls. Whether Barrett Browning's plea was heard, the poem at least achieved its expressed hope "to move the world, on a child's heart."

CHAPTER FIVE

Arguments

Jury Lawfinding and Constitutional Review in 1840s New Hampshire

K CROSBY

The Age of Reform 1820–1920 witnessed a significant move from popular constitutionalism, rooted in traditions of participatory democracy, to a much more exclusive, judge-centric, view of the law (Kramer 2004). This chapter explores this general development through detailed consideration of the particular case of *Pierce v State* (1843) 13 NH 536. The importance of the *Pierce* case, which concerned a conflict between the respective powers of judge and jury, has long been acknowledged. In the Supreme Court's 1895 rejection of jury lawfinding, it was one of the most influential cases cited by Harlan J; and in more recent academic literature its final appellate judgments have been described as "two of the most well-reasoned discussions opposing the jury's right to judge the law" (Conrad 1998: 69). But despite its foundational status within the judicial rejection of the jury lawfinding argument, little is known about the way the judgments were formed. The present chapter relies on contemporary newspaper reports and pamphlets to fill this gap in the cultural history of the case. In so doing, we will shed light on the popular cultural reception of constitutional developments in the Age of Reform.

The trial jury in America started the nineteenth century as an essential republican institution, with Thomas Jefferson having declared in 1789 that the jury was "the only anchor ever yet imagined by man, by which a government can be held to the principles of its constitution" (Jefferson 1853: 71). As the century continued, the judiciary increasingly came to view itself as a better, more legitimate constitutional anchor; and by 1895 the US Supreme Court, finally willing to sanction this significant reform of judge–jury relations, held that jurors should not be alerted to their power to find the law independently of the bench (*Sparf* 1895; Abramson 1994: 67–95). As several legal historians have shown, this transformation was (unsurprisingly) controversial, with some mid-century judges holding to the jury-centric view of the law, while others held to the now more familiar judge-centric vision (Alschuler and Deiss 1994: 902–921). Academic commentators exploring the shift to a judge-centric view of adjudication have often suggested that the most important transformation concerned the development of the American legal profession and, with it, American legal science. This view contrasts those "who were hostile to lawyers and to legal doctrine" to those "who understood that the intrinsic complexity of human affairs begets unavoidable complexity in legal rules and procedures. With legal complexity comes legal professionalism" (Langbein 1993: 566).

Pierce v State offers an early example of an American judge pursuing the judge-centric vision of jury trial, in which the jury is expected to simply follow the legal directions coming from the Bench. This case also allows us to see the development of a single set of arguments in various settings, for here we have a trial, a public debate, and then an appeal, all three of which centered around a dispute between the same two sets of people: the State's Chief Justice, and counsel for the defense. Drawing on pamphlets held at the Library of Congress, this chapter explores the three stages of the argument culminating in the appellate decision in *Pierce*, and finds that the sophistication of the Chief Justice's appellate judgment is vastly different to his more direct, and far less doctrinal, arguments in the debate's first two phases. Not only had the newspaper reports and pamphlets helped publicize the debate, but by giving the protagonists the opportunity to publicly air their views multiple times they had also helped to shape it. This is ironic, given that the Chief Justice's argument was largely based around a rejection of the claim that public debate might form a legitimate part of legal adjudication.

The media theorist James Carey once suggested there were two basic ways of conceptualizing communication: that it is either about the "transmission" of information or the "ritual" enactment of a shared view of the world (Carey 1989). Under a "transmission" view of communication, Carey argued, newspapers are simply concerned with the spread of knowledge, and analyzing them means questioning "the[ir] effects ... on audiences: news as enlightening or obscuring reality, as changing or hardening attitudes, as breeding credibility or doubt" (Carey 1989: 20). Understood as ritual, on the other hand, the act of reading a newspaper becomes "a situation in which nothing new is learned but in which a particular view of the world is confirmed" (Carey 1989: 20). The public debate between the Pierces' trial and their unsuccessful appeal included a meeting of local people, several letters in the press, and two opposing pamphlets, interventions which for the most part insisted that the Pierces' jury should have been permitted to determine the law's true meaning. Chief Justice Parker stands out in this debate as a lone voice against the jury's alleged lawfinding right, and it is notable in this context that much of his pamphlet was concerned with reporting information, explaining in an authoritative way what had happened at trial. But Parker ultimately played the same game as the others, setting out his perspective in a contentious print medium rather than waiting to deliver an authoritative appellate judgment. This indicates some level of agreement with the basic premise that constitutional questions, even if properly *settled* by judges, are at least the sort of thing which the whole community ought to be able to share in a discussion of. Even in his attempt to "transmit" accurate information about the trial, then, Parker CJ seems to have implicitly recognized the legitimacy of the "rituals" of popular constitutionalism.

JUDICIAL REVIEW AND POPULAR REVIEW

One of the more important ways in which it matters for the present discussion that the nineteenth century was an "age of reform" is through the development in America of the idea that adjudication should primarily be conducted by professionals, and that a lay jury ought therefore to be subordinated to a professional judge. It is well known that the post-Revolution judiciary was not always particularly professional, with many judicial seats filled by non-lawyers (Pound 1938: 91–92); although the federal judiciary, unlike the various state judiciaries, did become professionalized fairly quickly (Harrington 1999: 403–404). To take one particularly famous example of the early state benches' informality, the farmer-judge John Dudley (on the New Hampshire Superior Court 1785–1797) once encouraged his jurors to ignore the sophistication of the lawyers in reaching their verdict:

> You have heard, gentlemen of the jury, what has been said in this case by the lawyers, the rascals! … They would govern us by the common law of England. Trust me, gentlemen, common sense is a much safer guide for us—the common sense of Raymond, Epping, Exeter and the other towns which have sent us here to try this case between two of our neighbors. A clear head and an honest heart are worth more than all the law of all the lawyers. (Plumer 1857: 153–154)

Judicial decisions also tended not to be reported (Dudley's directions, for example, come to us third-hand, through a book written by a man whose father had heard the charge many years before). While the system of law reporting in England was notoriously inaccurate right up until the second half of the nineteenth century, there was at least a strong tradition of nominate law reporting as exemplified by Coke's seventeenth-century *Reports* (Baker 2007: 175–192). But in America, the system was not so well developed during the early years. Chancellor Kent, writing in 1828, reported that as late as the 1790s the New York Supreme Court had "no reports or State precedents" (quoted in Langbein 1993: 571); although during the early decades of the nineteenth century many states had started to hire official court reporters (Young 1975). By the time *Pierce v State* came to be decided, then, there were within living memory two broad schools of thought regarding the proper means of adjudication: that the law should be administered by experts, or that it should be administered, in Kramer's phrase, by "the people themselves" (Kramer 2004).

In his important work on the development of constitutional judicial review, Kramer has argued that for at least their first few decades, the state and federal constitutions of the United States were understood as a fundamental part of democratic self-rule; and that therefore the courts were not seen as the final, exclusive arbiters of constitutional disputes. In his subsequent work, Kramer has turned to the writings of James Madison for a detailed exposition of how such a model might work in practice and yet still be recognizably legal (rather than simply political), noting Madison's argument that various governmental departments should debate constitutional meaning, with the courts acting as neutral expositors and the people serving as the final judges of constitutional law (Kramer 2006). The examples given in the opening pages of *The People Themselves* are, however, a little more anarchic than this deliberative ideal would suggest. First, a federal jury refusing to convict a person of piracy, despite assurances from two Supreme Court justices that specific legislation was not constitutionally required. "Bonfires were lit and feasts held in cities and towns from Maine to Georgia" (Kramer 2004: 3–4). Second, a crowd of 5,000 New Yorkers, driving away (and throwing stones at) Federalists, led by Alexander Hamilton, who had spoken up in support of an unpopular treaty (Kramer 2004: 4). Third, a Congressional speech denouncing the proposed Alien Act (permitting the deportation of Aliens even in peacetime) and encouraging the people to refuse to enforce any such law. When supporters of the Act suggested the courts would be a better arbiter of its constitutionality than local militias, one outraged newspaper correspondent insisted that this "is removing the cornerstone on which our federal compact rests; it is taking from the people the ultimate sovereignty" (Kramer 2004: 4–5). What these examples illustrate is what Lord Mansfield had emphasized when, in his 1784 decision in *The Dean of St Asaph's Case*, he had rejected what he saw as an implicit appeal to jury lawfinding: that a strong popular element in legal questions necessarily puts rule-of-law values at risk (*Shipley* 1784: 1040). In this sense the history of constitutional judicial review in America is, as Kramer has argued, closely related to a tempering of what might be considered democratic excess.

Crucially, this democratic excess was not only about spontaneous mob action but also, as can be seen from at least one of Kramer's examples, involved public deliberations via the press. Building on Carey's claim (Carey 1997: 235–239) that newspapers necessarily take a form appropriate to their particular vision of public life, historians of the American press have concluded that the partisan nature of many of the nineteenth-century American newspapers deeply affected the ways in which information was conveyed. Ryfe in particular has argued that nineteenth-century American journalism generally, and not simply the partisan press, "expressed a public life in which values of affiliation, participation, and partisanship mattered most of all. When reading the news, nineteenth-century Americans participated in a ritual drama that confirmed and reconfirmed this conception of public life" (Ryfe 2006: 60–61). But while Ryfe reports (Ryfe 2006: 67) that newspapers tended to focus on readers' "feet," rather than their "heads" (reporting in particular on the movement of crowds rather than the spread of ideas), the lawyers' public pronouncements between the Pierces' trial and their appeal were unashamedly doctrinal in nature. The particular "conception of public life" at stake here, then, was one which concerned the precise legalistic details of government, rather than vaguer questions of participation through rallies and other such political events. What is most striking about all this is that even the State's Chief Justice, whose whole argument was built around a rejection of participatory constitutional decision-making in favor of judicial expertise, could not resist the urge to defend his views in public. In a pamphlet printed directly in response to criticisms launched against him in the local press, he, in turn, looked to the press as a way of circulating and developing his thoughts on the illegitimacy of this kind of public deliberation.

In order properly to understand the growth of the judicial power over constitutional interpretation, and the simultaneous decline of the equivalent jury power, it will be important to bear in mind these broader political shifts about the nature of the public space in which both deliberative democracy and judicial expertise were developing. As the judiciary (and the legal profession more generally) became ever-more professionalized, increasingly using the language of "science" to describe their work (Schweber 1999), they simultaneously extended their reach over the whole business of constitutional interpretation. By laying claim to legal (and therefore constitutional) expertise, decisions such as *Marbury v Madison* (1803) allowed the courts to present "the rule of law in general, and the role of judges in particular, as the principal means of protecting property and controlling the potentially rambunctious voice of the people" (Fritz 1997: 347). But this development in legal thought was at odds with an older tradition which had given colonial juries a much wider discretion. As Harrington has suggested, this earlier tradition can be accounted for or justified in two main ways: first, "many judges lacked formal legal training"; second, "many lawyers and judges were themselves convinced that juries possessed ultimate power to say what the law was" (Harrington 1999: 388). Furthermore, the fact many courts delivered *seriatim* directions to their juries would necessarily have made it difficult for judges to prevent juries deciding the law even if they had wanted to: by giving juries potentially conflicting directions, judges necessarily required juries to at least choose from among the legal positions presented by the various judges (Harrington 1999: 390). Judges wishing to establish their supremacy over juries regarding legal and constitutional interpretation had, therefore, to overcome both a political and a legal set of traditions.

But couching the development in terms of "overcoming" an earlier tradition runs the risk of misidentifying what the judges thought was at stake. Wilf, in particular, has sought to emphasize that the shift from revolutionary republicanism to learned law was not as simple as the federal judiciary returning to an earlier, English, common law tradition with a professional judiciary at its heart (Wilf 2000). Rather, republican ideas of public virtue and of public deliberation were caught up and developed in what Schweber has called the "'separation upward' and 'turning inward'" of nineteenth-century American jurisprudence (Schweber 1999: 431). Wilf has argued that the judiciary increasingly saw the public as corrupted by luxuries, and that the judges therefore came to see themselves as "the repository of virtue ... Legal deliberation, too, contracted as judges abandoned using the courtroom as a republican pulpit and, in its place, created a circumscribed learned law discourse primarily meant to address a professional elite" (Wilf 2000: 1678). The judicial rejection of jury lawfinding was, no doubt, a rejection in part of the idea, as Tocqueville memorably put it, that the jury box is "a free and ever-open classroom in which each juror learns his rights" (Tocqueville 2003: 320); but it is important to understand that this was likely only an effect of a more general process in which the judges increasingly came to see themselves as the guarantors of a republican tradition threatened by the specter of democratic excess. At stake in this change in the judge–jury relationship, then, were the wider questions of the legal profession's relationship to the public, including journalistic discussions of "legal" issues.

In the debates leading up to the appellate decision in *Pierce*, defense counsel appealed to the idea that the people themselves—constituted here in the jury—were the final arbiters of constitutional law. But while the argument was centered on the jury, it was not exclusively aimed at its members. More than this, particularly in the period between trial and appeal, the argument was aimed at a public readership. It seems defense counsel were hoping to participate in the maintenance of an "enlightened public voice" (Sheehan 2004: 406), persuading the wider newspaper-reading public of the justice of their claim that juries, and not judges, must ultimately determine constitutional meaning. But this argument was not merely political; rather, it took seriously the idea that popular constitutional judgment was also, in its own way, popular legal judgment. For this reason, the journalistic debate was heavily reliant on doctrinal argument of a much more detailed sort than that which had been presented at trial. This is something which is necessarily missed in standard accounts which focus solely on the final appellate decision of New Hampshire's Superior Court of Judicature: that the reported judgments are the product of a complex, technical public debate played out in local newspapers and pamphlets. In other words, despite the substantive conclusion of the New Hampshire courts that the people should not be directly involved in doctrinal questions of constitutional interpretation, this argument was an implicit response to the terrain which had been covered in exactly this sort of debate. And it was, paradoxically, this background which seems to have resulted in *State v Pierce*, unlike other earlier decisions to a similar effect, actually engaging in detail with jury lawfinding as a question suitable for serious doctrinal discussion.

THE LAW OF JURY LAWFINDING PRIOR TO 1842

Before we can explore the development of a set of clear doctrinal arguments in *Pierce*, it will be important briefly to survey the state of the doctrine in this area. The standard starting point was the *juratores non respondent* maxim drawn, in particular, from the seventeenth-century English judge and jurist Edward Coke (Coke 1629: 155b). This maxim, which held that judges must not answer questions of fact and jurors must not answer questions of law, was somewhat ambivalent, failing most importantly to describe the proper division of labor where a jury simply delivers a "general" verdict of "guilty" or "not guilty" (Sunderland 1920: 255–258). Does the fact that it is impossible to tease apart the factual and legal aspects of a general verdict mean a jury is *de facto* free when delivering such a verdict to decide legal questions, or even to ignore judicial directions on the law? The most common answer to this secondary question involved pointing to the thirteenth-century Statute of Westminster, which permitted general verdicts where the jury was willing to accept the "peril" of doing so, rather than finding the facts before requesting the "Aid of the Justices" (13 Ed I 1285: c30). This answer, which fails even to specify the "peril" being risked by such a jury (Whitman 2008: 154 n119), does little to give positive content to the *juratores non respondent* maxim, leaving it ripe for a variety of conflicting interpretations. Most significantly, it leaves open the extent to which a general verdict requires jurors to take on the whole responsibility for the decision in a particular trial and, therefore, the extent to which any judicial directions on the law might actually bind a jury. Even in a context such as late-eighteenth century America, where many commentators agreed that juries had a lawfinding right, it was "often difficult to determine whether it meant much more than the traditional ... right of the jury to apply the law, as stated by the bench, to the facts it had found" (Green 2015: 430). The claim that juries have a right to "find" the law, in other words, still leaves open the question of whether judicial directions on the law are better understood as advice or as a command.

One of the many colonial complaints in the dispute leading up to the War of Independence had been an imperial tendency towards undermining the local, independent character of juries in political trials (Reid 1986: 47–59); during the founding era there appears to have been a shift towards a greater local "capacity to resist the imposition of central government law" (Nelson 2010: 1029). By 1794, John Jay, one of the main contributors to the *Federalist Papers* and by then Chief Justice of the US Supreme Court, had imported some of these concerns into the new court's jurisprudence. In *Georgia v Brailsford*, a rare example of the Supreme Court presiding over a jury trial (Shelfer 2013), Jay encouraged his jurors to observe the *juratores non respondent* maxim, and therefore to respect the authority of the judges to rule on legal questions. But this standard common law statement of the judge–jury relationship was immediately followed by a concession that:

> it must be observed by the same law, which recognizes this reasonable distribution of jurisdiction, you have nevertheless a right to take upon yourselves to judge of both, and to determine the law as well as the fact in controversy. On this, and on every other occasion, however, we have no doubt, you will pay that respect which is due to the opinion of the court ... (*Brailsford* 1794: 4)

Jay, in short, was arguing that judicial directions, while doubtless an important part of the background to a jury's decision-making, were not strictly binding.

This idea, of judicial directions as non-binding advice, can be said to rest upon a "departmentalist" theory, giving "each institution of government" a duty to "interpret the Constitution for itself in the course of its own institutional responsibilities" (Young 2015: 845). Here, the shared judicial task of applying a general law to a particular set of facts creates a necessary tension between the role of the judge and that of the jury which, for Jay, could only be resolved by describing judicial directions as part of a dialogue between the two judicial bodies over the way a particular law should be understood. This

FIGURE 5.1 John P. Hale, head-and-shoulders portrait, facing front. Source: Library of Congress.

idea of legal directions as mere advice continued through the next few decades, with one federal judge even facing impeachment proceedings for, among other things, encouraging a jury to respect the value of certainty in the law, as expressed through the doctrine of precedent (i.e., that the jurors should think very seriously before departing from an earlier judicial interpretation of the law) (Harrington 1999: 406–414). And while civil juries had largely been tamed by the early nineteenth century, through the development of "special" pleadings, motions, and verdicts, all of which cleanly distinguished law from fact (Harrington 1999: 414–423), in the criminal law it had proved more difficult to quietly disempower juries. This meant an open debate was required before change could come; and this debate had to take place against a backdrop both of the political history of American juries and of the legal history of which *Georgia v Brailsford* was an important part. This particular part of the "age of reform" had therefore, despite the rejection of public debate the argument involved, to be publicly aired and openly debated. It is, therefore, unsurprising to find an aspect of this debate being played out in the press in the months leading up to the appellate decision in *Pierce*.

In 1851, Curtis J would draw on the known weaknesses in early American law reporting to argue that *Georgia v Brailsford* had simply been reported inaccurately (*Morris* 1851: 58); and in 1895 the US Supreme Court would eagerly embrace this possibility rather than openly overturn its own earlier decision (*Sparf* 1895: 64–65). But by 1842, when *Pierce* was decided, this strategy for dealing with the *Brailsford* decision had not yet been adopted, and as a result there was still a genuine ambivalence in the American authorities on the jury lawfinding question. In the seditious libel case of *Crosswell* (1804), for example, half the Supreme Court of New York, including James Kent, had followed Erskine's argument in *The Dean of St Asaph's Case* (rehearsed here by Alexander Hamilton acting as counsel for the defendant) that a properly constituted general verdict requires judicial directions on the law (*Shipley* 1784). But Kent had gone further than Erskine by adding that such directions were not strictly binding, echoing Jay's conclusion in *Brailsford* that juries could usually be trusted to respect the legal expertise of the judge but that they were not formally required to do so. The difficulty for those who sought to challenge the legitimacy of the jury lawfinding argument was not simply that there was clear Supreme Court precedent, but that those who had publicly supported the argument were often key figures in the development of American law and the constitution of the United States; men such as Hamilton, Jay, and Kent.

But while Hamilton, Jay, and Kent could all be used in support of the claim that the jury had a legitimate lawfinding role, Joseph Story, the "American Blackstone" (Newmyer 1985: 301), could be used as authority for the other side, Story having conclusively rejected the argument in a landmark decision in the 1830s (*Battiste* 1835). While he was unable to cite any authorities for his rejection of the jury lawfinding position, Story insisted that it was a point "upon which I have had a decided opinion during my whole professional life" (*Battiste* 1835: 243). Story's argument, however, appealed to his personal views rather than to the artificial, impersonal wisdom of more traditional common law constitutionalism (Boyer 1997); but it was not an entirely autobiographical argument. As Harrington, in particular, has emphasized, Story's argument placed heavy emphasis on legal certainty as a key juristic value which must necessarily be undermined by any concession to the jury's supposed right to find the law: "While constitutional considerations and the desire to protect the rights of the accused limited the extent to which judges might go in restricting the jury, these same concerns provided ammunition for the assault" (Harrington 1999: 428). Similarly, while the final reported decision in *Pierce* took a more recognizably common-law approach to the question of the jury's role in constitutional disputes, Parker CJ's initial decisions at the trials of Samuel Small and the Pierces was much more like Joseph Story's decision in *Battiste* in its lack of a clear focus on previously decided cases. It is therefore important to track the various uses of authority as *Pierce* went through its trial, journalistic, and appeal stages.

FIGURE 5.2 Portrait of John Jay. Source: Courtesy National Gallery of Art, Washington DC.

SMALL AND PIERCE: THE ARGUMENTS AT TRIAL

The trials of Samuel Small and of Alexander and Thomas Pierce formed part of a wider pattern of prosecutions, in which several people had been charged with breaching a legislative prohibition on selling spirits without a license. Defense counsel argued that the licensing requirement amounted to an unconstitutional restraint on interstate commerce, and furthermore insisted that it was for the jury, not the judge, to settle constitutional questions. Judicial directions on the law, they argued, were merely advisory, and so could not strictly bind a recalcitrant jury. But despite these claims, Parker CJ acceded to a prosecution request that the jury should be subjected to a *voir dire* examining them for their willingness to be bound by judicial directions. Despite this vetting, the defense team had sufficient success with Small's jury (the trial, on similar facts, which preceded the Pierces' trial) for them to fail to reach a verdict. The Pierces' jury convicted, however, and the prisoners appealed, citing the Chief Justice's directions (which had denied the jury's supposed right to determine legal, including constitutional, questions) and the decision to vet the jury for compliance with the judge-centric vision of constitutional interpretation. In the months between the trial and the appeal, Parker had become involved in a public debate with the Pierces' lawyers over his conduct in the trial, a debate which took on an added significance given the close relationship between the journalistic culture and mass democracy of the nineteenth-century United States (Ryfe 2006).

There were three main issues at the trials of Samuel Small and of Alexander and Thomas Pierce. First, was the licensing statute unconstitutional? Second, should the prospective jurors be subjected to interrogatories concerning their view of judicial directions (specifically, whether they should be understood as advice or as a command)? Third, what advice (if any) should the trial judge give the empanelled jurors on the jury lawfinding question? In addressing these points in the first of the two trials, defense arguments from general principle were met with judicial directions built upon an equivalent foundation. Neither side seems initially to have been particularly keen to explicitly draw on doctrine, but this quickly changed as the same core legal teams reassembled for the Pierces' trials. In the second trial, weaknesses in the earlier arguments were shored up through a greater focus on legal rules; although even here general principles were still of primary importance. And this is one of the more important features of the developing argument: rather than there being a particularly significant difference between the ways the parties' various positions were set out in a legal setting (at trial and appeal) and in an extra-legal, journalistic setting (between trial and appeal), each step in the debate was used as a way of developing a single set of arguments, gradually adding more doctrine with each iteration. Certainly, as far as the defense team were concerned, there appears to have been no meaningful difference between the arguments presented at court and those presented in the pages of local newspapers or pamphlets. Legal debate and public debate was one and the same thing, and so, of course, it was improper for the jury, as representatives of the public, to be commanded to reason in a particular way by mere judicial functionaries.

The first issue (whether the judge considered the alcohol licensing statute unconstitutional) was the most straightforwardly doctrinal part of the discussion at trial. J.P. Hale, arguing for the defense, began with the claim that the state law breached the commerce clause of the federal constitution (US Constitution: Art I.8), specifically the provision prohibiting individual states from laying "any imposts or duties on imports or exports" without prior Congressional authorization (US Constitution: Art I.10). In 1827, the US Supreme Court had held that a state law requiring dealers in foreign goods to purchase a license was an unconstitutional restriction on trade (*Brown* 1827). Hale sought to apply this case to the 1838 law which, while not specifically aimed at imported goods, would nonetheless have the effect of restricting imports. This argument did not particularly trouble the court, with Parker CJ noting there was no evidence that the alcohol in question had been imported, meaning the authorities cited by defense counsel did not apply (Parker CJ 1842: 19–20). But this conclusion was not fatal to the argument. Drawing on a still-fluid tradition of jury independence in the United States, Hale and his colleague B.F. Hallett sought to establish that it was the jury, not the judge, which ultimately had the authority to determine these and other constitutional questions.

But this position had been challenged before either trial had even begun, with Parker authorizing a prosecution request to ask the prospective jurors their opinion of jury lawfinding. Parker's record of Small's trial simply records that "JP Hale, Esq, for the defendant, objected" (Parker CJ 1842: 9), and does not mention any detailed basis for the objection. But by the time the Pierces were tried, the defense team seem to have been more organized. At the second trial, they pointed to the New Hampshire legislation which authorized *voir dire* procedures, noting that the legislation only permitted the process in order to ascertain whether a prospective juror had a financial or other interest in the case, and concluded that "if it shall appear to the court that such juror does not stand indifferent in said cause, he shall be set aside from the trial of that cause, and another appointed in his stead" (quoted in *Pierce* 1843: 554). This provision, Hale and Hallett concluded, did not extend to the jurors' approach to constitutional interpretation. Unfortunately for the defense team, Parker had also taken the opportunity to become better acquainted with the relevant law, and was now able to point to examples of jurors being excused for a general inability to "execute the laws of the state," even where this went beyond the wording of the relevant statute (Parker CJ 1842: 23–24). An earlier tradition of jury lawfinding had demanded a certain kind of virtue from all prospective jurors: that they come to court already educated about the broad workings of the legal system (Crosby 2012: 280–238). The New Hampshire statute had clarified this call to prior knowledge by insisting jurors must come with no specific interest in the case; but Parker's ruling entailed a qualitative shift, mandating that prospective jurors' prior view of the law must be restricted to a Socratic denial of all relevant knowledge. This marks an important shift in the virtuous juror's identity: from an already-engaged citizen to a neutral minister of the law.

At Small's trial, Hale argued that it was ultimately for the jury, not the judge, to determine constitutional questions, and that the judge's directions were therefore merely advisory. This claim had a strong doctrinal pedigree (in America, if not in England); but none of the relevant cases were drawn on in Hale's argument, and Parker also failed to engage with them in his rejection of Hale's claim. This suggests that the first rehearsal of the juror lawfinding arguments had been based on something like Joseph Story's "decided opinion" (*Battiste* 1835: 243) rather than judicial precedent. At the Pierces' subsequent trial, Hale's colleague B.F. Hallett drew on several relevant English cases. In most of these cases, however, the judges had decisively ruled that juries were not entitled to settle questions of law (*Lilburne* 1649; *Shipley* 1784); so even here, doctrine appears to have been used to draw on the authority of several significant figures (notably John Lilburne and Thomas Erskine), rather than for its strictly precedential value. Turning to American law, Hallett discussed *Brailsford* (1794), *Crosswell* (1804) and the Massachusetts decision in *Coffin v Coffin* (1808) that judicial directions should simply be considered advice. This doctrinal evidence was, however, extremely partial: Joseph Story's anti-lawfinding decision in *Battiste* (1835), for example, was described in Parker CJ's report of the defense's argument as one of only two "printed opinion[s] which *suggests* such a doctrine" (Parker CJ 1842: 29). The other such case, which Hallett obliquely referred to, was the decision of Baldwin J in *US v Shine* (1832); it is strange that Hallett did not follow the most recent edition of Conkling's *Treatise* by emphasizing that Baldwin J, the judge who had decided *Shine*, had in the same year as deciding *Shine*, also handed down a *Brailsford*-like decision (Wilson and Porter 1832; Conkling 1842: 425–426). While legal authority was used in the second defense argument, it was used in an extremely partial way.

Parker CJ began his direction to the Pierces' jury by recognizing that he was now engaged in an ongoing debate, noting that the jurors had all been present in court for Small's trial and therefore must have heard what he had said on that earlier occasion.

> But it cannot have escaped your observation, that the very able argument for the defendants has been, to some extent, a reply—urged in very respectful terms—to the charge delivered to the other jury, in the case of Small, which has just been tried. And the case may, therefore, require a charge which is, to some extent, a special notice of the argument. (Parker CJ 1842: 32)

Parker CJ's charge characterized the judge–jury relationship as a harmonious balance between two judicial offices, a harmony which the defense had sought to disrupt by urging the jurors to assert their "rights" against the Bench. Having argued generally that the legislature was a better check than the jury against a corrupt judiciary, the Chief Justice next went on to consider Hallett's doctrinal arguments. *Bushell's Case* (1670), he correctly noted, seems to have been more about a specific judicial attempt to compel a guilty verdict than the more abstract question of judicial directions (Parker CJ 1842: 35). This, however, was the only point in his judicial directions when Parker responded to the jury lawfinding argument with an unambiguously doctrinal argument. He next sought to establish that eminent American judges of the US Supreme Court tended to reject the jury lawfinding argument, referring, as Hallett had done (and with no less brevity), to decisions of Joseph Story and Henry Baldwin, as well as to a newspaper letter by the Supreme Court justice Smith Thompson (Parker CJ 1842: 47). The fact that an extrajudicial letter was cited suggests that Parker CJ was acknowledging the authority of the individual judicial personages and not simply the institutional authority of their judgments in keeping with the doctrine of *stare decisis*. As Howe has noted, "it was not unnatural that many Americans preferred to follow the constitutional opinions of Erskine and Fox rather than those of Jeffreys and Mansfield" (Howe 1939: 586). But what is notable in Parker's use of authority is how the opponents of jury lawfinding, no less than its proponents, were able use an appeal to personal authority as a partial substitute for the authority of past judicial decisions, and how that appeal to personal authority could include an implicit concession to the idea of legal argument being pursued in a public, journalistic, forum. This tension, between Parker's rejection of the jury's voice as a legitimate intrusion by the lay public into the professional courtroom on the one hand, and his willingness to cite extrajudicial letters to newspapers, and to publish his own views in pamphlet form on the other, is an unresolved tension at the heart of the decision in *Pierce*.

STATE V PIERCE: THE JOURNALISTIC ARGUMENTS BETWEEN TRIAL AND APPEAL

The reason such a detailed account of the arguments at trial exists is that the trial judge, Parker CJ, decided to publish his notes to defend his reputation. The reason for the publication was that his conduct had been called into question in several letters and reports in the local press, and the publication of his trial notes accordingly began with excerpts from these publications. From the outset, therefore, we can see how the judge, despite clearly rejecting the argument that a wider public debate might legitimately inform a jury's deliberative processes, nonetheless engaged with such a debate to justify the way in which he had tried to inform a particular jury's deliberations. A letter published in the *Boston Morning Post* had claimed that the juries in the trials of Small and of the Pierces had been packed, and had been instructed to "submit to judge law without an attempt to assert their independent rights" (Parker CJ 1842: 3). The *Dover Gazette*, meanwhile, had reprinted the *Morning Post* letter, along with a resolution of "the Farmers, Mechanics and Workingmen of Dover," resolving to instruct their state representatives to secure for juries "the right, which they have enjoyed since the first settlement of the Country, of judging of the Law and Fact" (Parker CJ 1842: 4). The *Gazette* had also published an article on "The Rights of Juries" signed "Mansfield" (Parker CJ 1842: 4–6), as well as a short report on Pierce and Small's trials detailing the steps by which the allegedly "packed" jury was obtained (Parker CJ 1842: 6–7).

The "Mansfield" letter—a strange pseudonym given Mansfield's anti-jury-lawfinding decision in *Shipley* (1784)—covered very similar ground to the letter in the *Morning Post*. This, together with the fact that all three complaints against Parker were printed by the same newspaper, suggests a somewhat orchestrated campaign. Furthermore, given that Hallett was based in Boston, it seems likely that the *Morning Post* letter was his, while Hale, who later published a pamphlet exploring closely related themes to the "Mansfield" letter, was responsible for the letter in the *Gazette*. Hale's letter directly appealed to the newspaper-reading public, asking them to "see where it will end" if "Judge Parker's novel doctrines are to become the judge law of this state" (Parker CJ 1842: 6); but it can hardly be described as a crude appeal to a democratic mob. Rather than directly accusing Parker of tyranny, the letter instead took the standard republican route of noting that the doctrine "puts it in the power of an arbitrary judge, *if we should ever have such on the*

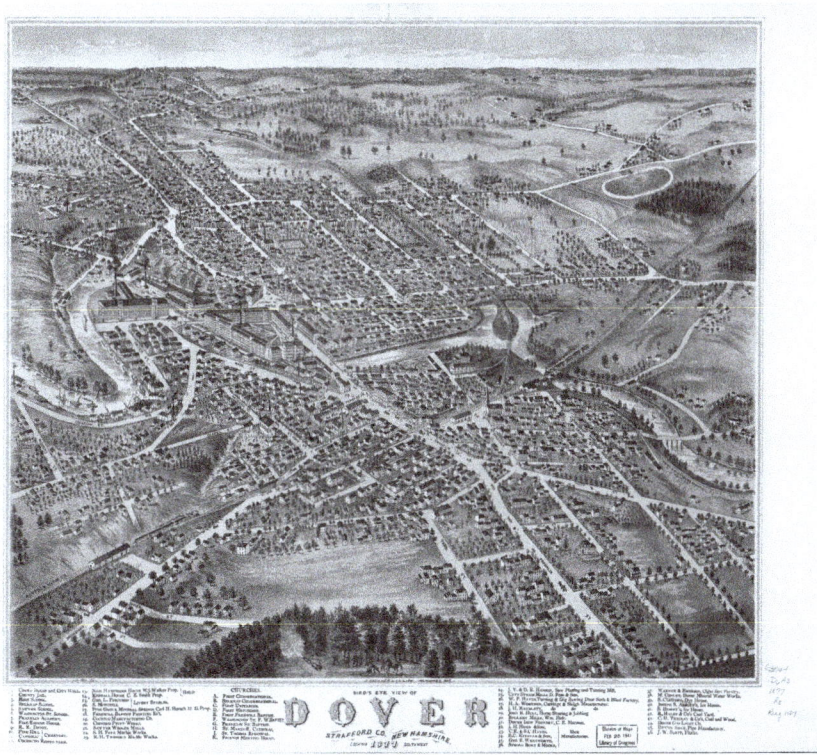

FIGURE 5.3 Bird's eye view of Dover, Strafford Co., New Hampshire 1877. Source: Library of Congress.

bench, to bend a jury to his purposes" (Parker CJ 1842: 5). And while the letter made several grand gestures regarding jury trial as a guarantor of republican liberty, it was also careful to rehearse in detail several doctrinal arguments against Parker's rulings. The literate public to which Hale was appealing was, therefore, expected to follow doctrinal argument; but more than this, it seems doctrinal arguments were expected to help the public as a whole to reach a reasoned decision on the justice of the judge's actions. In which case, the lawyers' interventions can be read as an attempt to maintain the legitimacy of the older view of public, deliberative, constitutional judgment.

It was against this backdrop of sustained public critique that Parker published an annotated version of his trial notes, explaining that the simplicity of some of his arguments at trial could be accounted for by the fact that he had not been expecting to have to deal with questions of jury selection and jury power: "The opinions expressed were those formed from general reflection, and from what occurred at the trials, and not from any special examination at any previous time, with a view to the settlement of such questions" (Parker CJ 1842: 7). Parker's account of the trials contained some eleven footnotes explaining his arguments in greater detail, as well as four pages of extracts from English and American cases, and a newspaper letter from a Supreme Court Justice (Parker CJ 1842: 45–48). The Chief Justice ended his introduction to his reports by declaring he had "abandoned, for the present at least," any plan to systematically discredit the arguments variously leveled against his treatment of Pierce and Small's juries. He was happy enough, however, to discredit his opponents: in language which a clearly wounded Hale constantly returned to in his subsequent pamphlet, Parker concluded that "no lawyer, who had any reputation to lose" (Parker CJ 1842: 37), would have made the arguments pursued by the defense. But despite the *ad hominem* attacks, Parker nonetheless provided more doctrinal support for his position than he had at trial, with a focus on those issues which had been called into question in the press. Parker, therefore, offered a greater level of doctrinal argument when addressing the general newspaper-reading public than he had done when making the same arguments before a jury.

The next stage in the public debate was for Hale to publish a fifty-page pamphlet, insisting, in the language of deliberative democracy, that "Justice require[s] that that Public to whom the Judge has appealed, should hear both sides in order to form an impartial opinion" (Hale 1842: 3). Hale began his examination of the relevant doctrine by describing (Coke and Blackstone's discussion of) the provision in the Statute of Westminster permitting jurors to deliver general verdicts if they were willing to risk the "peril" of doing so. Parker CJ, Hale concluded, was insisting that "the law of Democratic New-Hampshire" affords less power to juries than existed under "the Monarchy of England" (Hale 1842: 16). Having briefly surveyed the argument of Thomas Erskine in *Shipley* (1784), in which the future Lord Chancellor had argued that juries in trials for seditious libel were no less entitled than juries in other criminal trials to deliver general verdicts, he reprinted verbatim ten pages of Chancellor Kent's broadly similar judgment on New York's seditious libel laws in *Crosswell* (1804). In a wide-ranging survey of the available authorities, Kent referred to the practice of the eighteenth-century English legal profession and the fact that Parliament had described its own statute overruling Mansfield's decision in *Shipley* (1784) as merely declaratory as part of his argument. Clearly somewhat wounded by Parker's earlier criticism, Hale concluded by noting that Kent's judgment "leaves no room for addition or explanation by any one who would show what is the law, and by reason of the law, by an individual who will hardly be styled by Chief Justice Parker himself, 'a lawyer who has no reputation to lose'" (Hale 1842:

31). Having considered the English institutional writers Coke and Blackstone, and the two most important cases concerning the judge–jury relationship in cases of seditious libel, Hale concluded by exploring various other American decisions regarding the jury's supposed lawfinding right. In the Massachusetts cases of *Knapp* (1830) and *Kneeland* (1836) (remember that Hale had been assisted in the Pierces' trial by a Boston lawyer), as well as the 1841 Maine case of *Snow* (1841), Hale noted that various state courts had held that judicial directions on the law, while constitutionally required, did not strictly bind a jury. The Chief Justice, Hale was arguing, had erred in law, and it was ultimately the public who must—by reference to the relevant doctrine—judge the justice of his claim. And it was through the publication of his argument (sometimes in newspapers, sometimes in pamphlets) that Hale hoped to persuade the public to judge in his favor.

While Hale published a lengthy pamphlet setting out the doctrinal arguments against Parker CJ's behavior at trial, this was not the only way in which the defense team engaged with the various information networks of the antebellum USA. Hallett sent a letter to a newspaper in his native Boston and, according to Parker, the mechanics' motion reported in the local New Hampshire press had been instigated by discussions with Hale and Hallett (Parker CJ 1842: 4 n*). The two lawyers were therefore willing to engage with the networks with which, as Brown has shown, white northern men, and particularly those living in larger settlements, were able to engage in a relatively egalitarian way (Brown 1989: 218–244). Given Hale and Hallett were arguing for a more inclusive approach to constitutional interpretation, this strategy makes sense. What is perhaps more surprising is that their persistent public relations work was eventually sufficient to goad the Chief Justice into publishing a pamphlet of his own. Despite Parker's own clear preference for the "'separation upward' and 'turning inward'" of legal professionalization as described by Schweber, the republican idea of an enlightened public clearly retained enough vibrancy that it was not possible, when faced with sustained appeals to public wisdom, for him to ignore entirely the significance of public debate. In fact, the public debate between trial and appeal tacitly recognizes a residual idea that constitutional questions, however doctrinally dense, may (perhaps must) be properly submitted to the public at large for their consideration. Even Parker, despite his objections to juries settling questions of constitutional interpretation, seems to have accepted this point.

STATE V PIERCE: THE JUDGMENTS ON APPEAL

The first of the Court's two judgments came not from Parker, but from his colleague Gilchrist J. In a short twelve-page judgment, Gilchrist limited himself to the question "whether the jury possess the right to decide the law in criminal cases" (*Pierce* 1843: 542), and immediately set this question on a decidedly constitutional footing. Noting that New Hampshire's constitution had fully incorporated the common law, subject only to a general repugnancy clause, he approached his task in two parts. First, what was the common law prior to 1776? Second, was jury lawfinding "consistent with, or repugnant to, the spirit of the constitution" (*Pierce* 1843: 543)? Recognizing that the thirteenth-century Statute of Westminster was at the heart of much of the argument in favor of Hale's point of view, Gilchrist carefully explored Glanville, Coke and a number of English cases to glean the statute's meaning. Undercutting the political dimension of the argument, he dismissed John Hawles and Junius, who had both made important contributions to the debate in England, as being too tainted by their politics to qualify as any sort of "impartial legal authority" (*Pierce* 1843: 546); while the French constitutional theorist

FIGURE 5.4 Portrait of William Murray, 1st Earl of Mansfield. Source: Art Collection 2 / Alamy Stock Photo.

de Lolme "must be regarded simply as a learned foreigner, and sometimes showing that want of thoroughness and precision which even a learned man may display when writing on subjects which his previous education had not particularly fitted him to appreciate" (*Pierce* 1843: 546). The true content of the law, then, can only really be identified by lawyers; even then, these lawyers must be acting apolitically: even the future Solicitor-General John Hawles was tainted by "the heat of the party excitements of 1680" (*Pierce* 1843: 546). Gilchrist sought even to exclude history from his account of the English constitution: his reading of the Statute of Westminster was, to borrow from Maitland, structured around a "logic of authority," rather than a "logic of evidence" (Maitland 1911: 491). This judgment, then, was not particularly sympathetic to the wider argument about public, deliberative democracy.

Turning to more abstract principles of legality and of constitutionality, Gilchrist argued that those who insisted that the jury had a right to settle questions of law had

FIGURE 5.5 Portrait of Thomas Erskine, 1st Baron Erskine. Source: Art Collection 2 / Alamy Stock Photo.

fallen foul of thinking that the inscrutable general verdict "possess[es] some mysterious and inherent virtue, but it is difficult to perceive in what way it operates to relieve the jury from the duty of receiving the law from the court, and acting upon it, as it directs" (*Pierce* 1843: 549). While this argument ignores the actual traditions of the early republic, it is nonetheless internally sound: there is a difference between permitting a jury to apply the law, as defined by the court, and permitting it to define the law's contents for itself. And while he conceded the existence of American authorities on both sides of the jury lawfinding issue, Gilchrist preferred the anti-lawfinding authorities for two reasons. First, they "accord … with the best authorities in the common law," by which he meant English law prior to 1776. Second, accepting the alternative would undermine the rule-of-law values guaranteed by the state constitution, in particular the protection against retrospective law-making. Emphasizing his concern that jury lawfinding would necessarily destroy the rule of law, Gilchrist concluded by remarking that

We cannot think that the people or their representatives would be content with an exposition of the constitution which would cause the constitutionality of the license law to remain an open question, until it could be settled by the verdict of a jury ... And it is the opinion of the court, that it is inconsistent with the spirit of the constitution that questions of law, still less of constitutional law, should be decided by the verdict of the jury, contrary to the instructions of the court. (*Pierce* 1843: 553–554)

The rule of law, in short, can only be guaranteed by judicial control of legal interpretation, including constitutional interpretation.

Parker CJ began his judgment by discussing the New Hampshire statute which empowered trial judges to enquire of prospective jurors whether they "stand indifferent," and listed a set of particular interests which should be taken into account in determining this question (NH Laws 1830: 467). Turning to the rules of statutory interpretation, Parker simply noted that this "is not one of those cases where *expressio unius est exclusio alterius*" (*Pierce* 1843: 555). What if, he suggested, an otherwise qualified juror arrived drunk? Surely, he argued, the statute did not mean to exclude a judicial power to prevent such a person, in breach of their "ministerial" duties as a juror (Crosby 2016), from serving? Indeed, in several New Hampshire murder trials, prospective jurors had been asked whether they had conscientious objections to the death penalty. "If this is a correct practice in capital cases, it cannot be rejected in those of less importance; and it is believed to have been the uniform course of the court" (*Pierce* 1843: 556). While this is still a relatively simple argument, it is notable that Parker, as appellate court judge, engaged much more directly here with doctrine and with principles of statutory interpretation than he had done either as a trial judge or as a pamphleteer.

Turning to the wider question of whether New Hampshire juries have the right to settle questions of law, Parker took a notably less doctrinal line than Gilchrist, dismissing the earlier practice in the state as the product of an incompetent and corrupt Bench (*Pierce* 1843: 557). Even after the Revolution, those best suited to devise a rational plan for the state's governance were unable to do so, as they had only recently "relinquished the sword, and were absorbed in the arrangement of the first principles of free political institutions" (*Pierce* 1843: 558). Scholars exploring the legal history of the early republic have, indeed, noted the increasingly scientific approach of American lawyers in the "age of reform" during the early nineteenth century. Clearly a rejection of the earlier commitment to a tradition of jury lawfinding is part of this professionalization of American law. Nonetheless, there are several noteworthy features of Parker's rejection of the earlier tradition. First, the scientific approach being expounded here involves a rejection of history, particularly political history. Unlike the classical common law thought traced in particular by Pocock (Pocock 1957) which, although it dealt with history somewhat naively, nonetheless gave it an important part in the scheme, this is a thoroughly de-historicized version of the common law. Second, history is only permitted as part of the history of the new nation's search for independence, as part of the search for the "first principles of free political institutions." Law, it seems, was too scientific to be part of this process. Nonetheless, a scientific approach to law was essential for the liberty guaranteed by the rule of law: when the courts seized from the legislature the exclusive power to order retrials, for example, greater legal certainty was secured; and the supposed right of each jury to settle the law anew would fundamentally undermine the principle of legal certainty (*Pierce* 1843: 566–571).

If political and legal institutions are conceptually distinct, then an appeal to constitutional politics as a justification for jury lawfinding must necessarily fail; but this does not settle the purely doctrinal question of the jury's proper role. While he had addressed this doctrine in his pamphlet by printing a series of supportive extracts from various cases, in his appellate judgment Parker presented a fully reasoned rebuttal of the appellants' doctrinal argument. There is, again, a clear difference between Parker as appellate court judge and Parker either as trial court judge or as pamphleteer. He began by correctly noting that *Bushell's Case* (1670) and *Shipley* (1784) both had to be stretched quite far to make them say that juries had the power to settle questions of law. Turning to *Brailsford* (1794), he dismissed John Jay's attempt at combining the judge's ordinary power to interpret the law with the jury's extraordinary power to strike out on its own as incoherent. *Crosswell* (1804), he argued, was restricted to seditious libel trials; furthermore, the New York Supreme Court had actually been evenly split on the question of jury power. While the various other authorities cited by the appellants admitted the jury's *power* to depart from judicial directions on the law, they did not, he argued, establish its *right* to do so. In truth, Parker was probably stretching these American authorities no less than Hale had stretched the English authorities; although he did concede that the Maine judges in *Snow* (1841) had unequivocally held that the jury had a lawfinding right (*Pierce* 1843: 561–565).

At this stage, Parker introduced the American cases in support of his position, beginning with Joseph Story's decision in *Battiste* (1835). Given the significance this case would later acquire for those who denounced jury lawfinding, the case was covered with extraordinary brevity, with Parker simply quoting the following passage from the law reporter's headnote:

> The jury have not the right, though they may have the power, in rendering a general verdict, to determine the law in any case, civil or criminal. It is their duty to follow the law as laid down by the court. (*Battiste* 1835: 240)

Parker then cited a handful of other cases, again without any discussion, which may partly be due to the fact he confessed to not having read them (*Pierce* 1843: 566). So while he eventually condescended to engage with the appellants' own doctrinal arguments (and in a great amount of detail), he did not consider it important to do so until the case reached the state's supreme court. As for his own position, authorities were lined up, as they had been in his pamphlet account of the trials of Pierce and Small, but they were still not expounded or engaged with in detail. While this is a step beyond Joseph Story's bare reliance, in *Battiste*, on his life-long professional opinion, it is still apparent that Parker, for all his reliance on the idea of law as an expert, rarefied science, was nonetheless willing to rest in part on his own authority, ending his two-paragraph account of the cases which clearly supported his position with a simple "So much for authority" (*Pierce* 1843: 566).

CONCLUSIONS

In the mid-nineteenth century, the question of who should review the constitutionality of particular legislative or executive actions in the USA was not yet settled. Recent academic literature has emphasized the surprisingly late survival of a popular concept of constitutional review. This chapter has argued that the jury was still considered by many to be a legitimate means of review well into the nineteenth century, and has explored the arguments made for the jury and for the judiciary having this power in a pair of cases from 1842 New Hampshire. What these cases show is that neither side in the argument thought purely doctrinal arguments were particularly important until it looked likely that they might lose either in the public or in the judicial setting. When the jury's alleged right to ignore judicial directions on the law was finally rejected in 1895, the argument was heavily doctrinal, relying extensively on cases like *State v Pierce*. What the analysis in this chapter shows, however, is just how little doctrine was initially relied on by the judges in this case, with case law being used, at most, as a form of retrospective justification. At the root of the judicial rejection of the alleged jury power to review legislation, then, lies an attachment to certain principles justifiable by reference to precedent, rather than a set of principles flowing organically out of past judicial decisions.

But beyond the developing structure of the doctrinal arguments in *Pierce*, this chapter has also explored the public nature of the debate. Wilf has argued that the grand jury was considered by many antebellum Americans to be a means of constitutional dialogue, in which the judge would deliver his charge and the jurors would deliver their presentment; this institutional arrangement, he argues, served as "an alternative ... model for the diffusion of the rule of law. Instead of law reports and treatises, instead of creating a learned law rhetoric ... the Grand Jury as a method of communication directly addressed public opinion as a whole" (Wilf 2000: 1690). Equally, in his pamphlet appeal to the citizens of New Hampshire, Hale analogized between his audience and a grand jury, drawing on a strong tradition of republican virtue as developed through civic participation. In order to properly publicize their position, the defense lawyers had also drawn on the information networks of the time, most notably public meetings and newspapers. As their arguments passed through several levels of publicly circulated refinement, they steadily became more doctrinal, displaying a surprising confidence in the educated public's ability to follow dense legal argument, at least in a politically sensitive context such as the denial of the jury's alleged lawfinding right.

And this, ultimately, is the great irony of the decision in *Pierce*: that for all the rejection of the idea of legal directions as advice, and therefore as the start of an open-ended deliberative process, in short for all the insistence that judicial decision-making was distinct from any lingering republican sphere of deliberative public virtue, it was nonetheless through an engagement with this very public sphere that the arguments in *Pierce* came to take their final form. Earlier judicial decisions against jury lawfinding, most notably Joseph Story's decision in *Battiste*, had rested solely on abstract legal principles. What marks *Pierce* out as different is its status as one of the first American cases to give a thorough doctrinal basis for the rejection of the lawfinding argument. While it is clear that Parker had no less of a "settled opinion" on the subject than Story, the persuasive, authoritative nature of the final appellate judgment was based on much more than the judges' personal authority. And yet, paradoxically, the powerful doctrinal arguments in the appellate decision were drawn out of an engagement with precisely the kind of popular, republican discourse which it simultaneously helped to delegitimize. The legal proof against the jury as an agent of popular constitutionalism came, in large part, from an exercise in public constitutional debate.

CHAPTER SIX

Property and Possession

New Languages of Property

KIERAN DOLIN

> The possessive instinct never stands still. Through florescence and feud, frosts and fires, it followed the laws of progression even in the Forsyte family which had believed it fixed forever. Nor can it be dissociated from environment any more than the quality of potato from the soil. (Galsworthy *In Chancery*: 371)

In *The Forsyte Saga*, John Galsworthy attempted a sustained fictional chronicle of upper-middle-class life in late Victorian England, and identified property and "the possessive instinct" as one of its defining values. Like many a nineteenth-century writer, he recognized the reality of change, and the shaping influence of the surrounding environment on social and personal life, so approached his subject historically. Galsworthy's insight about the adaptability of the "possessive instinct" therefore provides a useful starting point for a cultural history of property law in the nineteenth and early twentieth centuries.

Echoing Galsworthy, the political theorist C.B. Macpherson wrote in 1978: "The meaning of property is not constant. The actual institution, and the way people see it, and hence the meaning they give to the word, all change over time" (1). This was emphatically the case during the nineteenth century, when the law of property expanded and developed in concert with industrial capitalism, but it is also important to recognize continuities, and the existence of factors that impeded reform and innovation in the law. The language of the common law, its inherited forms of action and remedies, its conceptual categories and specialized terminology, functioned as a force for continuity and resistance to change in the sphere of property law. Sir Henry Maine, who pioneered the cultural history of law in Victorian Britain, reflected on this dialectic: "Law is stable; the societies we are speaking of are progressive." He identified three mechanisms whereby "law is brought into harmony with society," namely legal fictions, equity and legislation (1861: 29). In what follows, I shall be interested in tracing some of the contexts in which the language of "property" was placed under pressure of change, not only in courts and "legislation," but in cultural texts and the broader society. My essential argument is that new kinds of property required new ways of speaking or writing, new "rhetorics of ownership," new languages of rights (Rose 1994). Carol M. Rose argues that claims of ownership are best understood as a kind of assertion or story, told within a culture that shapes the story's content and meaning. That is, the would-be "possessor" has to send a message that others in the culture understand and that they find persuasive as grounds for the claim asserted. (1994: 25)

This approach to property as entailing a communicative act includes specific, local assertions of ownership and the larger stories or meta-narratives that a culture tells itself about the very institution of property, its origins and ends.

After a short outline of key developments in the theory of property, this chapter will examine a notable campaign for law reform in which a new story was eventually accepted, the recognition of married women's rights over their own property, and then explore another contested area, the recognition of indigenous peoples' ownership of lands claimed as a result of Britain's imperial expansion. In many colonies the common law encountered radically different expressions of ownership, signs of property that it could not read or could not accept. These marked out a boundary of what Galsworthy called its "progression."

DEBATING AND DEFINING PROPERTY LAW

The importance of property as a topic in the legal history of the period was recognized by Dean G. Acheson, the future American statesman, in the *Harvard Law Review* in 1919. Acheson argued that:

> the all-absorbing legal conception of the [nineteenth] century [was] that of the property right. Everything was thought of in terms of property—reputation, privacy, domestic relations—and as new interests acquired protection, their viability depended upon their ability to take on the protective coloring of property. (330)

If we follow the metaphors in Acheson's account, property is the most fertile language of the law, "absorbing" other concepts, "colouring" new forms of value, and providing the currency ("terms") of legal argument. In essence, new interests tended to be translated into the language of property. However, this legal productivity, extending even into the private sphere, emerged out of a wider social ferment. As the historian and anthropologist Alan Macfarlane put it, in the nineteenth century "the law enshrined an obsession with property, which was conceived of as virtually private, rather than communal" (1986: 145). Private property was regarded as "sacred," that is, as the cornerstone and supreme value of this "capitalist and individualistic system" (158). A quotation from the robber baron turned philanthropist Andrew Carnegie suggests the stakes of this belief: "Upon the sacredness of property civilization itself depends—the right of the laborer to his hundred dollars in the savings bank, and equally the legal right of the millionaire to his millions" (1889: 654).

Carnegie's acceptance of the inevitability of inequality was not always shared. Throughout the century, the proliferation of forms of private property, and the social effects of capitalist individualism were contested as well as promoted. A line of eminent Victorian cultural critics, most notably Thomas Carlyle and John Ruskin, penned impassioned and eloquent challenges to the tendency within industrialism and laissez-faire capitalism to focus on economic considerations to the exclusion of other responsibilities, to make "the cash nexus" the primary form of human relationship, as Carlyle put it in "Chartism" (1839: 199). As a dominant ethos with roots deep in Protestant Christianity, industrial capitalism could call on writers as varied as Thomas Babington Macaulay and Samuel Smiles to articulate the social value of property accumulation and investment. Smiles's *Self-Help* with its exemplary lives of inventors and engineers found a ready audience for its gospel of hard work, thrift and self-belief throughout the latter half of the nineteenth century. In addition to such expository prose genres, poetry, fiction, and drama were also used as vehicles for exploring the inner life of property and possession. Benjamin Disraeli, the Tory politician who promoted his pre-industrial ideals in a series of novels, was a notable example, arguing in *Sybil* that "property has its duties as well as its rights" (1845: II.11).

Unsurprisingly, property became a subject of intense interest for new disciplines such as anthropology and sociology, and comparative or historical jurisprudence, as well as for law and economics. As a result, the cultural study of property began in earnest in this period. Lewis Henry Morgan, an American lawyer who conducted anthropological fieldwork among the Iroquois and other Native American peoples, offered a long historical perspective on the development of property:

> The growth of the idea of property in the human mind commenced in feebleness and ended in becoming its ruling passion. Governments and laws are instituted with primary reference to its creation, protection and enjoyment. It introduced human slavery as an instrument in its production; after the experience of several thousand years, it caused the abolition of slavery upon the discovery that a freeman was a better property-making machine ... Since the advent of civilisation, the outgrowth of property has been so immense, its forms so diversified, its uses so expanding and its management so intelligent in the interests of its owners that it has become, on the part of the people, an unmanageable power. The human mind stands bewildered in the presence of its own creation. ([1877] 2005: 27)

Morgan accepted that property had been a motive force in the development of civilization, but also thought that it had been deeply implicated in ethically questionable economic practices throughout history. He concluded that, as a social institution, its operation needed to be refined if the human race as a whole, and not just the class of owners, was to continue to progress. With its invocation of the mythic narrative of modernity, that history was an arc of progress towards ever-greater knowledge and freedom, and its identification of class as a key element in the ownership of property, there are indications of Morgan's awareness of the writings of Karl Marx and Friedrich Engels. Their critique in *The Communist Manifesto* and elsewhere of "modern bourgeois private property" as the expropriation of the labor of others, and the colonizing of all departments of life by economic relations, led them not to Morgan's bewilderment, but to a political program in which the abolition of private property would institute a new Communist society (Marx and Engels 1848: 485). In the literary sphere, Oscar Wilde combined his well-known aestheticism with a radical political vision, arguing in *The Soul of Man under Socialism* that, "If property had simply pleasures, we could stand it, but its duties make it unbearable. In the interest of the rich we must get rid of it" (1891: 1081). This text suggests there was a serious, critical undercurrent to the witty treatment of property and love in Wilde's upper-class comedies.

But what was property? How was it defined and understood in nineteenth-century law and society? As many previous commentators have noted, the word had, and still has, a popular usage and a legal sense. To quote Macpherson, "In current common usage, property is *things*; in law and in the writers, property is not things, but *rights*, rights in or to things" (2). The cultural critic Grace Kyungwon Hong elaborates the distinction:

> Rather merely than referring to things that are owned, property is better understood as describing a set of social relations. In other words, ownership describes not only the relationship between oneself and the thing one owns, but also a system in which the state protects one's right to own something by ensuring that no-one else does. (2007: 81)

Although this distinction is conceptually important for a cultural history, the fact that both meanings were in circulation in the period is equally significant, so both the popular and the legal senses of the word will be examined here.

In an influential argument, Kenneth J. Vandevelde surveyed developments in this area of the law in the nineteenth century, and concluded that a new understanding of property had arisen. Tracing the recognition of proprietary interests in business goodwill, trademarks and trade secrets, and in the ownership of oil and gas, Vandevelde argued that a "dephysicalized" and "limited" notion of property gradually emerged through the cases in response to new commercial activities and investments. As a result, the traditional theory expounded by Blackstone of absolute dominion and rights over things (or virtual things, such as "incorporeal hereditaments") no longer matched the state of the law. Vandevelde goes on to argue that in a series of papers from 1913 to 1917, the legal theorist Wesley Newcomb Hohfeld drew these various shifts in the law together, proposing that the traditional understanding of property as rights over land or other objects was misconceived, that "only rights could be property, [and] … [that] legal relations were between people" (1980: 360). Thus, Vandevelde argued, Hohfeld broke the concept into its constituent parts, and concluded that "property was a bundle of legal relations—rights, powers, privileges, immunities" (361). This image of property as a "bundle of rights" was widely adopted as a pithy expression, and remains current today, as the definitions by Macpherson and Hong quoted above show.

The contrast Vandevelde draws between the older theory and "the new property of the nineteenth century" may be drawn too starkly. As Macpherson argues, the idea that property consisted of limited rights was well understood until the seventeenth century, because it principally concerned land, "which was often not freely disposable" and where it was clear that "different people might have different rights in the same piece of land" (7). However, with the development of market capitalism, and the enclosure of the commons, "rights in land became more absolute, and parcels of land became more freely marketable commodities [and] it became natural to think of the land itself as the property." This usage was confirmed with the exchange of money and commodities in the market, and by the fact that rights such as those discussed by Vandevelde—goodwill, or the right to drill for oil on certain areas of other people's land—were increasingly regarded as saleable, and "the distinction between the right and the thing was easily blurred" (8). The accumulation of capital under the impetus of the industrial revolution was therefore accompanied by what Morgan called the "diversification of [the] forms" of property, and by what Charles Donahue called an agglomerative tendency in the law, that is, the "tendency to agglomerate" all property rights in a single legal person, the owner, and in particular "the exclusive right to possess, privilege to use, and power to convey" (1980: 32). Although this tendency is associated with property in the Western legal tradition, Donahue thinks it was "most manifest" in the nineteenth century. An example is the principle of testamentary freedom in the law of wills: the disposition of a person's property on their death was left to their individual will, the pun here capturing the fusion of psychological attribute and legal document to express the extent of property rights (Readman 2008: 110–111). As John Stuart Mill wrote,

> The ownership of a thing cannot be looked upon as complete without the power of bestowing it, at death or during life, at the owner's pleasure; and all the reasons, which recommend that private property should exist, recommend *pro tanto* [to that extent], this extension of it. (1848: 91)

Although Mill uses a bequest of a physical object as his example, his exposition centers on the rights of ownership, the "power" that property confers on owners, suggesting his awareness of the legal conception of property as rights and relations. The writings of Jeremy Bentham, on the editing of which Mill had worked as a young man, also advanced this idea. The utilitarian Bentham argued forcefully that, "There is no image, no painting, no visible trait, which can express the relation that constitutes property. It is not material, it is metaphysical; it is a mere conception of the mind." He went on to argue in terms that almost foreshadow those of Carol Rose, that this "idea of property consists in an established expectation; in the persuasion of being able to draw such and such an advantage from the thing possessed" (Bentham 1830: 51–52). It is the law that provides property holders with their assurance of the establishment and continuity of the rights they possess: "Property and law are born together, and die together. Before the laws were made, there was no property; take away laws, and property ceases" (52). Bentham's theory of property contests the idea expounded by Locke and Blackstone that property was a natural right, which originated when humans first added to the common resources of the earth through their own labor. Whereas this older narrative implied that law was instituted to ensure the preservation of property, Bentham radically reversed the order of precedence in holding that property was the creature of law, not its author. By the 1870s, this new jurisprudence of property was drawing widespread adherence (Maurer 2012: 1–4).

Bentham's dictum that "There is no image, no painting ... which can express the relation that constitutes property," may be strictly true in the legal sense, but certain cultural forms, such as landscape art, are deeply associated with ownership, while others explore the emotions associated with property or present narratives of contested title, illuminating the ethics and politics of an acquisitive society. Property relations also have a material presence and effect in the world; it is a "socially pervasive" discourse (Petch 2007: 380). Possession and dispossession both make for powerful images in the verbal and visual arts, images that in their turn contribute to the ideology of private property. Bentham's analytical legal positivism leaves out of account the influence of the cultural environment on the shape of all law, including property. Notoriously unsympathetic to poetry ("Prejudice apart, the game of push-pin is of equal value with the arts and sciences of music and poetry"), he believed there was no truth-value in images. Yet, as the literary and visual texts included in this chapter show, images can illuminate the conceptualization as well as the culture of property (Bentham 1825: III. 1. para. 8).

In George Eliot's novel, *The Mill on the Floss*, for example, the Tulliver family lose the mill that has been their home and livelihood for generations due to a legal dispute over their rights to the river water which powers the mill. Mr. Tulliver knows that "water's a very particular thing; you can't pick it up with a pitchfork," and yet believes that "it's plain enough what's the rights and wrongs of water," and that the mill "must have water to turn it" (Eliot 1861: 155–156). He is torn, irrationally and irritably, between a belief

FIGURE 6.1 Randolph Caldecott, The House that Jack Built. Source: Universal History Archive / Getty Images.

in property as an external object or as his relationship with it, and a realization that his property interests are non-material, like the water that runs through his pitchfork. His sense of entitlement is challenged when a newcomer, Pivart, buys land up-river, which he proceeds to irrigate using the flow of the river. Tulliver brings a case against him, and loses; the costs of the action bring the Tullivers to bankruptcy. The trial takes place offstage, so readers are not privy to the arguments or reasons for judgment. Jules Law has shown that the question whether the "riparian rights" of those who owned land along a river included a right to irrigate from it was moot at that time (1992: 59) and that the law was but one of many aspects of social reality experiencing the pressures of historical change.

A similar question was at the center of a major case in 1895, *Bradford v Pickles*, in which the courts found that the private owner of land in which an underground stream ran could divert that stream, despite the fact that it surfaced on neighboring land owned by the borough of Bradford, which used it for the town's water supply. For legal historian Brian Simpson, this decision was "a most striking illustration of the persistence ... of the individualistic conception of property rights" (Simpson 1995: 16). Tulliver's lawsuit is only one element in the culture of property that the novel reveals. Tom Tulliver accrues the funds to repay his father's debts by trading in the new forms of property. George Eliot represents the kinship network of the Tullivers and Dodsons as equally infused with property consciousness and family loyalty: "the family badge was to be honest and rich; and not only rich, but richer than supposed" (1860: 274). The author herself was born into this class, and so represents its ethos with intimate knowledge as well as ironic judgment.

Another work long regarded as a memorable distillation of this ideology is Tennyson's 1866 poem, "Northern Farmer—New Style." The central conceit of this poem is that the farmer hears his own beliefs echoed in the sound of his horse cantering, "Proputty, proputty, proputty":

> Doesn't thou 'ear my 'erse's legs, as they canters awaäy,
> Proputty, proputty, proputty—that's what I 'ears 'em saäy.
> Proputty, proputty, proputty—Sam, thou's an ass for thy paäins,
> Theer's moor sense i' one o' 'is legs nor in all thy braäins.
> ... Me an' thy muther, Sammy, 'as beän a-talkin' o' thee;
> Thou's beän talkin' to muther, an' she beän a tellin' it me.
> Thou'll not marry for munny—thou's sweet upo' parson's lass—
> Noä—thou'll marry for luvv—an' we boäth on us thinks tha an ass.
> Seeä'd 'er todaäy goä by—Saäint's daäy—they was ringing the bells.
> She's a beauty thou thinks—an' soä is scoors o' gells,
> Them as 'as munny an' all—wot's a beauty?—the flower as blaws.
> But proputty, proputty sticks, an' proputty graws ...

Repetition of the sound ensures that the "idea" of property is embodied in the rhythm of the farmer's everyday life, is uppermost in his mind. Spoken in the Lincolnshire dialect of Tennyson's birthplace, and based on a statement overheard and reported to him, the poem captures "the shrewd directness, the gruffness, the grim humour" of a lower-middle-class rural man of property (Ricks 1972: 291). Though not without tenderness, the rich farmer punctures the romantic illusions of his son with his astute perception of the importance of property at every level of society, including the parson's:

> Proputty, proputty 's ivrything 'ere, an', Sammy, I'm blest
> If it is n't the saäme oop yonder, fur them 'as 'as it 's the best.

Openly proud of the social status that ownership confers, the speaker urges his son to approach love without losing sight of practical, property considerations, reconciling love and money in a candid account of his own marriage:

> Luvv? What's luvv? Thou can luvv they lass an' 'er munny too,
> Maäkin' 'em goä together, as they 've good right to do.
> Couldn' I luvv thy muther b' y cause o' 'er munny laid by?
> Naäy—fur I luvv'd 'er a vast sight moor fur it; reäson why.

Although this blackly humorous rationalization reveals a mercenary element in the farmer's character, the idea that the lass and her money go together restates a general belief in Victorian Britain that property was an "index of identity" (Frank 2010: 6). More particularly, the "going together" conceals the custom and law whereby a wife's money became the husband's property upon marriage. The farmer unashamedly presents his personal history as a narrative of accumulation, of land and money. When the poem ends with his threat to disinherit his son, should he insist on marrying the parson's daughter, the depth of this society's "obsession with property," infusing even the relationship of marriage, is confirmed (Macfarlane 1986: 145).

REFORMING THE LAW CONCERNING MARRIED WOMEN'S PROPERTY

Under the social and legal tradition encapsulated in the monologue of the "Northern Farmer," a woman's personal property (including jewels, clothes, and household goods as well as money) passed absolutely to her husband once they married, and he held a freehold interest in her real property or land, while they were both alive. He also had absolute rights to any money she earned after the marriage, even if they had separated (Bodichon 1854). Sir William Blackstone in his *Commentaries* had explained this legal rule, known as coverture, as follows:

> By marriage, the husband and wife are one person in law: that is, the very being or legal existence of the woman is suspended during the marriage, or at least is incorporated and consolidated into that of the husband: under whose wing, protection, and *cover*, she performs every thing. (1765: I.430)

Blackstone, "the muse of the common law," incidentally reveals the extent to which marriage and property were intertwined institutions through his metaphors of incorporation and consolidation (Purdy 2010: 1). The idea of marriage as a contract in which one party's "legal existence" was "suspended" seems astonishing today, especially when set against John Locke's foundational principle of liberal property, that "every Man has a *Property* in his own *Person*. This no Body has any Right to but himself" (1689: 18). While reflecting the primacy of the biblical theory of marriage, in which the two become one, its material effect was to facilitate economic consolidation. In the early eighteenth century, notices of marriage published in the *Gentlemen's Magazine* often paired the name of the woman with her financial worth, as in the following example: "Sir John Glynne, of Hawarden in Flintshire, Bart—to Miss Conway, sole Heiress of Sir John Conway, Bart a Fortune of 50,000*l*" (1732: 588). The juxtaposition of the woman and her estate here make it clear that in this exchange a woman not only brought property, but *was* property. In the social vision encoded by the common law, wives became the property of their husbands upon marriage, and, as Tim Dolin has put it, "without any property of their own, they were prohibited any separate rights of action" (1997: 9). The loss of property rights upon marriage entailed a drastic reduction of women's sense of identity. In a discussion of gender difference and property today, Carol Rose echoes the insights of nineteenth-century feminists: "The inability to own property is a guarantor of some version of enslavement, however benevolent it may be in any particular instance" (1994: 253–254).

An assumption of domestic harmony and mutuality of interests underlay the doctrine of coverture, a theoretical ideal from which experience frequently departed. Writers in the nineteenth century began to analyze this law with increasing frequency and intensity, to expose its practical effects, and to urge its reform. In 1854 Barbara Bodichon saw the reformist projects of the past half-century as a favorable new legal mentality:

> It is not now as it once was, when all existing institutions were considered sacred and unalterable; and the spirit which made Blackstone an admirer of, rather than a critic on, every law because it was *law*, is exchanged for a bolder and more discriminating spirit, which seeks to judge calmly what is good and to amend what is bad. (129)

In this context, Caroline Cornwallis called the doctrine of coverture "the gentle dream of some Utopian legislator, who in his primitive innocence, had never heard of extravagant wives or brutal husbands" (1857: 313). Frances Power Cobbe, who became a member of the Married Women's Property Committee lobbying for new legislation, highlighted the one-sidedness of this law: "the husband and wife are assumed to be one person and that person is the husband" (Cobbe 1868: 111; Ferguson 2013: 97). In *The Subjection of Women*, John Stuart Mill noted that legal inequality led in practice to the "wife's entire dependence on the husband, every privilege or pleasure she has being either his gift, or depending entirely on his will" (1869: 1). After a detailed analysis, Mill concluded that wives had fewer rights than a slave under Roman law. Echoing one of Blackstone's metaphors he noted that "the absorption of all rights, all property, as well as all freedom of action, is complete" (37). He pointed to the ways that the terms of the law shaped social practices, giving husbands absolute power in the domestic realm, licensing authoritarianism and selfishness, and encouraging abusive behavior. As a result, for many people, he felt, the family was "a school of despotism" rather than "sympathy" (50; 42). Along with other feminist writers of the period, Mill believed that reforming the law of married persons' property in accordance with principles of equality would also reform the culture of marriage and family life, particularly the incidence of domestic violence. Property, therefore, betokened a network of personal rights and responsibilities, and was the key to an altered sense of legal personhood for women.

Mill reminded his readers that "laws and institutions require to be adapted, not to good men, but to bad" (40). Evidence of the presence of brutal husbands in society, and the outrages sanctioned under the principle of coverture were further revealed through press reporting of cases, most famously that of Caroline Norton, but also many others. Norton, who lost the custody of her children, was denied a divorce and had her earnings as a writer claimed by her estranged husband, decided to use her literary skills to bring about reform of the law, in both imaginative and expository forms: "I have learned the law respecting women, piecemeal, by suffering from every one of its defects of protection" (1855: 62). Advocates of reform focused on such limit cases, on Mill's "bad" men, for they sharply revealed the injustices caused by these "defects of protection." Norton's predicament inspired several fictional treatments, by Dickens, Hardy, and George Meredith among others (Dolin 2007; Craig 2009; Ferguson 2013). Indeed, poets and novelists took up the broader cause, seeking to provoke reform of the laws through narratives of fictional cases and by imagining the voices of women. The novels of the Brontë sisters, especially Anne Brontë's *The Tenant of Wildfell Hall* and Emily Brontë's *Wuthering Heights*, incorporate husbands who give effect to a cruel will to dominate through a deep knowledge of their legal rights (Ward 2012). In these novels, what Carol Rose called the "mystery of 'niceness' and trust at the center of economic transactions" is shown to be jeopardized within the institution where sympathy and trust ought to be at a premium by a Gothic realization of the extreme passions awakened by the "instinct for possession" (qtd. Purdy 2010: 4).

Kathy Alexis Psomiades has shown that the scope of this literary engagement with marital property was large, and its social implications profound:

> The language of women and property fills Victorian novels and the writings of Victorian feminists alike not because these are the existing terms through which the culture thinks gender difference, but because these terms themselves are a way of thinking through the increasing irrationality attached to the notion that men and women have different relations to property. (1999: 99)

Elizabeth Barrett Browning gives direct utterance to Victorian dissatisfaction with this inherited discourse in her verse-novel, *Aurora Leigh*. Rejecting a marriage proposal from her cousin, Romney Leigh, Aurora outlines the extent to which the property relation might be diffused through every aspect of marriage:

> This poor, good Romney. Love, to him, was made
> A simple law-clause. If I married him,
> I should not dare to call my soul my own
> Which so he had bought and paid for: every thought
> And every heart-beat down there in the bill;
> Not one found honestly deductible
> From any use that pleased him! (1856: II. 784–790)

Aurora's critique of this ideology implies the imagining of alternatives. John Stuart Mill underlined this point in the *Subjection*, taking note that "numbers of married people even under the present law ... live in the spirit of a just law of equality" (50–51).

Choosing to bind themselves to a different ethical principle, some couples took steps to dissociate themselves from the law of marital property. Not surprisingly, perhaps, given the sentiments expressed in *Aurora Leigh*, Robert Browning and Elizabeth Barrett were among them. As they planned their future together, he sought to bind himself to use her property in accordance with her wishes, and requested her to write a will-like document. Barrett duly complied, though the convolution of this plan produced some irony in the draft:

> In compliance with the request of Robert Browning, who may possibly become my husband, that I would express in writing my wishes respecting the ultimate disposal of whatever property I posses [sic] at the time, whether in the funds or elsewhere ... I hereby declare my wishes to be ... that he, Robert Browning ... having of course, as it is his right to do, first held and used the property in question for the term of his natural life ... should bequeath the same, by an equal division to my two sisters, or, in the case of the previous death of either or both of them, to such of my surviving brothers as most shall need it by the judgment of my eldest surviving brother. (Karlin 1990: 276–277)

Though honoring his motives, Barrett engages playfully in this act of quasi-legal drafting, noting her adeptness and women's exclusion from public, professional life: "Is this what is called a *document*? It seems to me that I have a sort of legal genius—and that I should be on the Woolsack in the Martineau-Parliament" (276). Five years later in anticipation of his marriage with Harriet Taylor, John Stuart Mill experienced a similar desire, to adopt the language of law and morality in an attempt to circumvent the existing legal concept of marriage in the name of a more just alternative:

> Being about, if I am so happy as to obtain her consent, to enter into the marriage relation with the only woman I have ever known, with whom I would have entered into that state; & the whole character of the marriage relation as constituted by law being such as both she and I entirely & conscientiously disapprove, for this among other reasons, that it confers upon one of the parties to the contract, legal power & control over the person, property, & freedom of action of the other party, independent of her own wishes and will; I, having no means of legally divesting myself of these odious powers (as I most assuredly would do if an engagement to that effect could be made legally binding on me) feel it my duty to put on record a formal protest against the existing law of marriage, in so far as conferring such powers; and a solemn promise never in any case or under any circumstances to use them. And in the event of marriage between Mrs. Taylor and me I declare it to be my will and intention, & the condition of the engagement between us, that she retains in all respects whatever the same absolute freedom of action, & freedom of disposal of herself and of all that does or may at any time belong to her, as if no such marriage had taken place; and I absolutely disclaim & repudiate all pretension to have acquired any rights whatever by virtue of such marriage. (Robson and Robson 1994: 47–48)

The adoption of a legal register in both these private texts suggests a respect for law, while the qualifications and negations they introduce reflect a sense of the limits of that language as it bears upon their vision of marriage. These factors indicate a wish to reform the laws relating to marriage rather than to reject them. If we read these exercises in legalese in the light of Wittgenstein's notion that "to imagine a language is to imagine a form of life," it suggests that they are acts of "legal imagination," (White 1973) in which Victorian writers extended their creativity into the language-game of the law to aid the emergence of a new language of property (1958: para. 19).

In the final version of *The Subjection of Women* that he published after Harriet Taylor's death, and in which he acknowledged her contribution to the development of his ideas, Mill articulated the ideals they had shared:

> I am one of the strongest supporters of community of goods, when resulting from an entire unity of feeling in the owners, which makes all things common between them. But I have no relish for a community of goods resting on the doctrine that what is mine is yours, but what is yours is not mine; and I should decline to enter into a compact with anyone, though I were myself the person to profit by it. (52–53)

In 1868, Mill co-sponsored a Married Women's Property Bill in the House of Commons (Shanley 1989: 68). In the form that passed into law, this statute provided for women to retain property in their own earnings after marriage, but did not dismantle the system of coverture. It required further lobbying, further pamphlets, further imagining of cases in fiction, to secure the passage of a law that inscribed the principle of equal treatment under law for husbands and wives. The *Married Women's Property Act* of 1882 conferred independent legal existence on married women, with full rights to hold, acquire, retain, and dispose of their separate property. For historian Mary Lyndon Shanley, these Acts were "arguably the single most important change in the legal status of women in the nineteenth century" (1989: 103).

COLONIALISM AND PROPERTY LAW

Soames Forsyte, the eponymous "Man of Property" in *The Forsyte Saga*, is presented as being immune to the reforming current we have been discussing: "Could a man own anything prettier than this dining-table with its deep tints, the starry, soft-petalled roses, the ruby-colored glass, and quaint silver furnishing; could a man own anything prettier than the woman who sat at it?" (Galsworthy *The Man of Property*: 70) His impulse to objectify, his powerful acquisitive desire, his self-regarding pleasure in ownership, meet their limit, however, in the independent existence of his wife Irene: he experiences "a sense of exasperation amounting to pain, that he did not own her, as it was his right to own her." In this relationship Galsworthy reveals a drive for mastery that lay concealed within the "possessive instinct" of modern English society, one that he represents as typical of the middle classes in the nineteenth century. This drive literally had a global reach and scope, enabled through the expanding British Empire. The house of Forsyte made its wealth importing high-quality exotic commodities for domestic consumption, so the characters in these novels are implicitly presented as participants in that "confident conquest of the globe by the capitalist economy" that was a central aspect of imperialism (Hobsbawm 1994: 9). Empire, then, is another significant context for the cultural history of property in this period.

More than a system that facilitated trade in goods, empire was at the heart of the liberal theory of property: John Locke and John Stuart Mill both had a close involvement in the imperial administration, Locke in drafting the constitution for the British settlement in Carolina in 1682, and Mill through his work in the India Office in London. The colonization of America is, in fact, the subtext of Locke's account of the origin of property rights, for his work justifies the appropriation of Native American lands (Arneil 1996). More broadly, David Spurr, in *The Rhetoric of Empire*, argues that during the epoch of imperialism there emerged a distinctive discourse, a "mode of thinking and writing wherein the world is radically transformed into an object of possession" (1993: 27). This argument links the appropriation of other lands as colonies with broader processes of exploration and "discovery," and with ideas about property. Spurr derives this argument from an insight expressed by André Malraux in his imaginary cross-cultural dialogue, *La Tentation de l'Occident* [*The Temptation of the Occident*]. According to Malraux, modern Western society

> wants to draw up a plan of the universe, to make of it an intelligible image ... It wants to subordinate the world, and finds in its own actions a pride that much greater for believing that it possesses the world already. (Spurr 1993: 27)

Malraux's diagnosis of Occidental hubris may be open to interpretation, but it rests on identifiable features of the intellectual history of Western modernity, such as the confident spirit of scientific progress, and the assumption of cultural superiority that characterized Enlightenment thought, justifying the annexation of other peoples' territories and proclamations of sovereignty over them. For Spurr, imperialist discourse fuses power and knowledge, for the study of new spaces is associated with a desire to order and control them. One of its most important textual manifestations is the "convention of the commanding view," in which authority is attributed to the perceptions of the Western observer, who is invested by the discourse with comprehensive vision and understanding of the scene laid out before them (15). Though Spurr is referring principally to verbal texts, his point holds equally strongly for landscape art.

FIGURE 6.2 Vase by Charles Frederick Hancock Set on Ebony Table. Source: V & A Collection.

In the colonial era, what Spurr calls "this proprietary vision" was first exercised through assertions of possession, ceremonies or formal procedures that varied according to the cultural tradition of the claiming nation (Seed 1995). In British colonies these involved the raising of the flag, the reading of a proclamation, the chopping down of a tree and other actions. Given the vast and complex history of empire, this chapter will largely confine itself to discussion of white settler colonies of the British Empire, particularly Australia. Under the common law, these acts of appropriation of the new lands took place in three possible ways: cession of the territory by its traditional owners under treaty, conquest, or settlement if the country was, in Sir Henry Maine's words, "newly discovered or never before cultivated" (1861: 259). In the case of Australia, on which most of this discussion will focus, the latter situation obtained: its nomadic inhabitants were believed not to have developed the social and political structures that would include a law of property, and the territory was deemed to be *terra nullius*, a land belonging to no one.

Carol Rose has analyzed this situation in terms of her theory of property as a rhetorical domain, a language of persuasion. She argues that the British colonizers were unable to recognize the signs of the local property language: trained in their own cultural system as defined by Locke, and expounded by Blackstone, and therefore expecting signs of agriculture, they failed to understand the very different system by which Indigenous people manifested their rights over the land. Drawing on the historical researches of Stuart Banner, who has studied the various forms of possession in the colonization of the Pacific, Rose summarizes the outcomes:

> Insofar as native peoples farmed, the English saw property, defined through crops, boundaries, fences. But insofar as native peoples did not farm, or did not farm in ways that resembled the English countryside, the English were much less likely to see property. In the most tragic case of all, they saw no property at all in native land uses in Australia, which the English viewed as up for grabs, terra nullius in the Latin phrase, land waiting to be reduced to property. (2006: 6)

Aboriginal law originated with the creator-spirits, who established sacred rights and duties with respect to the lands where a people live. These rights and duties were collective and inalienable, and were embodied in cultural practices, including story and songlines. Possession was manifested principally through the controlled firing of certain tracts of land, which promoted fresh vegetation and attracted animals for hunting (Gammage 2011). The acuity of Rose's insight into this tragedy lies in the fact that in Australia, as in other settler states, the land itself became the desired object, as economic prosperity was dependent on agricultural and pastoral activity (Wolfe 1994). In "taking up" of the land for these purposes, colonizers were also "taking" it from the original inhabitants. White possession entailed the dispossession of the Aboriginal people, a process that involved violent conflict. Some settlers were interested to observe the social organization of Aboriginal life, and to discern alternative signs of property. In the late 1830s, a campaign to recognize the rights of Aboriginal peoples across the Empire was mounted by humanitarian reformers, prompted by reports of violence, especially the Tasmanian genocide. Indigenous rights to land were debated in this context. At the inaugural meeting of the Aborigines' Protection Society in Sydney in 1838, a speaker urged: "By fraud and violence Europeans have usurped vast tracts of native territory, paying no regard to the rights of the inhabitants" (Anon 1838: 6). This view was disputed by a recently arrived barrister, Richard Windeyer, using Lockean principles: "It could not, he said, be supposed that the natives of this island had the exclusive right to all this land; he thought the right devolved on him who should first cultivate it" (*Sydney Gazette* 1838: 2). Edward Eyre, an experienced explorer, magistrate, and Aboriginal Protector in South Australia, forcefully argued that different groups had their own territories, the boundaries of which were known and respected by other groups:

> It has generally been imagined, but with great injustice, as well as incorrectness, that the natives have no idea of property in land, or of proprietary rights connected with it. Nothing can be farther from the truth than this assumption ... It is a feeling that

can only have originated in an entire ignorance of the habits, customs and ideas of this people. As far as my own observation has extended, I have found that particular districts, having a radius of from ten to twenty miles, or, in other cases, varying according to local circumstances, are considered generally as being the property and hunting grounds of the tribes that frequent them. (1845: II. 296–297)

Eyre is today best known for his controversial decision to declare martial law in Jamaica in 1865. The violence that followed led to his recall to Britain. Earlier in his career, however, he sought to formulate a more humane Aboriginal policy, although his recognition of Indigenous property in land did not derogate from the colonialist framework of sovereignty and possession (Evans 2005: 18–51). In the end, the evidence of Aboriginal proprietary interests adduced at this time was not sufficient to displace the imported story that Australia was *terra nullius*, and that property required cultivation of the soil. Material, as well as intellectual, factors were operative here: the economic success of the colony would have been "threatened by any official recognition that Aborigines might have a preexisting and superior claim of proprietorship over the continent" (Day 1997: 108). The availability of cheap land was a key element of this economy. So entrenched was this ideology that *terra nullius* remained Australian law until 1992, when it was overruled in the case of *Mabo v Queensland*.

Rose's statement that Australian land was treated as if it was "up for grabs" is no mere colloquialism. As the sovereign, the Crown claimed ultimate title to all lands, and allocated land to individuals and corporate entities through a system of grants. In the 1820s the government faced increasing demands for land, including pre-emptive occupancy by squatters in outlying districts, which it attempted to regulate by establishing "limits of location," an outer boundary of permissible settlement. This policy failed to deter squatting, and in fact may have promoted it. Squatters took their pick of the best land, capitalized on the suitability of the climate and country for wool-growing, and became the most wealthy and powerful sector of the community. In effect, squatting was a repetition of the original assertion of a right of occupancy by the Crown over the entire territory, performed on a local scale. Mark Twain, on visiting Australia, noted the distinctive social status and cultural identity of squatters, as compared with America:

With us, when you speak of a squatter, you are always supposed to be speaking of a poor man, but in Australia when you speak of a squatter, you are supposed to be speaking of a millionaire; in America the word indicates the possessor of a few acres and a doubtful title, in Australia it indicates a man whose landfront is as long as a railroad, and whose title has been perfected in one way or another; ... in America you take your hat off to no squatter, in Australia you do. (Twain 1897: 109)

In Britain, the lands of the Empire became symbols of renewal and opportunity for those with the skills and personal attributes to take advantage of them. In popular culture and public opinion, the colonies drew young men with a spirit of adventure and a desire for economic advancement, as Edward Eyre was drawn to Australia. The strength of popular investment in this idea of empire may be gleaned from the fact that two writers as different as Charles Dickens and Anthony Trollope both encouraged and supported their sons to emigrate to Australia, with a view to working in the wool industry, and becoming landowners. Readers will remember that feckless Mr. Micawber in *David Copperfield* makes good in the new society, both in terms of property and of citizenship, and that the convict Magwitch in *Great Expectations* makes the fortune that funds the hero's gentlemanly career back home. Trollope visited his son twice, helped him purchase a pastoral property, and wrote a travel book recommending emigration to Australia, and later a short novel centered on a sheep station very like his son's, *Harry Heathcote of Gangoil*. Adventure stories were one of imperialism's most popular and significant cultural forms, offering romanticized patterns of heroic masculine endeavor against the rigors of the physical world and the resistance of indigenous peoples to the urbanized readers of the mother country.

One of the most famous early novels set in Australia, *The Recollections of Geoffrey Hamlyn*, by Henry Kingsley, a failed colonist who returned to England, is an adventure story that is also a romance of property for England and the colony. Early in the novel, when the major characters are still in England, Australia is discussed in terms of a *terra nullius*:

> The land with millions of acres of fertile soil, under a splendid climate, calling aloud for someone to come and cultivate them. The land ... of deep forests and boundless pastures, which go rolling away westward, plain beyond plain, to none knows where. (Kingsley 1865: 19)

The image of the land crying out is an evasive trope of empire, a projection of the colonizers' desire for possession, which displaces the indigenous inhabitants from the scene. The impulse for emigration, and hence the motivating force of the story, are the social and economic pressures of life in England, where the leading families do not have sufficient funds to maintain their ancestral estate, though this is supplemented by a discourse of patriotic destiny, of participating in the imperial ventures of their "restless, discontented nation" (20). Hamlyn's first description of the Australian landscape after his arrival employs the device of the "commanding view" noted by Spurr:

> A new heaven and a new earth! Tier beyond tier, height above height, the great wooded ranges go rolling away westward, till on the lofty skyline they are crowned with a gleam of everlasting snow. To the eastward they sink down, breaking into isolated forest-fringed peaks, and rock-crowned eminences, till with rapidly straightening lines they fade into the broad grey plains, beyond which the Southern Ocean is visible by the great white sea-haze upon the sky. (149)

While this aesthetic response to natural beauty does not immediately reveal a possessory interest, in fact the characters Hamlyn meets are in search of good pastoral land that they can claim, and he himself is already a squatter with his own "property" nearby. He professes to be "writing a history of the people themselves, not of their property," but gives priority to a statement of their assets, both the extent of the lands they have "taken up" and the number of sheep they carry. Both run into many thousands! And the getting is represented as easy: "in a very few years, both the Major and Troubridge, by the mere power of accumulation, became very wealthy people" (165). This idyllic picture of the English propertied class transplanted to Australia means that the adventure plot is not mobilized in the quest *for* property, but in defense of property recently acquired. The second half of the novel is dominated by a series of challenges presented to the characters by Aborigines, fire, and bushrangers. These hazards are conventional in the colonial adventure genre, but the protagonists' power to overcome them reveals the "proprietary vision" of colonialism. The characters struggle and win out against threats to their persons and to their expectations with regard to the objects they have put under their control. Not only are these depredations repelled, the characters return home to England, and reclaim their true inheritance, the original family seat of Clere.

FIGURE 6.3 John Everett Millais, "Lucius Mason, as he leaned on the gate that was no longer his own" from *Orley Farm* by Anthony Trollope. Source: University of California Libraries.

This ending suggests that *The Recollections of Geoffrey Hamlyn* is a conservative property narrative in both the Australian and the English contexts. In unselfconsciously celebrating the colonization of Australia, through the "taking up" of supposedly vacant land, it failed to recognize the language of property of the people being dispossessed. This failure was, of course, the condition precedent to the colonial enterprise, and so Kingsley's novel, which has always been deeply unpopular with Australian nationalists and progressives due to its privileging of English class values, in fact articulated the founding principle of Australian legal culture. In relation to England, its ending demonstrates an ideological preference for the inherited forms of landed society and law, and eschews the new market-based understanding of property as dephysicalized and fungible that emerged in nineteenth-century England and America. Some characters, however, cannot return to England, including a woman whose marriage to a criminal disgraced her family. Thus *Geoffrey Hamlyn* also fails to imagine the reforming of property and identity in the law of marriage that was slowly emerging at this time. In adhering to a Blackstonian vision of property, this little-known novel illustrates how legal language permeates the cultural realm, and how stories of property in their turn can shape the legal imagination in various ways.

*****

In a rare judicial comment on the nature of the language of property, Baron Bramwell wrote in 1865:

> Property is not a term of art but a common English word, which must be taken in an ordinary sense, and any ordinary person would certainly think it strange, if he were told that a debt due to him were not part of his property. (*Queensbury* 4)

Given the technicality and complexity of property law in the nineteenth century, this dictum may seem a little disingenuous. However, in bridging the common usage and the legal meaning of the word, it rightly recognizes that property was a "socially pervasive" discourse, one spoken by "ordinary persons" like Tennyson's northern farmer and not just by lawyers (Petch 2007: 380). It was part of the ordinary culture, a source of meanings and an "index of identity" (Frank 2010: 6). Although property was and is usually understood in terms of individual rights, the cultural history of this institution reveals the unequal access of different groups to property rights, and their sometimes successful struggle for proper recognition.

FIGURE 6.4 Skinner Prout, On the Plenty, near Melbourne. Source: Antiqua Print Gallery / Alamy Stock Photo.

CHAPTER SEVEN

Wrongs

Negligence, Neighborliness, and the Duty of Care in Nineteenth-century Narrative

JAN-MELISSA SCHRAMM

> As a behavioural science law is understood to be a response to values created in the thousands of interactions between people in a community … As a result, the building blocks used to construct the legal edifice are social, not legal, and the law is built from the bottom up rather than the top down. We ought not look for a legal principle to apply to a particular situation, we ought instead to look for the maxim that people must be applying when they decide how to behave, and we must construct the law in response to that maxim. (Gerhart 2010: 239)

The idea that a man owed a "duty of care" in law to his neighbor was first expressed by Francis Buller in 1768:

> Every Man ought to take reasonable Care that he does not injure his Neighbour; therefore, wherever a Man receives any Hurt through the Default of another, though the same were not wilful, yet if it be occasioned by Negligence or Folly, the Law gives him an Action to recover Damages for the Injury so sustained … However, it is proper in such Cases to prove that the Injury was such, as would probably follow from the Act done. (Buller 1768: 35–36)

Buller's *Introduction to the Law relative to Trials at Nisi Prius* was expanded and reprinted in several further handbooks in the second half of the eighteenth century, with this passage reprinted verbatim (see e.g., Onslow 1789: 22–23). But the belief that tort law as a field might be organized by duties owed to one's neighbor did not seize the legal imagination of the day. Searches for phrases including the "neighbor principle" and "duty of care" do not return more than a handful of results on the extensive digital site *Eighteenth-Century Collections Online*, and for the next fifty years, handbooks of tort law simply listed the facts of cases in which liability was established: there was no attempt to articulate more comprehensively the principles on which such a "duty of care" might depend; subsequent commentators have concluded that duty-biased definitions of liability in tort were "slow to take hold" (Lunney and Oliphant 2010: 105). A coherent articulation of neighborly "duty" could not, it seems, take place in the absence of a rich seam of complementary public opinion.

Yet within a hundred years, jurists asserted with confidence that the liabilities which arise in tort law could best be understood as failures to discharge one's duty to one's neighbor. For Frederick Pollock, the relevant moral injunctions were Roman in origin:

> Can we find any category of human duties that will approximately cover [all definitions of tort] and bring them into relation with any single principle? Let us turn to one of the best-known sentences in the introductory Chapter of the *Institutes*, copied from a lost work of Ulpian. "Iuris praecepta sunt haec: honeste vivere, alterum non laedere, suum cuique tribuere." "Honeste vivere" is a vague phrase enough: it may mean refraining from criminal offences, or possibly general good behavior in social and family relations. "Suum cuique tribuere" seems to fit pretty well with the law of property and contract. And what of "alterum non laedere"? "Thou shalt do no hurt to thy neighbour." Our law of torts, with all its irregularities, has for its main purpose nothing else than the development of this precept (Pollock. 1887: 11–12)

This is a typical manifestation of the nineteenth-century impulse to trace points of continuity between the Golden Age of the Greco-Roman past and the less heroic alloy of the industrial present, but other historiographers were uncertain whether the genealogy of the maxim was, in fact, classical or Christian. For Lord Atkin, offering the most famous articulation of the duty fifty years later in *Donoghue v Stevenson* [1932] AC 562, the maxim was Scriptural in origin: "You must take reasonable care to avoid acts or omissions which you can reasonably foresee would be likely to injure your neighbour. Who, then, in law is my neighbour?" This question was asked of Christ by a lawyer in the parable of the Good Samaritan in Luke 10 of the New Testament, and it is the argument of this chapter that law was one discourse among many participating in the formulation of an answer to this question amidst the social and economic upheaval that characterized the nineteenth century. Literary and theological contributions to public debate sharpened legal understandings of neighborly duty: in fact, as Henry Sumner Maine observed (speaking of the idea of equality before the law), many a legal maxim was at best "languidly assented to and suffered to have little influence on opinion and practice until it passed out of the possession of the lawyers and into that of the literary men ... and of the public which sat at their feet" (Maine 1861: 95). In this chapter, then, I want to probe literary contributions to the domain of public opinion on which the burgeoning jurisprudence of tort law seemed to depend, and to suggest that law and literature's mutual preoccupation with definitions of "neighborliness" in the nineteenth century tells us much about cultural and political anxieties in an age of rapid social change.

"WHO IS MY NEIGHBOR?"

As numerous critics have noted (for example, Gribble 2004; Colón 2012; Schramm 2012a; Gibson 2015), the parable of the Good Samaritan enjoyed extraordinary prominence in nineteenth-century discourse, with countless digests of Christian behavior and sermons pondering the moral relations encouraged by the narrative:

> And, behold, a certain lawyer stood up, and tempted him, saying, Master, what shall I do to inherit eternal life? He said unto him, What is written in the law? How readest thou? And he answering said, Thou shalt love the Lord thy God with all thy heart, and with all thy soul, and with all thy strength, and with all thy mind; and thy neighbour as thyself.

And he said unto him, Thou hast answered right: this do, and thou shalt live.

But he, willing to justify himself, said unto Jesus, And who is my neighbour?

And Jesus answering said, A certain man went down from Jerusalem to Jericho, and fell among thieves, which stripped him of his raiment, and wounded him, and departed, leaving him half dead. And by chance there came down a certain priest that way: and when he saw him, he passed by on the other side. And likewise a Levite, when he was at the place, came and looked on him, and passed by on the other side. But a certain Samaritan, as he journeyed, came where he was: and when he saw him, he had compassion on him, And went to him, and bound up his wounds, pouring in oil and wine, and set him on his own beast, and brought him to an inn, and took care of him. And on the morrow when he departed, he took out two pence, and gave them to the host, and said unto him, Take care of him; and whatsoever thou spendest more, when I come again, I will repay thee.

Which now of these three, thinkest thou, was neighbour unto him that fell among the thieves?

And he said, He that shewed mercy on him. Then said Jesus unto him, Go, and do thou likewise. (Luke 10. 25–37, KJV)

Susan Colón has suggested that the popularity of the parable form in the nineteenth century can be attributed partly to the rise of Tractarianism, which privileged the doctrine of "reserve" (the process by which a richly ambiguous text reveals its meaning in a degree proportionate to the reader's moral preparation and diligent labor), partly to the parable's interest in teaching by emplotment (through the literary representation of action, plot reversal, and recognition which shared clear affinities with the aims and objectives of the realist novel in English), and partly to the ways in which the parable uses a largely non-supernatural register to illustrate its moral truths (2012: 15–16). Victorian re-readings and re-writings of the parable form exploit these traits: in Jennifer Gribble's terms, "[e]xpressing one story in terms of another, the parable form is perhaps the most accessible example of the cultural role of the Bible as infinitely reinterpretable text" (2004: 431), and as William Twining observes, "[a] parable may be intentionally polyvalent: the audience is deliberately left to draw its own moral or point from the story" (1990: 403). Many Victorian novels shared a similar commitment to ethical instruction through the engagement of the reader, and a similar immersion in the world of empirical evidence, thus appropriating the parable's conceptual and imaginative claims to probe the complex and often conflicting interests at stake in any moral transaction. Some novels imitated Scriptural precedents to such an extent that Colón describes them as "extrabiblical parables" (e.g., Charlotte Yonge's *Heir of Redclyffe* (1853), and Margaret Oliphant's *The Perpetual Curate* (1864), *The Prodigals and their Inheritance* (1885), and *Who Was Lost and Is Found* (1894) while George Eliot's *Felix Holt* (1866) also draws extensively upon the story of the prodigal son). Other texts are seasoned with allusions to the parables of mercy, repentance, and stewardship (e.g., Charles Dickens's *Oliver Twist* (1837–1839), *Bleak House* (1852–1853), *Hard Times* (1854), *Little Dorrit* (1857), *A Tale of Two Cities* (1859), *Great Expectations* (1861), and *Our Mutual Friend* (1865)). And while Dickens shared Eliot's interest in prodigal sons, he was drawn most compulsively to transactions that brought strangers into relations of mutual help, thus demonstrating for modernity what mercy should look like in action.

For Dickens's radical political sympathies, the appeal of the parable of the Good Samaritan was precisely its call to confront what Gribble has called "the stereotyping assumptions that derive from class, gender, and ideology" (2004: 433). And the nation had a tremendous need for narrative to bridge social divides in the 1830s and 1840s when a perfect storm of factors—economic deprivation, Chartist protest, mass immigration from an Ireland devastated by famine—left England on the brink of the same sorts of class-wars and revolutions that were engulfing other European countries. Writing in his novel *Sybil* (1845), Benjamin Disraeli noted that England was now a land of two nations—"rich and poor" (Disraeli 1845: 65–66). In her famous "Preface" to *Mary Barton*, composed only a few years later in 1848, Elizabeth Gaskell followed Thomas Carlyle's request that authors speak up on behalf of the working class, "giv[ing] some utterance to the agony which from time to time, convulses this dumb people; the agony of suffering without the sympathy of the happy, or of erroneously believing that such is the case" (Gaskell 1848: xxxvi). This altruistic agenda extended also to visual art (see Figures 7.1, 7.2 and 7.3). Such aesthetic manifestos served a dual purpose, advancing what authors saw as the legitimate claim of the poor for inclusion in the "common interest" of the nation, and simultaneously attempting to raise the status of the novel by positioning it as uniquely able to advance an agenda of social reconciliation (see Schramm 2012a: 1–32).

FIGURE 7.1 This engraving of the "Arrival of the Good Samaritan at the Inn" by Gustave Dore, is taken from an illustrated Authorized Version of the Bible published *c.* 1885 by Petter & Galpin, London. Source: Jan-Melissa Schramm.

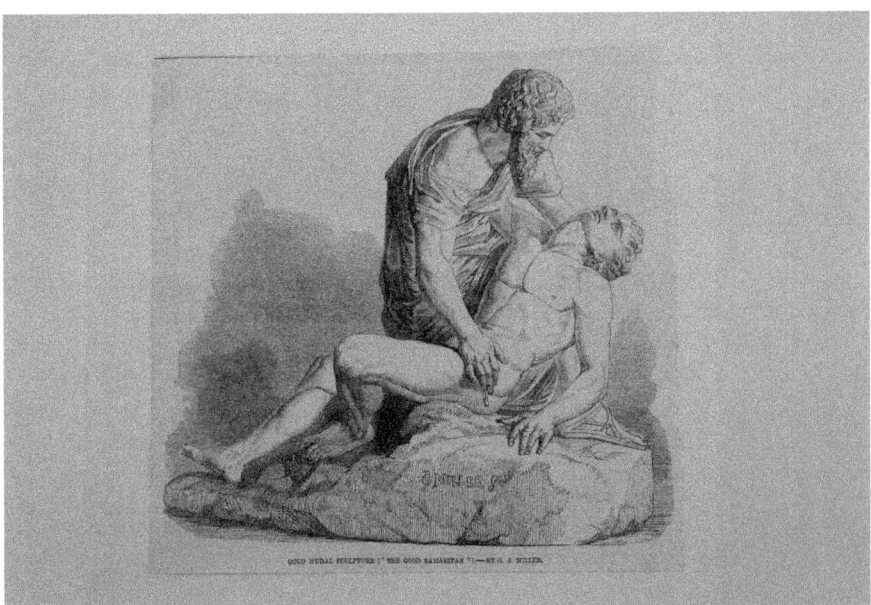

FIGURE 7.2 This image depicts the sculpture by George James Miller which won the Gold Medal for "Best Historical Sculpture" at the Royal Academy of Arts in 1858: from the *Illustrated London News*, January 9, 1858. Source: Jan-Melissa Schramm.

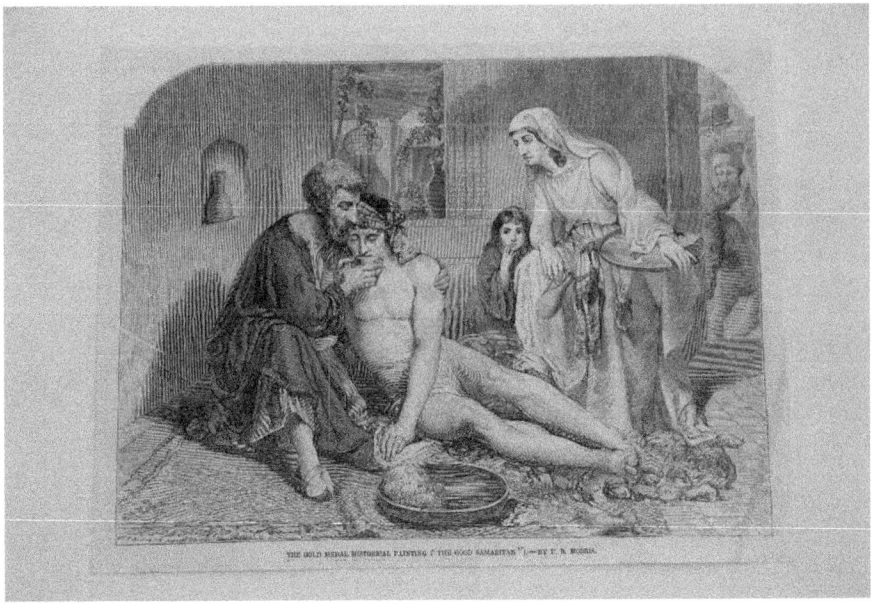

FIGURE 7.3 This image depicts the painting by Philip Richard Morris which won the Gold Medal for "Best Historical Painting" at the Royal Academy of Arts in 1858: from the *Illustrated London News*, January 9, 1858. Source: Jan-Melissa Schramm.

In order to promote ethical action, Victorian fiction—like the biblical parable—used portraits of individual lives and choices to illustrate the consequences of adhering to various moral philosophies. And such a reliance on instruction through particularity positioned itself directly in opposition to the governance of all moral thought by abstract precepts that sought to cater for the "many" but not always the individual "one." In Dickens's *Hard Times*—the most parabolic of his works, offering "a network of intersecting versions of the Good Samaritan" tale (Gribble 2004: 432)—Jeremy Bentham's thought is cast as the necessary adversary: duly exaggerated for comic effect, utilitarianism becomes the enemy Dickens would have otherwise had to invent in order to demonstrate the higher pedagogic and ethical claims of a literary aesthetic dependent on particularity. Among the many "anti-types of the Samaritan and parodies of his saving action" on display in *Hard Times* (Gribble 2004: 433), Stephen Blackpool stands out as the man of perfect integrity, the Christ-like figure who invokes assistance only to be rejected by all before dying for the villainy of another in imitation of the Christian atonement. In his refusal to join the trade union (for complex personal reasons), Stephen understands that he will forfeit all relations of neighborliness: no one will choose to act for him as the Good Samaritan did—"I know weel that if I was a lyin paristh in th' road, yo'd feel it right to pass me by, as a forrenner and stranger" (Dickens 1854: 145–146). Dialect speech serves here as the marker of social "otherness." What Dickens seeks to do is make it less likely that his readers will in turn "pass by" their own neighbor when he lies injured, physically or otherwise, in need of communal help.

According to Aristotle, the plight of the marginalized "one" in such cases is addressed by equitable thought, which seeks to correct the abstraction of universal laws by drawing attention to particular features of hard cases that might necessitate more individualized treatment (Aristotle 2002: 1137b). In *The Mill on the Floss* (1859–1860), for example, George Eliot's narrator observes that "moral judgments must remain false and hollow, unless they are checked and enlightened by a perpetual reference to the special characteristics that mark the individual lot:" to be guided by general rules "and formulas of that sort is to repress all the divine promptings and inspirations that spring from growing insight and sympathy." Instead of seeking "justice by a ready-made patent method, without the trouble of exerting patience, discrimination, impartiality," the person of integrity and compassion must seek out "a life vivid and intense enough to have created a wide fellow-feeling with all that is human" (Eliot 1860–1861: 628). According to Adam Smith, in his influential *Theory of Moral Sentiments*, this is the very definition of "imagination"—the capacity by which we "change places in fancy with another," and extend thereby our capacity for compassion (Smith 1759: 11–12). And the pedagogic agenda of the Victorian novel was precisely this—to encourage, through reading, the education of our sympathies through the practice of imaginative identification, firstly with individuals, and then (insofar as such ties extend outward in ever-increasing circles) with the wider polis. For Victorian authors, the generation of feeling was habitually elicited by attention to the plight of those on the margins of society—to the condition of the vulnerable but worthy "one" who was at risk of being sacrificed to the well-being of the "many," the one who required a show of "mercy" in order to be incorporated within the wider body politic (see Schramm 2012a: 1–32, 255–267). As a consequence of this prolonged narrative attention to disenfranchised individuals, both the novel and the long poem found themselves empowered to intervene in public debate, shoulder to shoulder with public moralists such as Thomas Carlyle and J.S. Mill and Broad Churchmen such as F.D. Maurice and Benjamin Jowett, and against the exponents of self-interest and laissez-faire economics. Unlike other forms of public discourse (such as legal evidence, the de-particularized language of precedents, statistical records, or *Hansard*), "aesthetic teaching," in George Eliot's phrase, could make a claim to being "the highest of all teaching because it deals with life in its highest complexity." If it remained a "picture" and didn't lapse into being solely a "diagram" (Eliot August 15, 1866 in Haight 1954–1978: vol. IV: 300), the capacity of narrative art to work on the emotions made it a powerful vehicle for the paralegal advocacy of social equality and the inalienable dignity of the human subject.

In its emphasis on the moral re-education of Louisa Gradgrind through her friendship with Stephen Blackpool, *Hard Times* replicates the standard trajectory of many Victorian novels in which a middle-class, largely sympathetic, protagonist journeys across a rapidly industrializing landscape to acquire first-hand knowledge of their "social other." Before she meets Stephen personally, Louisa notes that she had known of the existence of the workers in the "hundreds and thousands," but "she had scarcely thought more of separating them into units, than of separating the sea itself into its component drops" (Dickens 1854: 160–161). Louisa learns much about virtue and duty from her encounters with Stephen, and at the end of the novel, Dickens calls upon his reader—addressed in singular terms—to do likewise: "Dear reader! It rests with you and me, whether, in our two fields of action, similar things shall be or not" (Dickens 1854: 298). The novel's plot is more than a call to personal charitable action: it also modeled for the attentive reader the process by which wider social reconciliation might occur. In an age of individualism and self-interest, competition and laissez-faire capitalism, the cultural work of literature was to place corrective emphasis on altruism, to re-position the best moral action as self-less rather than self-ish, and to show that the wisest decision-making also took account of the goods of others (see Collini 1991: 63–65):

> Other-regarding behaviour therefore becomes the glue that holds communities together; it is the essence of community. And other-regarding behaviour does not necessarily require an external monitor to force the behaviour. It only requires each member of the community to make decisions giving appropriate weight for the well-being of those who might be affected by the decision, relying on others to reciprocate and on reputational sanctions to enforce the reciprocity. (Gerhart 2010: 10)

But imaginative literature, and the theology of the New Testament on which it so frequently drew, were not approaching this task alone: in the words of the legal philosopher Peter Gerhart, "tort law exists to define the extent to which an actor is expected to incorporate the well-being of others into the actor's choice set" and "[w]hen it is successful, tort law works in tandem with social practice to shape and enforce shared values and understandings" (2010: 12). For the law,

> [t]he relevant prescriptive issue is what forms of other-regarding behavior a person should follow in a particular context in order to make a socially appropriate decision. Tort law defines behavior as reasonable when it is appropriately other-regarding. (Gerhart 2010: 10–11)

Consequently, both legal and literary texts had to grapple with the definition of "other-regarding" moral choices, and both discourses found themselves compelled to ask, "Who, then, is my neighbour?" The answer afforded by literature is often expansive: our relations—and thus perhaps our duties and obligations—were potentially limitless. As Henry James observed in his famous "Preface" to the New York edition of *Roderick*

Hudson [1907], "[r]eally, universally, relations stop nowhere, and the exquisite problem of the artist is eternally but to draw, by a geometry of his own, the circle within which they shall happily *appear* to do so" (James 1907: 5). Dickens, the pre-eminent artist of the age of democratization, was intrigued by precisely these relations—these connections between individuals and classes at a time when the nation was especially sensitive to the definition of "the people." *Bleak House* exemplifies this fascination (Dolin 1999: 1–32; Watt 2009b):

> What connexion can there be, between the place in Lincolnshire, the house in town, the Mercury in powder, and the whereabouts of Jo the outlaw with the broom, who had that distant ray of light upon him when he swept the church-yard step? What connexion can there have been between many people in the innumerable histories of this world, who, from opposite sides of great gulfs, have, nevertheless, been very curiously brought together! (Dickens 1852–1853: 272)

Authors were more aware than ever of the new political pressure exerted by the masses—with their demands for greater representation in the House of Commons and for universal male suffrage. The test was how far the mechanism of neighborliness would hold in performing the work of keeping these disparate individuals together. If Dickens in *Hard Times* wants to show his reader that the working-class operative is her or his neighbor, the same claim is made for socially disadvantaged women, and poor and illegitimate children throughout the corpus of Victorian writing (from Charlotte Brontë's *Jane Eyre* (1847), Gaskell's *Mary Barton* (1848) and *Ruth* (1853) to long poems like Barrett Browning's *Aurora Leigh* (1857)). How far could the politics of sympathy be made to stretch?

The law, however, was compelled by its institutional constraints to approach the subject in a different way: to acknowledge a duty was to create an obligation, and "[o]nce a contractual obligation was held to give rise to a duty in tort which extended beyond the parties to the contract, what other limitation was there?" (Lunney & Oliphant 2010: 105). As Brett MR articulated in the case of *Heaven v Pender* (1883) 11 QBD 503:

> The questions which we have to solve in this case are—what is the proper definition of the relation between the two persons, other than the relation established by contract, or fraud, which imposes on the one of them a duty towards the other to observe, with regard to the person or property of such other, such ordinary care or skill as may be necessary to prevent injury to his person or property.

Fifty years later, Lord Atkin's initial attempt to formulate the "neighbor principle" as the foundation of tort law was generous in its ambit:

> It is quite true that law and morality do not cover identical fields. No doubt morality extends beyond the more limited range in which you can lay down the definite prohibitions of law; but, apart from that, the British law has always necessarily ingrained in it moral teaching in this sense: that it lays down standards of honesty and plain dealing between man and man.
>
> [A man] is not to injure his neighbour by acts of negligence; and that certainly covers a very large field of the law. I doubt whether the whole of tort could not be comprised in the golden maxim to do unto your neighbour as you would that he should do unto you. It imposes standards ... and it is of the utmost importance to the community that those standards are maintained; and it teaches a man to respect his neighbour's right of property and person ... (Atkin 1932: 27)

But upon the adjudication of the facts in dispute in *Donoghue v Stevenson* [1932] AC 562, Lord Atkin answered the question in a way that circumscribed indirect responsibility and limited the sorts of eternal and universal relations which James had imagined in his expansive "Preface":

> Who, then, in law is my neighbour? The answer seems to be—persons who are so closely and directly affected by my act that I ought reasonably to have them in contemplation as being so affected when I am directing my mind to the acts or omissions which are called in question ... "If one man is near to another, or is near to the property of another, a duty lies upon him not to do that which may cause a personal injury to that other, or may injure his property" ... I think that this sufficiently states the truth if proximity be not confined to mere physical proximity but be used, as I think it was intended, to extend to such close and direct relations that the act complained of directly affects a person whom the person alleged to be bound to take care would know would be directly affected by his careless act.

Literary texts with no mandate for intervention in the affairs of the litigious world saw such attempts to delimit moral responsibility as cowardice on the part of the law, and a particularly vicious discursive battle along these lines plays out in many mid-Victorian novels. Esther's narrative in Dickens's *Bleak House* offers perhaps the best example of this dynamic: in a sophisticated critique of the rigid and petrified form of the Equity law applied in the Court of Chancery (historically a flexible court of the King's conscience but inefficacious and rule-bound by the nineteenth century), Dickens prises the work of equity away from institutions and restores it to its Aristotelian fullness, locating it within the compassionate heart of his female narrator whose self-sacrificial benevolence is upheld as a model of Christian devotion (see Dolin 1999: 71–86). Denied participation in her mother's legal proceedings by virtue of her illegitimacy, Esther is accorded status within the text as a faithful spokesperson on behalf of the wider social group she represents. Dickens allows her to articulate his wider moral manifesto: "I thought it best to be as useful as I could, and to render what kind services I could, to those immediately about me; and to try to let that circle of duty gradually and naturally expand itself" (Dickens 1852–1853: 154). Dickens here positions the novel as a class action on behalf of that part of the population which Thomas Malthus, in his *Essay on the Principle of Population* (1798), had been prepared to describe as "surplus" to the nation's economic requirements (Schramm 2012b: 219–244). As Simon Petch has observed, the mid-Victorian generation of authors—the novelists Dickens, Eliot, and Gaskell, but also the poets Alfred, Lord Tennyson, in *The Idylls of the King* (1859–1885), and Robert Browning in *The Ring and the Book* (1868)—were active participants in these conversations about how conscience and equitability should manifest themselves in public discourse at precisely the point in time when national institutions were being reorganized (Petch 1997: 123–139). And while new discoveries in science undermined traditional understandings of moral law as divinely ordained revelation (and, by implication, exposed the ideas of ritual vengeance underpinning criminal law and capital punishment), private law was increasingly positioned as "the institution society has created to work *within society* by recognizing and endorsing forms of interpersonal decision-making that seem to be good for the community and correcting those that do not" (Gerhard 2010: 237, my italics). "Duty" and "conscience" thus became the catchphrases of the new (and quasi-secular) gospel of nineteenth-century English literature in a complex response to changing demographics of readership and the increasing prominence of a middle-class culture of politeness.

WHAT IS MY DUTY?

The late eighteenth and early nineteenth-century popular imagination was bloodthirsty and many novels addressing legal themes in the 1810s–1830s concerned violent crime. Although literature had always been implicated in the vicarious consumption of passionate transgression, the Romantics and early Victorians took this interest to new heights (empowered by modern technologies of print culture and the public appetite for news in all its forms: see Collins 1962; Hollingsworth 1963; Brantlinger 1998). When barristers became entitled to address juries on behalf of people accused of felony after the enactment of the Prisoners' Counsel Act in 1836, the scene was set for conflict between the culturally preferred forms in which such transgression could be represented and consumed, culminating in the journalistic and fictional "Murder Mania" of the late 1830s (Schramm 2000: 100–144, 2004: 285–303). While historians remind us that such violence—and its language of carnivalesque excess—remained a feature of popular and literary culture as the century progressed, the nineteenth century was also an age of increasing civility and public decorum as the middle-classes gained political prominence: after mid-century, explicit crime and guilt were increasingly displaced to the literary margins (e.g., in the genres of gothic and sensation fiction) while realism by definition increasingly positioned itself as concerned with wrongs and errors, rather than original sin and inherited guilt (Lacey 2008; Crone 2012). While the fiction of Dickens, Eliot, Gaskell, Thackeray, and Trollope successfully combined ingredients from both the melodramatic tradition and the realist interest in the psychology of the ordinary man, it is nevertheless true to suggest that novels became less and less concerned with the figure of Cain, for example, and more interested in the wrongs of omission which anyone could potentially commit against the counsel of their better judgment. These wrongs were not salacious criminal acts in which guilt was flagrant, but complex grey areas of moral action, questions of negligence and breach of duty, the domain of tort law.

The extent of a defendant's guilt for something which he or she may have wished for, but played an ambiguous role in bringing about, is something Eliot returns to time and time again in her fiction: to resort to deliberate violence is to be obviously culpable, but what is Hetty's guilt in *Adam Bede* (1859–1860) for abandoning a child when she seems herself incapable of effective moral discernment? What is the extent of Arthur's guilt for taking advantage of Hetty's youthful vanity? In *Felix Holt*, what is Felix's culpability for the manslaughter of a policeman when the death was the unintended consequence of an attempt to lead a rioting mob away from peoples' homes? In *Middlemarch*, what is Bulstrode's guilt for allowing an alcoholic to be treated in accordance with the "standard" medical practice of the day? Is this complicated by the fact that Lydgate had alerted him to the potentially fatal risks of this "standard practice"? And in *Daniel Deronda*, does Gwendolen have an obligation to attempt to rescue her brutal, drowning husband? Is an *omission* to act as morally or legally wrong as some kind of more decisive culpable behavior? Tort law was wrestling with the same questions: for example, as Baron Alderson reasoned in *Blyth v Birmingham Waterworks* (1856) 11 Exch. 781:

> Negligence is the omission to do something, which a reasonable man, guided upon those considerations, which ordinarily regulate the conduct of human affairs, would do, or doing something, which a prudent and reasonable man would not do. The standard demanded is thus not of perfection but of reasonableness. It is an objective standard taking no account of the defendant's incompetence—he may do the best he can and still be found negligent.

To be reasonable is to give due consideration to the interests and claims of others, but was altruism required or only prudence? Eliot was fascinated by the ethical value of intention (Rodensky 2003: 88–170): while she recognized that our bad deeds "carry their terrible consequences" which must be weighed independently of any moral vacillation that preceded their commission (Eliot 1859: 218), she also acknowledged what Mr. Lyon in *Felix Holt* calls that "invisible work of the soul whereby the deeds which are the same in the outward appearance and effect yet differ as the knife-stroke of the surgeon, even though it kill, differs from the knife-stroke of the wanton mutilator" (Eliot 1866: 548). Aligning her fiction with the emergent science of moral psychology, Eliot created many of the period's most compelling portraits of the complexities of human intention and agency (Lynch 1998: 25–27).

TORT LAW AND PARODIES OF NEIGHBORLINESS

That Dickens in particular was aware of the tortious parallels with his own fascination with neighborly relations can be seen in his encyclopedic study of legal forms, *Bleak House*. In a novel obsessed with the connections between characters, the forces which propel them all on a journey from strangerhood to intimacy, and the contrasting duties they owe to one another along the way, Dickens does not neglect the role that tort law plays in the protection and perhaps even the construction of neighborly relations. In fact, as part of his overall commitment to the literary and charitable recuperation and restoration of relations that have been hollowed out by litigious conflict, Dickens depicts two neighbors at war over a disputed right of way. The litigants are the inflexible peer of the realm, Sir Leicester Dedlock, and John Jarndyce's volatile but admirably radical childhood friend Lawrence Boythorn, "a true gentleman in his manner, so chivalrously polite," with a face 'lighted by a smile of so much sweetness and tenderness." Although his language is intemperate and his judgments extreme (he describes Chancery as an "infernal cauldron" that should be blown "to its father the Devil" and Sir Leicester as "Sir Lucifer" (Dickens 1852–1953: 168–169)), it is Boythorn's judgment of the law which is vindicated in the course of the novel. And for Boythorn, the bad-tempered dispute between neighbors serves as a synecdoche for parliamentary reform in the nineteenth century as he asserts his right of way against older feudal entitlements. As he explains to Mr. Jarndyce, this fierce rhetorical contest exposes the fragility of neighborly relations—civility is revealed to be, at best, a thin veneer of cordiality inadequately masking genuine differences of self-interest—and the verbal cut and thrust soon gives way to comic acts of violence on both sides:

> "By my soul!" exclaimed Mr Boythorn, suddenly firing another volley, "that fellow is, and his father was, and his grandfather was, the most stiff-necked, arrogant imbecile, pig-headed numskull, ever, by some inexplicable mistake of Nature, born in any station of life but a walking-stick's! The whole of that family are the most solemnly conceited and consummate blockheads!—But it's no matter; he should not shut up my path if he were fifty baronets melted into one, and living in a hundred Chesney Wolds, one within another, like the ivory balls in a Chinese carving. The fellow, by his agent, or secretary, or somebody, writes to me, 'Sir Leicester Dedlock, Baronet, presents his compliments to Mr. Lawrence Boythorn, and has to call his attention to the fact that the green pathway by the old parsonage-house, now the property of Mr Lawrence, is Sir Leicester's right of way, being a portion of the park of Chesney

Wold; and that Sir Leicester finds it convenient to close up the same.' I write to the fellow, 'Mr Lawrence Boythorn presents his compliments to Sir Leicester Dedlock, Baronet, and has to call his attention to the fact that he totally denies the whole of Sir Leicester Dedlock's positions on every possible subject, and has to add, in reference to closing up the pathway, that he will be glad to see the man who may undertake to do it.' The fellow sends a most abandoned villain with one eye, to construct a gateway. I play upon that execrable scoundrel with a fire-engine, until the breath is nearly driven out of his body. The fellow erects a gate in the night. I chop it down and burn it in the morning. He sends his myrmidons to come over the fence, and pass and re-pass. I catch them in humane man traps, fire split peas at their legs, play upon them with the engine—resolve to free mankind from the insupportable burden of the existence of those lurking ruffians. He brings actions for trespass; I bring actions for trespass. He brings actions for assault and battery; I defend them, and continue to assault and batter. Ha, ha, ha!" (Dickens 1852–1853: 170)

Although tort law exists to arbitrate between such competing claims to the satisfaction of both parties, Boythorn delights in the perpetuation of the dispute, with the rhetorical sparring imitating the very actions which it is failing to eliminate—"[h]e brings actions for assault and battery; I defend them, and continue to assault and batter." Such vicarious violence seems to ensure that proper neighborly relations cannot be fostered: Boythorn can only suggest that Ada and Richard keep that "distant relation [Sir Leicester] at a comfortable distance" (Dickens 1852–1853: 169)—common interests must not be allowed to develop. When Esther, Ada, and Richard visit Boythorn's home, he again demonstrates the ways in which a lack of affective proximity plays out in spatial terms: "I am sorry, ladies ... that I am obliged to conduct you nearly two miles out of the way. But, our direct road lies through Sir Leicester Dedlock's park; and, in that fellow's property, I have sworn never to set foot of mine, or horse's foot of mine, pending the present relations between us, while I breathe the breath of life!" And as he tells Mr. Jarndyce, "if you call upon the owner [of Chesney Wold], while you stay with me, you are likely to have but a cool reception ... he will have some extra stiffness, I can promise you, for the friends of his friend and neighbour, Boythorn!" (Dickens 1852–1853: 298). Lurking beneath this is the ineradicable gulf of class: Boythorn "is not the man to be walked over" either literally or politically—as Sir Leicester observes in conversation with Tulkinghorn, Boythorn is a "levelling person. A person who, fifty years ago, would probably have been tried at the old Bailey for some demagogue proceeding, and severely punished—if not ... hanged, drawn and quartered" (Dickens 1852–1853: 213–214). Mr. Jarndyce's party sees new performances in the farce on arrival in Lincolnshire:

[Mr Boythorn's] house, though a little disorderly in comparison with the garden, was a real old house, with settles in the chimney of the brick-floored kitchen, and great beams across the ceilings. On one side of it was the terrible piece of ground in dispute, where Mr Boythorn maintained a sentry in a smock-frock, day and night, whose duty was supposed to be, in cases of aggression, immediately to ring a large bell hung up there for the purpose, to unchain a great bull-dog established in a kennel as his ally, and generally to deal destruction on the enemy. Not content with these precautions, Mr Boythorn had himself composed and posted there, on painted boards to which his name was attached in large letters, the following solemn warnings: "Beware of the bull-dog. He is most ferocious. Lawrence Boythorn." "The blunderbuss is loaded with slugs. Lawrence Boythorn." "Man-traps and spring-guns are set here at all times of the day and night. Lawrence Boythorn." "Take notice. That any person audaciously presuming to trespass on this property, will be punished with the utmost rigour of the law. Lawrence Boythorn." (Dickens 1852–1853: 301)

It is the thoughtless, superficial Mr. Skimpole who interrogates Boythorn as to the symbolic meaning of such efforts:

> "But this is taking a good deal of trouble," said Mr Skimpole in his light way, "when you are not in earnest after all?"
>
> "Not in earnest!" returned Mr Boythorn, with unspeakable warmth. "Not in earnest! If I could have hoped to train him, I would have bought a Lion instead of that dog, and would have turned him loose upon the first intolerable robber who should dare to make an encroachment on my rights. Let Sir Leicester Dedlock consent to come out and decide this question by single combat, and I will meet him with any weapon known to mankind in any age or country. I am that much in earnest. Not more!" (Dickens 1852–1853: 304)

The provocation arises from the way in which Sir Leicester contemplates the members of his local community as if his social status was divinely assigned and protected—he thinks of himself "as if he were a considerable landed proprietor in heaven:"

> "He believes he is!" said Mr Boythorn. "He firmly believes it. So did his father, and his grandfather and his great-grandfather!"
>
> "Did you know," pursued Mr Skimpole, very unexpectedly to Mr Boythorn, "it's agreeable to me to see a man of that sort."
>
> "Is it!" said Mr Boythorn.
>
> "Say that he wants to patronize me," pursued Mr Skimpole. "Very well! I don't object."
>
> "I do," said Mr Boythorn, with great vigor.
>
> "Do you really?" returned Mr Skimpole in his easy light vein. "But, that's taking trouble, surely. And why should you take trouble? ... I say 'Mighty potentate, here is my homage!' It's easier to give it, than to withhold it ... I take it that my business in the social system is to be agreeable; I take it that everybody's business in the social system is to be agreeable. It's a system of harmony, in short." (Dickens 1852–1853: 305–306)

To which Boythorn can only reply "Is there such a thing as principle, Mr Harold Skimpole?" In Boythorn's terms, neighborly civility to the proprietor of a grand estate is not only an individual example of spineless submission, but an act of collusion in the perpetuation of wider patterns of social inequality. The idea that all are equal before the law is at best a fiction when access to justice is dependent upon pecuniary means and social status.

In this often overlooked strand of one of the novel's many sub-plots, Dickens also shows his awareness of the ways in which tortious litigation creates the very idea of neighborliness. If as Buller observed, "[e]very Man ought to take reasonable Care that he does not injure his Neighbour" and if one's neighbours in law are "persons who are so closely and directly affected by my act that I ought reasonably to have them in contemplation as being so affected when I am directing my mind to the acts or omissions which are called in question," then it is perhaps logical to argue in reverse that, inter alia, he whom my acts injure must by definition be my neighbour. Dickens is aware of the extent to which litigation is thus constitutive of the very definition of "neighbor," and case reports evidence the ways in which harm retrospectively creates the category:

by the very act of succeeding in a complaint, parties are identified as "neighbors" of the defendant even where no personal or contractual relation existed between them beforehand. This might seem a perversion of the term "neighbor," and almost a parody of the caring actions which demonstrate neighborliness in the parable of the Good Samaritan. Dickens was more than prepared to critique the law with savage indignation: for example, perhaps motivated by his own experiences as a litigant in Chancery in 1844, Dickens was prepared to expose Chancery's administration of Equity law as warped and hollow, the exact opposite of the flexible, sympathetic reasoning which the Court of the King's Conscience had historically been created to demonstrate. As mentioned previously, Dickens consequently undermines Chancery's alleged monopoly on the spirit of equity and re-invests it in the work of individuals like Esther and Mr. Jarndyce, who become alternative practitioners of mercy and charity in its truest Christian sense (Petch 1997; Dolin 1999; Watt 2009b; Schramm 2012b). Yet in a masterly display of his fictive inventiveness, Dickens permits an affirming resolution of Boythorn's and Sir Leicester's tortious battle of wills. After Lady Dedlock's death (which elicits a compassionate gesture of forgiveness from Sir Leicester, albeit one expressed in formal economic terms), Boythorn wishes in turn to show mercy to his antagonist:

> War rages yet with the audacious Boythorn, though at uncertain intervals, and now hotly, and now coolly; flickering like an unsteady fire. The truth is said to be, that when Sir Leicester came down to Lincolnshire for good, Mr Boythorn showed a manifest desire to abandon his right of way, and do whatever Sir Leicester would: which Sir Leicester, conceiving to be a condescension to his illness or misfortune, took in such high dudgeon, and was so magnificently aggrieved by, that Mr Boythorn found himself under the necessity of committing a flagrant trespass to restore his neighbour to himself. Similarly Mr Boythorn continues to post tremendous placards on the disputed thoroughfare, and (with his bird upon his head) to hold forth vehemently against Sir Leicester in the sanctuary of his own home; similarly, also, he defies him as of old in the little church, by testifying a bland unconsciousness of his existence. But it is whispered that when he is most ferocious towards his old foe, he is really most considerate; and that Sir Leicester, in the dignity of being implacable, little supposes how much he is humoured. As little does he think how near together he and his antagonist have suffered, in the fortunes of two sisters; and his antagonist, who knows it now, is not the man to tell him. So the quarrel goes on to the satisfaction of both. (Dickens 1852–1853: 928–929)

The litigation has become a source of comforting continuity for the bereaved Sir Leicester, and at novel's end Dickens reintegrates the legal and theological meanings of "neighborliness:" in his willingness to commit "a flagrant trespass to restore his neighbour to himself," Boythorn demonstrates genuine Christian love. By acknowledging that charitable care can coexist with the terms of tort law, Dickens effects a rare comic conclusion to one of his many fictional skirmishes with the law.

LIMITATIONS OF SYMPATHY AND THE "VEIL OF IGNORANCE"

Despite Dickens's confidence in the ways in which Christian values could be expressed in literature at mid-century, by fin-de-siècle this consensus had largely broken down: the vocabulary of duty, "goodness," and self-sacrifice was increasingly interrogated, and while some commentators stressed that neighborly duty could be sustained by agnosticism or even atheism, others were less sure. And while many mid-Victorian writers seem to have felt that literature was some kind of ethical laboratory in which new visions of social organization might be imagined (even if they disagreed about the exact architecture of the newly imagined arrangements), subsequent authors and critics expressed increasing skepticism about the power of sympathy as an educative tool. In the face of intensifying attacks on received religion, public sages like George Eliot and Matthew Arnold had held even more tightly to the rhetoric of para-Christian duty and "ardentness" of purpose: as Friedrich Nietzsche registered so insightfully in his note on Eliot in *The Twilight of the Idols*, "[i]n England, in response to every little emancipation from theology, one has to reassert one's position in a fear-inspiring manner as a moral fanatic" (Nietzsche 1888: 80). But, by 1895, Eliot's emphasis on *earnest*, sincere self-sacrifice gives way to witty word play on *The Importance of Being E(a)rnest*, in Oscar Wilde's astute dramatization of the changing moral field.

What, then, did Christian neighborly sympathy as a foundational principle of ethics achieve in the nineteenth century? Critical consensus seems to suggest, for example, that *Bleak House* played no direct role in the demise of the Court of Chancery as a separate jurisdiction in the radical overhaul of the judicial system a few years later with the passage of the Judicature Acts between 1873 and 1875. While the philosopher Martha Nussbaum argues that reading is "structurally isomorphic to lived experience"—a virtual thought experiment, which, by imagining equality, can thus effect social and eventually legislative change (Nussbaum 1990: 125)—difficulties remain for those who want to argue that the effect of reading is inevitably liberal and progressive. Philosophers and public moralists increasingly acknowledged that sympathy has many limitations in terms of how far it can extend, and even those nineteenth-century novelists who extolled its virtues often revealed (though sometimes inadvertently) that readers sympathize with people most like themselves—witness, for example, the communal rejection of Mary Shelley's monster in *Frankenstein* (1818), the incarceration of Bertha Mason in Charlotte Brontë's *Jane Eyre* (1847), and even Dickens's treatment of Jo in *Bleak House* (when he positions him as an object of charitable pity in other people's narratives but not an agent of active self-determination in his own). In his famous *Lectures on the Relation between Law and Public Opinion in England during the Nineteenth Century* (1905), the jurist and constitutional theorist A.V. Dicey observed that while English law was highly responsive to the increasingly compassionate tone of social opinion in the Victorian period, the primary engines of social reform were Benthamite utilitarianism and the Evangelical revival. Dicey did, however, offer some acknowledgment of the social role of literary art: it facilitated the movement from individualism to collectivism by century's end:

> For the last sixty years and more, the needs and sufferings of the poor have been thrust upon the knowledge of middle-class Englishmen. There are persons still living who can recall the time when about sixty years ago the *Morning Chronicle* in letters on "London Labour and the London Poor" revealed to the readers of high-class, and then dear, newspapers the miserable condition of the poorer wage-earners of London. These letters at once aroused the sympathy and called forth the aid of Maurice and the Christian Socialists. For sixty years, novelists, newspaper writers, and philanthropists have alike brought the condition of the poor constantly before the eyes of their readers or disciples. The desire to ease the sufferings, to increase the pleasures, and to satisfy the best aspirations of the mass of wage-earners has become a marked characteristic of the wealthy classes of Englishmen. This sentiment of active goodwill, stimulated no

doubt by ministers of religion, has spread far and wide among laymen, e.g., lawyers, merchants, and others not specially connected with any one religious, theological, or political party ... It may be expected that, as has happened again and again during the history of England, the power of opinion may, without any immense revolution in the institutions of the country, modify and reform their working. (Dicey 1905: lxii)

Sympathy, or narrative works promoting sympathy, played a role in enhancing the visibility—and by extension, the political recognition—of those marginal figures who paid the price for social progress, and for those "neighbors" whose rights were harmed in the course of industrial or commercial activity. But by the time Dicey was writing, in the early twentieth century, other mechanisms were rising to prominence as the best means for the protection of vulnerable groups.

In essence, the idea of "sympathy" seems to have run aground against the idea of impartiality. Take Leslie Stephen's famous assessment of George Eliot's artistic achievements:

The ethical value of artistic work, she held, is simply its power of arousing sympathy for noble qualities. The artist, if we must talk about that personage, must of course give true portraits of human nature and of the general relations of man to the universe. But the artist must also have a sense of beauty; and among other things, of the beauty of character. He must recognise the charm of a loving nature, of a spirit of self-sacrifice, or of the chivalrous and manly virtues. He shares, indeed, with the scientific observer the obligation of seeing things as they are ... He must be as absolutely impartial as the physiologist describing the physical organisation. (Stephen 1902: 116)

Eliot was not naïve: she acknowledged the existence of prejudice. As her forensically minded narrator had observed in *Felix Holt*, "[e]ven the bare discernment of facts, much more their arrangement with a view to inferences, must carry a bias: human impartiality, whether judicial or not, can hardly escape being more or less loaded" (Eliot 1866: 377). But on other occasions she expressed a hope that an attitude of impartiality would arise from ever-expanding sympathy with the particularity, the thickness and granularity of our knowledge of our neighbors' stories (Eliot 1860–1861: 628). This was perhaps too idealistic. As Ryan Balot observes:

Impartiality and sympathy are strange bedfellows. Impartiality, in essence, calls on human beings to adopt a "view from nowhere," to reason morally in an abstract way, unencumbered by emotions or partisan ties or particular loyalties. Impartial individuals must appreciate that they are single agents among many fundamentally similar or equal agents, without morally substantive distinction. In the Kantian conception, indeed, "impartiality demands that the moral agent reason in detachment from her own loyalties, projects and emotions;" ideally the moral agent is motivated by a sense of duty toward rationally legislated categorical imperatives. But sympathy, like love, is an emotion of caring and attachment that makes impartial acts, at least in the traditional philosophical sense, impossible. Hence, ostensibly, a major conflict exists between the two. (Balot 2014: 174–175)

Narrative art, which conducts its ethical experiments through representations of chosen individuals, is not then uncomplicatedly democratic or scientifically objective in its treatment of its chosen subjects. In *The One vs the Many: Minor Characters and the Space of the Protagonist in the Novel*, Alex Woloch argues that the politics of the novel form is always compromised by its very structure: because it chooses to prioritize some characters above others—because it simply cannot give equal narrative space to the claims of all the minor characters—its critique of prevailing political structures is automatically blunted (2010: 32–33). Despite its democratic pretensions, then, the novel is always implicated in aristocratic power structures in ways that render sympathy an immature medium for effecting wider political change. Paul Ricoeur, too, questions the extent to which acts of imaginative projection and emotive identification can bring strangers into just social relations with one another:

> However wonderful the virtue of friendship may be, it is not capable of fulfilling the task of justice, nor even of engendering it as a distinct virtue. The virtue of justice is based on a relation of distance from the other, just as originary as the relation of proximity to the other person offered through his face and voice. This relation to the other is, if I may so put it, immediately mediated by the institution. (Ricoeur 2000: xiii)

For Ricoeur, impartiality is practiced not by benevolent individuals but by just institutions, such as the judiciary, the collective body against which so much of Dickens's satire is directed. That too great a knowledge of individual particulars might generate not justice but *bias* has become an increasingly prominent concern. In *Tort Law and Social Morality*, Gerhart acknowledges that while empathy plays an important part in the agent's decision-making process—the actor "must be able to stand in the shoes of others and try to appreciate the world as those people understand it"—it is tempered by a requirement "to evaluate the interpersonal claims of injurer and victim from a neutral position (i.e., without regard to the actor's circumstances that are extraneous to the appropriate balance between injurer and victim)" (2010: 38). So while Gerhart acknowledges that "[t]ort law revolves around a modified golden rule: Do unto others as you would have them do unto you if you had their projects and preferences," he imports John Rawls's idea of "the veil of ignorance" (a "thought-device" designed to filter out knowledge of extraneous particulars) to refine the decision-making procedure (Rawls 1990: 118–125). To be reasonable, an agent must consider what "course of action she would choose if she understood the trade-off between the projects and preferences of injurer and victim but did not know which characteristics she had and whether she was injurer or victim" (Gerhart 2010: 38):

> The idea is to task each actor in a community to make decisions under conditions of equality and under constraints that forbid the actor from finding a maxim that is neutral and universal ... The device of the veil of ignorance works because it forces the decision maker to eliminate reasons or reasoning that would bias the decision in his or her favour. (Gerhart 2010: 95)

Gerhart's line of argument is persuasive, but at the same time it expunges from legal consideration all the emotions which Eliot hoped to generate from sympathy with the particulars of an individual's circumstances or details of his life story. While sympathy was a prominent part of the nineteenth-century public discourse that promoted the initial transition towards collective ideals, it has been superseded in the century that followed by various forms of rights-based legislation (addressing, for example, workers' compensation for injury, and matters of health and safety in the wider community: see Dicey 1905: 259–302). The performance of our duty to our neighbors has become, at least in part, the state's business.

In conclusion, imaginative literature often sought to instill virtue into its nineteenth-century readership, performing valuable cultural work at a time of enormous social and cultural upheaval. Over the course of Victoria's reign, literature and the law mutually addressed the Scriptural question—"Who is my neighbor?"—and although their answers expressed themselves in very different formal shapes (novels, precedents, parables, plays, poems) they ultimately worked together to clarify the issues at stake. Each of these formal choices illuminated the relationship between the general and the particular, asking whether, in Twining's terms, a parable (or, by implication an extrabiblical parable) can express a *ratio decidendi* and how much detail is necessary to arrive at a propositional maxim or a precedent that might guide subsequent decision-makers (see Twining 1990: 404–411, and also Ben-Yishai 2013, *passim*). If literary contributions to that debate have now been largely forgotten by legal practitioners, it remains important to understand the jurisprudence of tort law in the wider cultural context from which it emerged.

CHAPTER EIGHT

The Legal Profession

Dickens, Daumier, and The Man of Law

GARY WATT

a painter and a black-and-white artist ... His figures are resurrections.
—Vincent Van Gogh, letter to Anthon G.A. Ridder Van Rappard (March 1883)

INTRODUCTION

This chapter is concerned with the forms of the legal profession at the start of the Age of Reform (1820–1920) as represented by Charles Dickens (1812–1870) and Honoré Daumier (1808–1879). It is a tale of two cities, London and Paris, and of the legal professions practiced in these two cities, and it is a tale of two art forms, text and image, and how those two forms combined in print publications to represent the legal profession in the popular imagination. Dickens's first novel developed from a commission to supply literary illustrations to accompany another artist's comic drawings, whereas Daumier's major professional output was the production of images to be accompanied by text legends written by his editors. The present chapter is also a tale of two sexes, of men and women in art and law. The single most significant legislative reform to occur in the legal profession across the Age of Reform was the admission of women to the ranks of practicing lawyers. In France, a law of 1900 opened the way for the first women to enter the profession that year. In England, the Sex Disqualification (Removal) Act 1919 was followed in 1920 by the first admission of women to the Inns of Court (the traditional site of education in English law), and in 1922 the pioneers were at last called to the bar and the first woman entered legal practice. As this chapter goes to print, with the centenary of the 1919 statute on the horizon, it is notable that in England today the majority of new entrants to the traditional legal professions are female.

    Our window on the cultural history of the legal profession in the Age of Reform opens at the end of the first decade of the nineteenth century where we see a baby boy born to parents of modest means in a town on his country's south coast. When still young, he is uprooted to the capital and there, pressed by his father's financial difficulties, takes humble paid work, including, in his early teens, employment as a junior clerk at the fringes of the legal profession. A theater enthusiast and a keen observer of the quotidian drama of urban life, his early sketches led to a lifetime of work and immense popularity as a result of publications in journals and other print periodicals. To say that he was a caricaturist is the truth, but it is not the whole truth. He has left us with many a masterpiece and his legacy is undoubtedly the oeuvre of an artistic genius. I am talking of Charles Dickens, but also of his contemporary Honoré Daumier. The Frenchman Daumier is justly celebrated for his drawing and painting, but it was to Dickens that Van Gogh was referring in the quotation set out at the top of this chapter.[1]

Accidental coincidences in the backgrounds of the two artists cannot justify their pairing for present purposes, but what makes them compelling as subjects for comparison is the similarity, and the undoubted popularity, of their visual imagination as it is expressed in satirical mode. Gordon McKenzie concludes his article "Dickens and Daumier" with the observation that "[i]n both men the art of caricature was expressed at its highest level, and as artists in this field there is little to choose between them" (McKenzie 1941: 298) Dickens and Daumier produced memorable critiques of many walks of metropolitan life, including that of the banker and the politician, but the legal profession in all its varieties and ranks was among the most significant stimuli for both artists. Indeed, they have been called "The two great popularizers of legal themes and attitudes toward lawyers in the nineteenth century" (Chase 1986: 536) and Geoffrey-Dechaume said of Daumier that he "knows lawyers, and above all the lawyer, better than they know themselves" (Catalogue 1999: 271). The series of lithographs for which Honoré Daumier is best known today, *Les Gens de Justice* (most of which were published first in the Parisian satirical journal *Le Charivari* between March 21, 1845 and October 31, 1848), depicts a wide range of participants in the legal profession. Those represented include the judge,

FIGURE 8.1 Honoré Daumier, "La Caricature Provisoire" Types Parisiens No.15 (LD568), for *Le Charivari*, 10 February 1839 (author's copy) [Clients by-passing their lawyer: *He bien! Tant pis! ... nous plaiderons ... j'aime mieux ça!! ...* ("Well, nevermind, we will plead ... that's better")]. Source: Gary Watt.

the court usher, the witness, the defendant and oppressed citizens who are reluctant participants in the law and those already so impoverished that they are excluded from recourse to law when they most need it. Dickens's first novel, *The Posthumous Papers of the Pickwick Club* ("*The Pickwick Papers,*" serialized April 1836 to November 1837), and his longest, *Bleak House* (serialized March 1852 to September 1853), present compelling studies of the legal profession in all its shades from farcical to fearful. One commentator suggests dryly that "the novels of Charles Dickens and the etchings of Daumier make plain" that "Contempt for lawyers ... transcends national borders" (Schechter 1996: 368), but arguably the artists' barbs are aimed more at faults in the systems of law and the institutions of the legal profession than at individual lawyers. Even if lawyers are the intended targets of the satire, they rarely feel it as a personal attack. It has been noted by more than one observer that "even the targets of such humor will likely join in the good-natured irreverence" (Chase 1986: 536). Howard Vincent attributes the fact that Daumier's *Les Gens de Justice* has "always been a favourite among the lawyers themselves" to lawyers' narcissism (Vincent 1968: 111).

Dickens and Daumier lived and worked in a culture in which the legal profession was exclusively male. The art of Dickens and Daumier is to some extent an unreformed depiction of an unreformed profession in which women are cast as outsiders—for the most part vulnerable and pitiful, occasionally exotic and wily, but always excluded and dependent. It is debatable whether our two artists and their arts merely reflected and confirmed the forms of the legal profession or whether they contributed to its reform. Dickens's *Bleak House*, for example, first appeared in the same year as the Chancery Reform Act 1852 and so cannot claim to have instigated the improvements to the administration of the old High Court of Chancery that were heralded by that statute (culminating in the Judicature Acts 1873–1875). The novel can nevertheless claim to have spurred the reforms on to completion and to have prevented any sliding back into old errors. Even if it is difficult to demonstrate that Dickens and Daumier made any decisive and direct causal contribution to law reform, there is no doubt that in general terms they contributed to the reforming spirit of their time. They did this most obviously through their overt engagement with themes of social and political justice,[2] but they also made a more subtle and distinctively artistic contribution to the prevailing spirit of reform by reason of their irreverent playfulness with simple, stereotypical polarities. Daumier even manages to disrupt the polar distinction between male and female, on which the law at the time set such store, by depicting a woman in full beard and full female dress.[3] Whether his intention was subversive or supportive of the polarity at that time, what matters is that that the image endures and that it still unsettles established states.

REFORMING ARTS OF COLOR AND MOVEMENT

There are two features of Daumier's art, and of Dickens's too, that especially evidence a reforming influence in their treatment of lawyers. The first is that both men worked on the page in black and white with such a refined level of skill and visual imagination that they were capable of finding and presenting the nuance and greyscale of human individuality within the absolutism of binary stereotypes. They were not postmodern artists. Dickens unashamedly sets his binary novel *A Tale of Two Cities* (1859) in "the season of Light ... the season of Darkness" (1). Dickens and Daumier worked with and within the binary modes of modernity (there is certainly nothing radically reforming in the attitude of either Dickens or Daumier to suffragettes and women's place in traditionally male spheres of social life), but within those constraints they sought to give rich expression to the diverse shapes and subtleties of human individuality. Dickens's depiction of Esther Summerson, for example, can be criticized as being not radical enough in the way it depicts her gender in relation to legal institutions, but in symbolic terms she stands to law as Florence Nightingale would stand to war: holding up a critical light to its darkest corners and challenging its intransigent, systemic neglect.[4]

Howard Vincent, commenting on the reasons for Daumier's attraction to the lawyer as artistic subject, attaches appropriate weight to Daumier's personal experience of lawyers, law and the courts (to which we will return shortly); but he also acknowledges Daumier's "aesthetic reason for drawing lawyers"; namely that such features as lawyers' dress "played into his talent for handling contrasts of black and white, of chiaroscuro" (Vincent 1968: 111). Daumier and Dickens painted pictures in black and white, but their shading and detailing introduced a tonal range of such fine nuance that they might be said to have expressed true colors within the confines of a polarized palette. This is how Charles Baudelaire, the French prose-poet and critic (who is credited with coining the term "modernity") saw it.[5] For him "the great colourists know how to produce colour with a black dress, a white cravat and a grey background" (Baudelaire 1992 [1846]: 155) (throughout this chapter translations from French are my own unless otherwise stated). He develops the same idea specifically in relation to Daumier; observing that "his drawing is naturally coloured. His lithographs and his etchings on wood evoke ideas

FIGURE 8.2 "Light" by "Phiz" (Hablôt Knight Browne) for *Bleak House* ch.51, "Enlightened" (1853). Source: Gary Watt.

of color. His pencil contains more than mere delineating black. Color comes to him instinctively" (Baudelaire 1992 [1846]: 217). Like Baudelaire, the English artist John Ruskin considered that "the romantic artist must use color, the element of feeling, to combat the inherent greyness of the times in which he lives" (Landow 168: 300). Despite Dickens's supposedly limited palette of black and white, Ruskin was satisfied that he painted his scenes to perfection. In his autobiography *Praeterita* he wrote that "Dickens taught us nothing with which we were not familiar,—only painted it perfectly for us" (Ruskin 1949 [1885–1889]: 275). Ruskin seems to have been content that Dickens's reforming achievement did not lie in his political and social subject matter, but in the more romantic accomplishment of his painterly perfection. At least one academic authority on the period concurs, writing that Dickens's "significance is not that he propounded any program of social reforms or political improvements, but simply that he painted, for all to appreciate and enjoy, a vivid picture of working class folk" (Thomson 1950: 114).

Related to the possibility of color in black-and-white images is the possibility of truth in caricature. Dickens is said to have had "a nervous dread of caricature" (Leavis 1970: 348), but what is really meant by this is that he feared that his work might be characterized as caricature of the clumsy and overblown kind. Dickens was happy to claim the name of caricature for his work provided it was understood to be caricature of the closely colored variety that attains the level of fine art. In the preface to *Martin Chuzzlewit*, he writes that "What is exaggeration to one class of minds and perceptions, is plain truth to another" (Leavis 1970: 349). John Harvey might have been recalling this when he wrote that "In a fine caricature, the exaggeration still creates in the mind a real human face, and not an impossible mask" (Harvey 1970: 63) or perhaps he was recalling a similar sentiment expressed by Baudelaire in relation to Daumier's works: "It is not so much caricature as the mundane and monstrous story of reality" (Baudelaire 1992 [1846]: 212). Caricature indicates a thing that carries a cargo or charge and some complain that the art of Dickens and Daumier is overloaded—that it is "exaggerated" (in the etymological sense of that word, which is from the Latin *aggerare*; "to heap"). I prefer to think that their satire is not so much over-loaded as super-charged with life. In the creation of artistic images, bright line certainty is not a fault. We have just noted how Ruskin admired Dickens for the precision of his images. Daumier was equally exact in the execution of his artistic performance, thus Henri Frantz opined that Daumier engraved his characters "with marvellous exactitude upon the mind of the observer" (Holme 1904: D vi). In law, the broad brush strokes of generic laws cannot achieve a just representation of an individual's humanity, which is why we need "equity" (Watt 2009a), but in art, when the artist's hand and eye is true enough, lines can be drawn with a certainty that is just.

The second reforming feature of Dickens's art and Daumier's art is that it brings movement to seemingly static states. It has been said that the best rule for Victorian lawyers who wished to be retained as family solicitors was "Don't just do something; stand there" (Shaffer 1978: 733). Dickens was passionately opposed to the immovable state that is inherent in the noun and nature of "institution." He regarded the institution of the law and the state of the legal profession as stubborn obstacles to social progress. He hoped to move them (and to remove them if needs be) by the force of his emotive prowess. He was, in this sense, a master rhetorician, but of the romantic and poetic sort rather than the parliamentary or legal breed: "the evidence for Dickens as a rhetorician, a man constantly aware of and in touch with his audience, is, as has often been recognized, very strong" (Kincaid 1971: 18). Daumier knew as well as Dickens how to exploit pathos to advance the rhetorical power of an image; witness his lithograph depicting the massacre of a working-class family by government troops ('*Rue Transnonain, le 15 Avril 1834*' [LD135]). Daumier understood the arts of rhetoric (witness Plate 33 [LD1369] of *Les Gens de Justice* in which an audience of lawyers admire one of their colleagues presenting a peroration in the style of Demosthenes), but his rhetorical power to move resides not so much in artificial attempts to induce pathos as in the essential fluidity of his artistic execution and the flowing lines of his figures. Baudelaire sensed this stirring in the stones of Daumier's lithographs, diagnosing that "All his figures are sustained with true movement" (Baudelaire 1992 [1846]: 217). Referring to Daumier's black-and-white palette, Vincent concludes that "[t]he very medium is here part of the meaning" (Vincent 1968: 111). So it is, but in more material ways than the mere contrast of tone. The fact that a lithograph is, as the very word tells us, "drawn on stone" has significance in an aesthetic and allegorical sense. Daumier moves his lithographic stones to strike us and stir us with a weight that is almost tangible. One even feels the frenetic pace with which his images were performed on the slab. They seem to live. Michelangelo famously said that "Every block of stone has a statue inside it and it is the task of the sculptor to discover it," in other words, that the sculptor's art is to reveal the human form trapped within the stone. Daumier draws stones to the same end. Balzac is said to have declared that Daumier had "something of Michelangelo under his skin" ("Ce gaillard-là a du Michel-Ange sous la peau!").

In one of the most striking images in the series *Les Gens de Justice*, Daumier presents two lawyers walking down the stony steps of the grand staircase of the Palais de Justice (LD1372, Le Charivari, February 8, 1848).[6] Howard Vincent comments that "[t]he picture is as hard as granite in its satire, and moving in its certainty, in its compositional simplicity and perfection. It is one of Daumier's finest achievements" (Vincent 1968: 113). The reference to granite shows that Daumier has succeeded in his aim of communicating the stoniness of the lawyers and the sort of stately stability that they profess to be a virtue. What Vincent does not spell out is the fact that the whole study is an architectural joke. The lawyers' faces are stony and cold as if presenting an architectural face-on profile of the legal edifice. The clue is in the legend: "Grand Escalier, Palais du Justice: Vue de Faces." The lines of the clothing are rigid and regulated. The robes and collar tabs fall straight down. The faces are inanimate. The lawyers' feet are hidden. The absence of humanity in the image prompts the viewer to supplement it with a humane response. In other images Daumier sets up his statuesque lawyers to emphasize the dramatic contrast between the inanimate lawyer who is unpaid and the absurdly excessive gestures of the lawyer who has his fee. In some images we see the lawyer who is stonily unmoved when an impecunious client seeks his professional assistance; and in several others we see the lawyer who, like an automaton sparked into life by the drop of a coin, performs a frenzy of forensic flourishes for the client who has means to pay. In one such (LD1342), the lawyer is a very whirlwind of facial gymnastics, gesticulating limbs, swishing gown and well-placed props of paper, hat, and client. The legend informs us, though the information was hardly needed, that this fully engaged lawyer is someone "who is eminently convinced of his client's … ability to pay!". Similarly animated is the lawyer in Plate 11 (LD1347) who confronts a three man panel of sleeping judges with the claim that "Justice always has her eyes open." (Compare Dickens's *Bleak House*: "then there were the gentlemen of the bar in wigs and gowns—some awake and some asleep" [1].)[7]

Daumier revisited his lawyers on the steps of the Palais de Justice some years later, this time in watercolor. The composition is very similar in broad outline to that of the earlier

THE LEGAL PROFESSION   153

FIGURE 8.3 Honoré Daumier, "Le grand escalier du Palais de Justice" *c.* 1864; watercolor, detail. Source: Gary Watt.

lithographic plate, but the lawyers' feet can be seen and the robes and tabs are ruffled. One lawyer ascends the stairs in the background; another descends in the foreground. The latter is the main focus of the image and there, on his chest, near his heart, is the smallest square of red—the ribbon of la Légion d'honneur. Where the lawyers of the lithograph were lifeless stones, Daumier here adds movement and a hint of human spirit.

PERFORMING THE LEGAL PROFESSION

"Performance" is perhaps the key word that connects Daumier and Dickens to the profession of the lawyer. Like lawyers, the artists were paid to perform to a brief and to a deadline. Dickens's first novel, *The Pickwick Papers*, was first published on a periodic basis; as was every one of his subsequent novels. This episodic mode of production had its counterpart in the publication of the major caricature series of the period—for example, Daumier's illustrations to James Rousseau's *Physiologie du Robert-Macaire* (Dixon 1971: 131)—indeed, *The Pickwick Papers* emerged from a project which had begun when Dickens agreed to supply text legends to accompany a series of "Cockney sporting plates" by the ill-fated illustrator Robert Seymour (Seymour committed suicide early in the series). Gordon McKenzie rightly observes that "[c]ircumstances of publication forced Dickens into structural defects. But those same circumstances brought his work closer to Daumier's by sharpening the spatial and visual quality of his writing" (McKenzie 1941: 126).

What is it about the legal world that so especially appealed to the aesthetic sense of both Dickens and Daumier? One answer is that the drama of the legal world has all the physical elements essential to theater, which was a great passion of both men.[8] In the world of law we have the contrast of shadows and bright lights, we have the dramatic action of the stillness and movement of the actors, we have the physical edifices and environs of the legal profession to set the backdrop to the scene and we have costume (Watt 2013: 101–109). Theatrical subjects were a favorite of Daumier and by that light we can see that "the impressive neo-classical edifice of the Palais de Justice ... provided a kind of stage setting for his legal subjects" (Laughton 1996: 89). *Les Gens de Justice* contains numerous plates satirizing the theatrical nature of legal performance. In Plate 7 (LD1343) one among a coterie of lawyers cautions the others not to argue outside of court, for the effort is wasted without an audience to impress. Plate 8 (LD1344) depicts two lawyers joking about how they insulted each other in court without really getting angry at all. In Plate 14 (LD1350), opposing advocates "robing up" joke that they were on opposite sides of the same argument some weeks before. Laughing, they suggest that they can prompt each other if they forget their lines. Compare this with the anonymous 1841 publication *Physiologie de l'Homme de Loi*, illustrated by Louis Trimolet and Théodore Maurisset, in which a mother prompts her son, a newly fledged lawyer, during his first audience in court, and where it is said that for two brothers at the bar to be in perfect agreement, it is only required that they be opponents in the same case (Trimolet and Maurisset 1841: 21, 54). In Daumier's Plate 21 (LD1357), the lawyer whispers an aside advising his client to shed tears for good effect and in Plate 30 (LD1366), where a lawyer feigns illness in court, we are told that this is the last resort when his case is in bad health.

Dickens was a great lover of theater and a devoted amateur performer. He had immense affection for Shakespeare. Daumier's affection for the dramatist Molière was no less. Molière's depiction of lawyers in his farce *Les Fourberies de Scapin* (known in English as *That Scoundrel Scapin*) is uncannily close to Daumier's depiction of lawyers in *Les Gens de Justice* and elsewhere. Daumier advertises the connection in the close similarity between some of his theatrical and legal images. For example, his many images of scheming lawyers whispering secret asides to each other bear a striking resemblance to *Crispin et Scapin*; his painting of Crispin or "Crespin" (valet de Dom Pedre in Paul Scarron's *L'Écolier de Salamanque*) bending the ear of Molière's Scapin (valet to Leander in *Les Fourberies de Scapin*). John Wood's translation of Molière's *That Scoundrel Scapin* warns that it is "hell on earth to be mixed up with the law—the very idea of a lawsuit would make me pack up and fly to the ends of the earth" (Wood 1953: 86). In Dickens's *Bleak House* the lawyers themselves advise that claimants should "[s]uffer any wrong that can be done you rather than come here!" (1). Dickens and Daumier prompt our visual imaginations to see that lawyers are always performing, and that every trial is a show trial. They helps us

> to see all that full dress and ceremony and to think of the waste, and want, and beggared misery it represented; to consider that while the sickness of hope deferred was raging in so many hearts this polite show went calmly on from day to day, and year to year. (*Bleak House*, 24)

Daumier's *Les Gens de Justice* shows us, as does Dickens's *Bleak House*, that the legal show goes on only so long as there is clients' money to pay for it. The first plate in the series (LD1337) depicts the defeated lawyer who expresses his readiness to take the client's case to appeal, subject to further payment. Plate 4 (LD1340) mocks a judicial judgment so complex that a lawyer must be paid to explain it. In Plate 6 (LD1342) an advocate is shown to perform well because he believes his client can pay well and in Plate 20 (LD1357) a lawyer says it is impossible to act for the client because he is missing the most important evidence—"money down!" (those words are spoken as a theatrical aside ["à part"]). The legend to Plate 38 (LD1374), which might be translated "when crime doesn't pay," depicts two lawyers playing dominoes while a third sleeps.

An accusation leveled at Daumier is that he only observed the legal theatrical scene from the wings. One French lawyer complains that he merely peeped into the advocates' robing room (le Foyer 1958: 9). This, one suspects, is a lawyer's instinctive defense of his profession. The complaint is certainly a very partial view of Daumier's immense artist achievement. More generous is Julien Cain's suggestion in his introduction to an English language edition of Daumier's *Les Gens de Justice*, that Daumier's satire "has become a means of self-examination which reveals the innermost being of us all" (Cain 1959: 25). At an even higher pitch of eulogy, the French poet and dramatist Émile Bergerat wrote of Daumier that "nobody has served justice and liberty more than this great honest man" (Bergerat 1878: 4453–4455).

Daumier's experience of the law, and that of Dickens, was not the experience of an intimate insider to the legal profession, but neither was it superficial. Daumier's first employment (1820) was as an office lad to a bailiff or notary (he also lived for two years (1829–1831) in La rue de la Barillerie, near Le Palais de Justice). He revealed his fondness for the autobiographical subject of the junior office lad, errand-runner, or clerk after censorship forced him away from his primary interest in political satire. His first series of this new era was of the *Types francais* and the first plate in the series was *Le Petit Clerc* (*Le Charivari*, September 23, 1835, LD260). Clerks and other peripheral figures of the legal profession also feature in *Les Gens de Justice*. Plate 2 (LD1338) shows a bailiff taking an inventory. Plate 3 (LD1339) depicts a debtor apprehended by a bailiff or sheriff and his men, with the legend "quarry that can be hunted all year round"; in Plate 5 (LD1341) a poor couple wonder if they will need a letter of introduction to meet the court usher; and Plate 10 (LD1346) depicts an old woman who is bamboozled by the bailiff's legal jargon.

Dickens had insider knowledge of the law at a similar low degree to Daumier. Frank Lockwood QC recites that "[a]t the age of fifteen we find Dickens a bright, clever-looking youth in the office of Mr. Edward Blackmore, attorney-at-law in Gray's Inn, earning at first 13*s*. 6*d*. a week, afterwards advanced to 15*s*" (Lockwood 1894: 17). This was

1827. Lockwood attributes Dickens's detailed knowledge of the ranks of legal clerks to his eighteen months' experience in the firm of Ellis and Blackmore. That knowledge is displayed in the pages of the *Pickwick Papers*, where Dickens explains that:

> There are several grades of lawyers' clerks. There is the articled clerk, who has paid a premium, and is an attorney in perspective, who runs a tailor's bill, receives invitations to parties, knows a family in Gower Street, and another in Tavistock Square; who goes out of town every Long Vacation to see his father, who keeps live horses innumerable; and who is, in short, the very aristocrat of clerks. There is the salaried clerk—out of door, or in door, as the case may be—who devotes the major part of his thirty shillings a week to his personal pleasure and adornment, repairs half-price to the Adelphi Theatre at least three times a week, dissipates majestically at the cider cellars afterwards, and is a dirty caricature of the fashion which expired six months ago. There is the middle-aged copying clerk, with a large family, who is always shabby, and often drunk. And there are the office lads in their first surtouts, who feel a befitting contempt for boys at day-schools; club as they go home at night for saveloys and porter: and think there's nothing like "life." (31)

In the hierarchical chain of legal beings, Lockwood speculates that Dickens never rose above the status of office lad (Lockwood 1894: 19). Dickens's portrayal of the solicitor's clerk William Guppy in *Bleak House* shows that, like Daumier, he retained a degree of fellow feeling for those in the junior echelons of legal practice, even though Guppy seems to have gained more seniority in the ranks of lawyers' clerks than Dickens ever attained. Guppy is by no means a paragon of fairness and justice. He already displays the taint of legal habits of thought and speech. His pursuit of Esther Summerson is disconcertingly reminiscent of Mr. Tulkinghorn's pursuit of Esther's mother Lady Dedlock, and when Guppy proposes marriage to Esther he addressed her in inappropriately formal legal terms. Yet Dickens shows sympathy for the young man by depicting him as one still full of color, or as one who has yet to have the color completely washed out of him, at least when relaxing at home in his mother's house. There we find him "dressed in a great many colours" (38).

Lockwood writes that, according to his son Henry Fielding Dickens QC, Charles Dickens had "kept a term or two at one of the Inns of Court" and "eaten the five or six dinners which is part of the necessary legal education for a barrister" (Lockwood 1894: 20). The Inn in question was the Middle Temple. There were other dimensions to Dickens's association with the Inns and courts, including the fact that his good friend John Forster lived in Lincoln's Inn gardens. Dickens also lodged for a period as a paying tenant of Furnival's Inn. Dickens's first sustained employment, commencing November 1828, was as a legal reporter in the Consistory Court of Doctor's Commons (this curious court supplies the topic of one of the *Sketches by Boz*). Like Daumier, he had reason to thank the legal profession for employment, and like Daumier he had personal cause to begrudge its blight upon his life. When Dickens was a teenager, his father had been imprisoned for debt and, as an adult, Dickens had suffered an unpleasant experience as a suitor in the Court of Chancery when seeking to defend his exclusive rights to publish the story of *A Christmas Carol*.[9] Daumier's adult experience of the law was no less sharply felt. His political satire, and in particular the famous "Gargantua" caricature of Louis-Phillipe "King of the French" published in *La Caricature*, December 16, 1831 (LD34), led to a six-month prison sentence (February 23, 1832). The sentence was suspended, but Daumier continued with his political caricature—including the lithograph *Masks of 1831*

FIGURE 8.4 "Magnanimous conduct of Mr. Guppy" by "Phiz" (Hablôt Knight Browne) for *Bleak House* ch. 54, "Esther's Narrative" (1853). Source: Gary Watt.

that appeared in print just a few days after his suspended sentence had been handed down (La Caricature, March 8, 1832)—and he was inevitably incarcerated (he spent August 31, 1832 to January 27, 1833 in Sainte-Pélagie prison).

How to judge our artists' attitude to lawyers is a moot point. In Dickens's case contrasting opinion is as sharply drawn as any of his characters. On the one hand a leading literary scholar, Professor J. Hillis Miller, can assert with confidence at some 150 years remove from the publication of *Bleak House* that "Dickens detests lawyers" (Miller 2001: 56), whereas Dickens's own son, Henry Fielding Dickens, by this time a very senior barrister of the rank of Queen's Counsel, claimed that his father "was very fond of lawyers" and that he "numbered among his intimate friends Lord Denman, Lord Campbell, Mr. Justice Talfourd, Chief Justice Crockford." Lockwood reported these facts in a lecture attended by Henry Fielding Dickens QC, adding that "it is difficult to name any eminent lawyer who could not claim acquaintance, at any rate, with our great author" (Lockwood 1894: 23). To this we might add the fact, often overlooked, that Dickens's father-in-law, George Hogarth, had been a practicing lawyer for many years before he and Dickens met at the *Morning Chronicle*. Lockwood ventured to claim that "in Dickens we have a great literary man who has been impartial in his treatment of lawyers" (Lockwood 1894: 12). Lockwood and Henry Fielding Dickens might have been, as lawyers, less than impartial on the question of Dickens's like or dislike of the members of their profession, but Lockwood's next observation seems a fair judgment of the moot issue. Dickens, he stated, "has seen both the good and the bad" in lawyers (Lockwood 1894: 12). Dickens seems to have been, on the whole, rather more sympathetic to individual lawyers than to administrative systems and institutions of law. It is true that some individual lawyers come off badly in *Bleak House*—he paints a pretty damning portrait of Mr. Tulkinghorn (an attorney-at-law and solicitor in Chancery) and Mr. Vholes fares little better—but others (such as Kenge and Guppy) are painted with a more even hand. The theory that Dickens was more tolerant of the individual than the institution is borne out by his humane depiction of the judge whom we find relaxing in the vicinity of the Inns during the vacation. The black-clad specter now wears contrasting white:

> There is only one judge in town. Even he only comes twice a week to sit in chambers. If the country folks of those assize towns on his circuit could see him now! No full-bottomed wig, no red petticoats, no fur, no javelin-men, no white wands. Merely a close-shaved gentleman in white trousers and a white hat. (19)

The Lord Chancellor receives the same even-handed treatment. He is portrayed as an obfuscating demon within the forum of the High Court of Chancery, but as something more like a concerned father when conversing with Richard, Esther, and Ada in the privacy of his chambers. It is telling that, in this private episode, the Lord Chancellor is described as "plainly dressed in black and sitting in an arm-chair" while his "robe, trimmed with beautiful gold lace, was thrown upon another chair. He gave us a searching look as we entered, but his manner was both courtly and kind" (3). Whatever he thought of lawyers, Dickens's view of law as an institution seems to have been cynical to the end. In the last year of his life he explained in a letter To "Mrs Frederick Pollock" (wife of the politician and lawyer Sir Frederick Pollock) that he had "that high opinion of the law of England generally, which one is likely to derive from the impression that it puts all the honest men under the diabolical hoofs of all the scoundrels."

Daumier seems to have remained similarly cynical in his dotage. Just nine days before his death he was assisted in scrawling a weak and straggling signature on a sketch he had executed many years before. The sketch was a rendition of Paul-Pierre Prud'hon's painting *La justice et la vengeance poursuivant la crime*, which Prud'hon had produced in 1808, the year of Daumier's birth, to be hung in the courtroom of the Palais de Justice as a replacement for a painting of a crucifix which had previously hung there (Weston 1975). In Daumier's version, the place and pose of the criminal has been taken by the figure of a judge in robe and hat. Daumier was nearly blind by this stage so perhaps he did not appreciate what he was signing, but that seems improbable. We can conclude, I think, that Daumier's youthful cynicism in relation to the legal profession was something he never sought to distance himself from.

Certainly Daumier's cynicism (combined with that of his editors) shows through strongly in *Les Gens de Justice*. The reader can easily locate all of Daumier's images online by searching for the relevant Loÿs Delteil (LD) number, but for present purposes we will rely on the legend to the plates to give a faint flavor of what is conveyed by the lithographic image. On the self-serving or self-indulgent nature of the legal profession, we have Plate 12 (LD1348) in which a prosecution lawyer confides in his wife: "Think of it, that's three of my defendants in a row that were not found guilty! I will lose my reputation!"; and Plate 13 (LD1349) in which the lawyer reassures his client that he will have better luck proving his innocence the next time the client commits a theft; also, Plate 16 (LD1352) in which the judge applauds the advocates and everyone in court is perfectly satisfied, except the accused; in Plate 18 (LD1354) a lawyer reads in the newspaper an eulogy to himself—written by himself; Plate 19 (LD1355) reads *"twelve* thefts—even better—I can plead compulsive obsession!" and Plate 23 (LD1359) shows us an advocate

THE LEGAL PROFESSION 159

dining on steak and fries at his client's expense; in Plate 25 (LD1361) the female parties to the cause are clearly not happy, but are deemed to have been reconciled by a rather self-satisfied *juge de paix* (a few months earlier Daumier had produced a similar scene as plate 63 in the series *Les Beaux Jours de la vie* [LD1151] *Le Charivari*, May 15, 1845); Plate 26 (LD1362) depicts another "unsatisfied litigant" (this plate did not appear in *Le Charivari*, but appeared in the specially published collector's edition of the series); Plate 29 (LD1365) depicts a lawyer urging his client to sue a neighbor so as to make him eat up his wealth, but the client refuses because he has no appetite for his own legal bill; in Plate 34 (LD1370) a lawyer, joking with a colleague, is amused to see that his client (presumed to be a self-portrait of Daumier) is so sad at losing his case, as if unaware that he could appeal to another court; in Plate 35 (LD1371) a smug lawyer comforts the widow and orphan with the thought that, though they have lost their case, they at least had the pleasure of hearing him plead; and in Plate 37 (LD1373) the lawyer is delighted that his client is so villainous—all the more of an achievement if he can secure his release from custody.

On the inhumane or unemotional nature of the profession, we have Plate 9 (LD1345) in which a lawyer, who has been upbraided by a well-dressed civilian, assures the citizen that he has enough civil courage never to respond to provocation. This recalls the *Physiologie*, where we learn that the civil lawyer is not a man of law as the criminal lawyer is, but is rather a "gentleman of law"(Trimolet and Maurisset 1841: 46). Dickens's Mr. Tulkinghorn is a gentleman lawyer of this sort, and it may be observed that in Victorian England, real-life lawyers of that breed held positions of great trust and sometimes rose to very high social standing (Luxon 1983). Daumier's Plate 15 (LD1351) depicts a self-satisfied lawyer boasting to his client that he also goes hungry most days but does not turn to theft; in Plate 22 (LD1358) the lawyer is said to defend the orphan and widow graciously ... when he's not attacking them; Plate 28 (LD1364) shows a lawyer in cahoots with his criminal client; Plate 31 (LD1367) presents the thoroughly hideous notion of the day's big case being savored as a great performance—murder garnished with rape! In Plate 32 (LD1368), the lawyer promises his client that if the opposing advocate dares say anything against the client, the lawyer will malign the entire family of his client's adversary; and Plate 36 (LD1372) is the plate of the lawyers on the "*Grand escalier du Palais de Justice*" discussed earlier. Plate 17 (LD1353) seems less severe at first sight, for it depicts a witness whose only agony is his attempt to recount in exact detail the events of a single day nine months ago; such discomfort and inconvenience may be relatively mundane, but it is rendered institutionally fearful by the fact that it is the perennial experience of witnesses in court even to the present day.

DID DAUMIER INFLUENCE DICKENS?

John Harvey writes that "the possibility that Dickens knew Daumier's work and found it suggestive is worth investigation" (Harvey 1970: 134). A brief digression to carry out that investigation might not solve the case, but it will have the merit of taking us deeper into the impressive similarities between the two artists' cultural background and to their flourishing at the same time in such coincident ways at the heart of the Age of Reform. Daumier is mentioned on two occasions in Dickens's journal *Household Worlds*. The references appear on March 12, 1853 and April 12, 1856. For present purposes, the 1853 reference is the most interesting; in part because it appeared while *Bleak House* was still being published in serial installments, and in part because the reference to

Daumier too casually lumps the French artist in the clichéd category of over-the-top caricaturist. The article refers to "Figures such as, were you to see them in the drawings of Leech, or Daumier, or Gavarni, you would pronounce exaggerated and untrue to nature."[10] It cannot be said for certain that these words were written by Dickens, but it seems inconceivable that he could have been unaware of Daumier's work. Dickens was an enthusiastic Francophile and he undertook his first long stay in Paris between November 1846 and February 1847, which was right in the middle of the period in which Daumier's *Les Gens de Justice* was being published at irregular intervals in the Parisian journal *Le Charivari*. *Le Charivari* is itself mentioned in several articles in Dickens's *Household Words* that appeared late in 1851, which is precisely as *Bleak House* was taking shape in Dickens's mind.[11] An article of November 15, 1851 specifically refers to *Le Charivari*'s caricatures. The fact that no plate was published in *Les Gens de Justice* between November 18, 1846 and the summer of 1847 is inconvenient to the possibility that Dickens saw them during his stay in Paris, but it is by no means fatal. The November plate was the twenty-ninth in the series, so earlier plates would have been in circulation in Paris at the time of Dickens's visit; Dickens visited Paris twice more before he began to write *Bleak House* in November 1851.[12]

Daumier produced a striking series of four plates in 1848, presumably intended to relate to *Les Gens de Justice*, but they were not published until November–December 1851, when they appeared under the heading *Les Avocats et les Plaideurs*. This means that they appeared in print at precisely the time that Dickens, back in England, began to write *Bleak House*. Two of that set of four plates, sequentially the first and third, were published in *Le Charivari* on November 12, 1851 (LD2185) and December 3, 1851 (LD2187) respectively. They have legends that are particularly evocative of the fictional Chancery case "Jarndyce and Jarndyce" that Dickens erected as the legal scaffold for the plot of *Bleak House*. Two core characteristics of that case are, first, that it drags on and on: "Jarndyce and Jarndyce still drags its dreary length before the Court, perennially hopeless" (1); and, second, that in the course of its so-called "progress," it ruins people both personally and financially. When a resolution of the legal issues is finally reached in the case, there is no money left to allocate between the parties. The coincidence with Daumier's 1851 plates is conspicuous, for the legend of the lithograph of 12 November reads (in my translation): "'The case is running along! The case is running along!' / The client: 'You said that four years ago. If it runs much longer like this I won't have shoes left to pursue it with!'" *Bleak House* expressly refers to the "ruined suitor with his slipshod heels and threadbare dress" (1). Equally evocative of the Jarndyce case (in which legal costs ultimately consumed the disputed estate), the legend to the lithograph of 3 December records a conversation between two lawyers:

1st lawyer: "Finally! We have achieved a division of the spouses' assets."
2nd lawyer: "That's good timing, for the trial has ruined them both!"

These two lithographic legends are clearly written in the same spirit as the satirical text of the *Physiologie*, which "Daumier certainly knew" (Cain 1959: 12). There, we read that "a well-managed case can sometimes outrun the lifetime of the client and his lawyer—but only the client will waste away and die in a garret on a bed of straw" (Trimolet and Maurisset 1841: 42–43). Coincidentally, the "most serious and pathetic point" (as Dickens described it in a letter of December 20, 1852) that he had tried to make in *Pickwick* "was the slow torture and death of a Chancery prisoner" (Storey 1987: 1). That point was revisited in *Bleak House* in the slow demise of Mr. Gridley, following Dickens's acquaintance with a pamphlet account of the case of a real-life "prisoner" in Chancery (Challinor 1849: 4). The historical picture that emerges as most plausible is one in which Dickens and Daumier flowered in similar ways and at the same time, not because of any direct influence that one had upon the other, but because they were working in, and growing out of, a common tradition of graphic and literary satire that had been fertile since the days of Voltaire, Swift, Goldsmith and Hogarth (Marten 1974, 1976). As John Dixon Hunt writes, we "can stress only parallels between Dickens's imagination and that of the graphic artists rather than exact sources" (Hunt 1971).

If we struggle to show that Dickens was influenced by Daumier's legal caricatures and even that he had detailed direct knowledge of them, it is nevertheless reasonable to speculate that he was aware of Daumier in general. There is even a possibility, perhaps a strong likelihood, that Dickens's would have learned about Daumier through his illustrator Hablôt Knight Browne (known by the sobriquet "Phiz," which is short for "physiognomy") (Stein 2001: 168). Browne illustrated the periodic installments of *Bleak House*. As early as 1839, the author and illustrator William Makepeace Thackeray had advised Browne to look

FIGURE 8.5 Honoré Daumier, *Les Gens de Justice* Plate 24 (LD1360) 14 October 1846. Source: Gary Watt.

to the inspiration of Daumier. It seems that he took that advice at once, for John Harvey sees the influence of Daumier's caricatures of Robert Macaire in Browne's illustrations of George Reynolds' 1840 novel *Robert Macaire in England*; and Harvey demonstrates an undeniable similarity between Browne's nurse Mrs. Gamp (*Martin Chuzzlewit*, 1842) and Daumier's nurse or "La Garde-Malade" (*Le Charivari*, May 22, 1842) (Harvey 1970: 132–133). It is highly likely that Browne, commissioned with the task of illustrating Dickens's great legal masterpiece *Bleak House*, would have sought further inspiration from Daumier and especially from his two recently published series *Les Gens de Justice* (1845–1848) and *Les Avocats et les plaideurs* (1851). Consider Plate 24 (LD1360) in *Les Gens de Justice*, which was published on October 14, 1846 (Dickens arrived in Paris that November). It depicts in the background a young bonneted woman with her back to the viewer while in the foreground a group of three lawyers leer at her. The legend accompanying the image adds very little—a complaint leveled by Baudelaire against all the legends accompanying Daumier's lithographs (Baudelaire 1992 [1846]: 216). (The same has been said about the illustrations accompanying Dickens' works [Leavis 1970: 361]). What is interesting for present purposes is that Daumier's figure of the bonneted female is highly evocative of Browne's illustrations of Esther Summerson which accompany *Bleak House* (Richard L. Stein notes that Esther Summerson is frequently depicted bonneted, or with her back to the viewer; noting that *Bleak House* concludes with Esther's self reflections on her own face, and therefore "ends at the point its principal subject recognizes herself as an object in visual culture, at the moment narrative acknowledges its own inescapable place in a world of images" [Stein 2001: 186]). To enjoy the coincidence between Esther and Daumier's bonneted young woman is not to say that one artist inspired the other. It is at least as likely that they were both inspired by some other source in common, such as contemporary prints of fashionable ladies of the sort Dickens mentions in *Bleak House* as "copper-plate impressions" from the series "The Divinities of Albion, or Galaxy Gallery of British Beauty" (20). More interesting than any direct connection between Daumier and Browne is the fact that the female figure of Esther is frequently effaced in Browne's images. The illustration titled "Magnanimous Conduct of Mr Guppy" (54) depicts a jolly social gathering in which Esther's is the only face turned fully away from the viewer. She is self-effacing throughout the novel, and her selflessness at one point exposes her to a disease (probably smallpox) that literally obscures her facial features. Her mother is correspondingly and repeatedly effaced by a veil, which is clearly intended to be symbolic: "If you hear of Lady Dedlock, brilliant, prosperous, and flattered, think of your wretched mother, conscience-stricken, underneath that mask!" (36). When Dickens was writing, the law went to great lengths (including the length of stovepipe police hats and judges' full-bottomed wigs) to fashion a face in the world that was distinctively male (Watt 2013). The image of the effaced female thus becomes a face excluded from the legal world. The law made itself a face for public encounter. There it was seen by, and only saw, the masks of legal personality that the law had created for the purposes of social and political interaction. Women had to make up their faces in private.

CONCLUSION

Earlier, I suggested that the art of Dickens and Daumier exhibits two significant reforming qualities. The first is that it is somehow able to color humanity with (and despite) a palette of black and white. The second is that it moves the state of stones and institutions and other static things. Their art is therefore inherently critical of the law's habitual error of thinking in simple black-and-white contrasts and adhering stubbornly to strict rules and routines. Another contemporary form of cultural expression that added color to bright lights and movement to static images was the so-called "magic lantern." The sequential passing of tinted transparent plates before the beam of the projector produced a distinctly modern sense of progress. Like lithography, the lantern was an example of science and art plowing forward in harness. Dickens experienced the magic lantern and greatly enjoyed it. He was generally excited by the facility and opportunity of new technologies.[13] He thrilled to travel by the new fast trains to France—witness his short essay "Railway Dreaming" published in *Household Words* on May 10, 1856—in which the frame-by-frame flashing by of window scenes must have sparked his imagination like a sort of magic lantern or proto-cinema (Kirkby 1997; Smith 2003). Certainly the lantern itself served as an allegory for his artistic acquisition, and representation, of the sequential passing before his eyes of the scenes of city life. Writing from Switzerland on August 30, 1846, Dickens described London as his lantern, reporting that: "the toil and labour of writing, day after day, without that magic lantern is IMMENSE!!" (Smith 2003: 27). Many years earlier, Voltaire had described Paris with the same metaphor: "the life of Paris disperses all one's ideas, one forgets everything, one is diverted only momentarily by everything in that great magic lantern, where all the pictures pass as rapidly as shadows" (Smith 2003: 25). Baudelaire adapted the metaphor somewhat when he wrote of the "vast picture gallery which is London or Paris" (37) and, again referring to Paris, we read elsewhere that "Daumier saw this 'magic lantern of black figures' performed before his very eyes" (Cain 1959: 13). That thought might have been inspired by the *Physiologie de l'Homme de Loi*, which concludes with the metaphor: "*Ami lecteur, tu as vu passer devant tes yeux cette lantern magique de figures noires*" (Trimolet and Maurisset 1841: 112).

Daumier's *Les Gens de Justice* flashes by from plate to plate like a proto-cinematic slideshow of images. As we watch the magic lantern at work, we become aware that it is we, especially those of us who perpetuate the law, who are being watched by the artist's critical eye. When Dickens's Mr. Tulkinghorn is murdered in his law chambers (which, in keeping with a common practice at the time, was also his home) the painting of Allegory on the ceiling is said to point at his corpse. The image accuses him. He was killed by the French maid Hortense, so perhaps Allegory alleges that an intransigent law devoid of passion will be killed by an excess of the passion it has tried to exclude and repress (Fradin 1966: 104) and perhaps it alleges, in similar vein, that an exclusively male law and legal profession sows the seeds of its own destruction in the figure of the excluded female. In one of Daumier's later pencil drawings we see the lawyer pointing back at allegory. *La Defense* is a sketch in ink and charcoal with a grey wash in which a defense lawyer is looking back at his client in the dock while pointing in the opposite direction to where a painting hangs high on the wall of the court above a bench of three of judges. The painting he is pointing to is Pierre-Paul Prud'hon's *Allegory of Justice and Crime*. Daumier's lawyer, and through him Daumier himself, is quite literally pointing to allegory. He is also reflexively alerting the viewer to his own art. If lawyers care about the image of their profession, even today, they might start by approaching Dickens and Daumier. It is remarkable to think that in both academy and practice the appreciation of the legal profession as a culture of rhetorical and performative arts continues to be considered a strangely exotic way to color law's black-and-white world, and that the innovation of approaching law from the perspectives of creative art, culture, and the humanities is considered still to be a new movement.

The reforming power of the artistic picture, whether created directly or through the medium of words, was already plain enough in Dickens's day. His contemporary Anthony Trollope certainly had Dickens in mind when he wrote in reference to Mr. Popular Sentiment (the author of serialized novels who is depicted in Trollope's 1855 novel *The Warden*) that "[t]he artist who paints for the million must use glaring colours" (15). This is a moderate version of the familiar complaint that Dickens lacked subtlety in his literary efforts to reform such social institutions as workhouses, schools and the Court of Chancery, but Trollope is generous enough to acknowledge in the same breath that "the radical reform which has now swept over such establishments has owed more to the twenty numbers of Mr Sentiment's novel, than to all the true complaints which have escaped from the public for the last half century." According to Dickens, "the wisdom of our ancestors is in the simile" (Dickens 1843: 1), so let us agree with Trollope that "sweeping" reforms is as good a picture as any. The point is that it is a moving picture. Satirists and caricaturists at the beginning of the Age of Reform enjoyed the fact that one of the new "brooms" sweeping for change was Henry Brougham (pronounced "broom") who on February 7, 1828 (the date of Dickens's sixteenth birthday) spoke in the House of Commons for six hours (still a record) on the subject of law reform.[14] Two years later Brougham was appointed Lord Chancellor and thus swept into the dusty heart of the Court of Chancery that Dickens would soon condemn to universal and perpetual infamy in *Bleak House*. Brougham's speeches finally came to an end and are now all but forgotten, for it is generally the fate of "true complaints" of the political and legal sort that they move only for a short time. The satirical art of Dickens and Daumier, on the other hand, is still sweeping and swiping with timeless force, as only great art can.

NOTES

Preface

1. Laurence Rosen, *Law as Culture: An Invitation* (Princeton: Princeton University Press, 2006), 199–200.
2. Pierre Legrand, *Fragments on Law-as-Culture* (Deventer: W E J Tjeenk Willink, Schoordijk Institute, 1999), 5.
3. Malcolm Andrews, *Landscape and Western Art* (Oxford History of Art) (Oxford: Oxford university Press, 1999), 53.

Justice

1. For a fuller explanation of the complex history of the invention see Edwards (2006).
2. Meier and Wolfensberger (1998) suggest that a collection of police photographs of Swiss itinerants from 1852 to 1853 constitute the earliest preserved collection of police photography. Baylis (2014) dates the Larcom albums of 1857 and 1866 as the earliest prison photographs in Ireland and Britain.
3. A daguerrotyupe was one of the earliest photographic processes, first published by Daguerre of Paris in 1839, in which the impression was taken upon a silver plate sensitized by iodine, and then developed by exposure to the vapor of mercury (Oxford English Dictionary online, last accessed August 2015).
4. See https://sites.google.com/site/newzealandpolicemuseum/home/online-exhibitions/mug-shots/invention-2 (Last accessed August 2015).
5. As modified by the Prevention of Crimes Act 1871 and the Penal Servitude Act 1891. Other jurisdictions introduced similar legislation. For instance, in New Zealand, the Prisons Amendment Act of 1912 officially sanctioned the use of mug shots, by declaring that all accused or convicted prisoners incarcerated for the first had to submit to being photographed and fingerprinted, including by use of "reasonable force" if necessary (Nichols 2012).
6. This front-and-side-view pose was either achieved by two photographs being taken or by taking one photograph in which the prisoner held a mirror showing their profile.
7. The poses described can be traced back to prevailing practices in the art of portraiture and continue to occupy a sub-set of this genre commonly referred to as "identification photography" (Jackson 2009). For some commentators only "the gaze, stance and impoverished appearance indicate any difference from well-arranged bourgeois portraits" (Meier and Wolfensberger 1998: 281). It appears that some sections of the middle classes were rather concerned about the association of mugshots with the genre of the family photograph. It was argued that by using the portrait for "common purposes" like criminal portraits would rob photography of it's "art" (New Zealand Police Museum 2015).
8. "Forensics: The Anatomy of Crime," Wellcome Collection, London. 2015.
9. Images taken at Newcastle city jail and house of correction collection between December 1871 and December 1873 also illustrate frontal photographs of prisoners with their hands on their laps, There are numerous copies of Victorian mugshots on the internet. See, e.g., http://arnesvenson.com/prisoners.html.

10. See, e.g., records from Wandsworth prison dated 1873: National Archives (1897) and National Archives (1873).
11. For a full explanation of the Bertillon system see *Scientific American* (1904).
12. Galton and Lombrosso (Hagins 2013).
13. The voyeuristic potential of displays of mugshots did not come to an end when rogues' galleries became unfashionable. An article in the *Smithsonian Magazine* (2007) referred to the fact that the exhibition of mugshots on the photosharing website Flickr.com has produced a new generation of postmodern voyeurs.
14. Boyce (2000) points to instances such as prison riots and the survival of ego in concentration camps as examples of counter-cultural constructions of non-docile identities in total institutional contexts.
15. In *The Disciplinary Frame,* Tagg (2009) provides another example of a sketch of a prisoner being held in place while their photograph is taken.
16. This is probably motivated by the fact that, for many in the period, the Fenian call for self-determination was based on Catholic and Protestant unity under an Irish identity. Attempts to link criminal activity to Catholics was considered to undermine this goal.
17. Accounts of challenges to the disciplinary apparatus of the state have also emerged in other accounts of the identification photograph genre. Rizzo (2013), for instance, has drawn attention to the ways in which men and women applying for travel documents in colonial Southern Africa used portrait photography as a way of challenging discriminating notions of nationality enforced by a segregationist state. By commissioning their own passport photographs in the style of white bourgeoisie photography that was popular in the region from the 1870s, the politically alienated introduced a genre of honorific images for the marginalized into the application process as a visual counter practice to that fabricated in the other bureaucratic processes of the state.
18. Reproduced in Byrnes (1866), 52.
19. See p. 83. Doyle's (2007) book on Sydney police photographs contains an image of a man screwing up his eyes accompanied by a note that "This man refused to open his eyes" (p. 189).
20. See, e.g., entries 68, 90, 92, 136,160,178, 181, and 185. See also the image of Jim O'Brien (p. 25); Unknown prisoner p. 87; "27309" p. 143 and "7900" (p. 271) in Kasher, Michaelson and Kasher 2006.
21. See, e.g., Ellis p. 65; Unknown sitter p. 210; Unknown sitter p. 213 in Doyle (2005).
22. Welch (2012) refers to this as a form of "penal tourism."
23. See further Battersby (2012) 'Victorian mugshots reveal nineteenth-century interest in criminal anthropology' *The Independent online*, Wednesday June 27, 2012. Available at: www.independent.co.uk/life-style/history/victorian-mugshots-reveal-nineteenth-century-interest-in-criminal-anthropology-7892823.html.
24. This is a focus that lawyers have also tended to adopt. For one of the seminal article sin the field see Mnookin (1998).
25. Other more specialist exhibitions in police museums are even more common. See for instance the Ontario Provincial Police Museums "Arresting images" exhibition 2009–2015. Available at: www.opp.ca/museum/current.php.
26. Private conversation with Peter Doyle. See further Doyle (2005).
27. See www.stevenkasher.com/exhibitions/least-wanted-a-century-of-american-mugshots.
28. Lashmar (2013) has argued that many early mugshots had a "'painterly'" quality. In turn, it is worthy of note that mugshots have also been known to act as the inspiration for fine art depictions of criminals. Possibly the best example is the minor scandal provoked by Andy Warhol at the 1964 New York World's Fair when he enlarged thirteen mugshots from a New

York police department booklet featuring the most wanted criminals of 1962: See www.queensmuseum.org/2013/11/andy-warhols-13-most-wanted-men-and-the-1964-worlds-fair. For a more recent example of art inspired by mugshots see www.bbc.co.uk/news/uk-england-birmingham-30280240. Artist Michaelson has also admitted to enlarging mugshots, stamping them with a number, signing them, and making successful sales.

Constitution

1. The starting point for the plot summary is Frederic Lloyd's politically-oriented synopsis issued with the LP recording made by the D'Oyly Carte Opera Company in 1976 (SKL 5225/6, Decca Record Company Ltd). Reissued on CD in 1993 (436 816-2 LM2, London Records) and 2003, and available as an MP3 download, this is one of only two commercially available audio recordings of *Utopia, Limited*, the other being by the Ohio Light Opera from 2001 (NPD85659/2, Newport Classic).
2. Subsequent page references will appear bracketed in the text and refer to the annotated libretto in Bradley 1996.
3. Joint Stock Companies Act 1856.
4. Anon (ed.) 2007: 4–5.
5. Ibid., p. 9.
6. Ibid., pp. 104–105.
7. Ibid., pp. 105–108.
8. Ibid., pp. 109–117.
9. Ibid., p. 1047.
10. Ibid., p. 72.
11. Ibid., p. 84.
12. Ibid., pp. 83–84.
13. Ibid., p. 87.
14. Ibid., p. 60.
15. Co-authored by Gilbert à Beckett, *The Happy Land* was a highly targeted satire on popular government (specifically, on William Gladstone's 1868 administration): "Caricatures of Gladstone, Ayrton, and Lowe enter fairyland singing: "Oh, we are three most popular men! / We want to know who'll turn us out … " (Sutton 1975: 89).
16. See Oakeshott 1975: 268, rhetorically: "Utopia has no lawyers but it bristles with inspectors and overseers."
17. But see Gordon 2015, ch. 12.
18. This proved prophetic, because Companies Act 2006, s. 7(1), allows for single-member companies!

Agreements

1. For more on Carlyle's view on utilitarianism, see Morrow 2007: 149. For more on Ruskin's critique of utilitarianism, see Landow 2015: 68–69.
2. *The First Report of the Commissioners: Mines* was published in May of 1842. *The Second Report, on Trades and Manufactures* was published early in 1843, although the publication date is 1842.
3. In a letter to Richard Hengist Horne, dated May 29, 1843, Barrett Browning tells him that she has been reading him in *Illuminated Magazine*. See Hudson and Kelley 1989: 154–156.
4. Thank you to my colleague Dr. Pauline Uchmanowicz for her insightful comments on the poem.

5. For a concise summary of reception see the headnote to "The Cry of the Children," in Stone and Taylor 2010: 433–435.
6. The epigraph from *Medea* does not appear in the original publication of "Cry of the Children" in *Blackwood's*; it appears only in the version published in *Poems* (1844).
7. In a note to lines 1029–1031 of *Medea*, Collier and Machemer observe that Medea sends her children off "as sacrificial animals" and that "[t]he language reflects the often-heard formula warning the profane or impure to keep away from sacred rites, whose performance their presence would invalidate or corrupt" ([*c.* 431 BCE] 2006: 102).
8. Steve Dillon notes that Barrett Browning often "articulate cries" for those who have no voice. See Dillon 2001. Peaches Henry observes that the cry serves as a unifying theme, and she detects seventeen instances, in a variety of forms, of crying in the poem. See Henry 2011: 545.
9. The report reads: "'Many of the children,' continues Mr. Horne, 'told me they always said their prayers at night, and the prayer they said was, 'Our Father.' I naturally thought they meant that they repeated the Lord's Prayer, but I soon found that few of them knew it. They only repeated the first two words: they knew no more than 'Our Father!' These poor Children, after their laborious day's work, lying down to sleep with this simple appeal, seemed to me inexpressibly affecting. Having nothing but harsh task-masters in this world, or 'working under their father,' it was probably the only true sense in which they could use the words'." See [Report, p. Q18, §215]. *Second Report of the Commissioners: Trade and Manufactures*
10. Henry is quoting from *Aurora Leigh*, Book 1, line 859.
11. For further discussion on the curse see Stone 1986: 160–161.

Legal Profession

1. "For me the English black-and-white artists are to art what Dickens is to literature" (Vincent Van Gogh, letter to Amice Rappard, The Hague September 18–19, 1882).
2. Daumier suffered censorship and a prison sentence for his art. Dickens wrote critical essays on a wide range of reforming issues including the slavery of blacks in America, the plight of women in prisons and capital punishment.
3. For example "La Femme à Barbe" (*Le Charivari* February 16, 1867; LD3555).
4. See Gary Watt, (2009c). David Parker considers it significant that Dickens "locates desirable young women within" the inns of court "amid the drab lawyers' tenements" ("Dickens, the Inns of Court, and the Inns of Chancery" *Literary London: Interdisciplinary Studies in the Representation of London*, 8(1) (2010). Available online: www.literarylondon.org/london-journal/march2010/parker.html.
5. The essay *La Modernité* appears in Baudelaire's *Le Peintre de la vie moderne* ("The Painter of Modern Life") (1864).
6. The most comprehensive catalog of Daumier's works was by the lithographer and collector Loÿs Henri Delteil, hence plate numbers are prefixed with the initials LD.
7. In relation to novels, parenthetical references are to the relevant chapter.
8. See, generally, Carol Hanbery MacKay (ed.), *Dramatic Dickens* (Basingstoke: Palgrave Macmillan, 1989).
9. *Dickens v Lee* (1844) 8 Jurist 18.
10. "Perfidious Patmos" *Household Words* No.155, March 12, 1853, p. 27.
11. Examples include "More French Revolutions" *Household Words*, September 13, 1851, p. 5 87; "Thirty Days of Pleasure for Fifteen Francs" *Household Words*, October 11, 1851, p. 72.

12. He visited Paris again by the overnight train on June 22–23, 1850, staying until July 1, and stayed again between February 10 and 15, 1851.
13. For example, in a personal book of memoranda commenced in January 1855 he imagined narrating a story from the point of view of a message sent by electric telegraph.
14. See, for example, the 1825 plate "Buy a Broom?!!" by Dickens's friend, and illustrator, George Cruikshank.

BIBLIOGRAPHY

CASES

Bushell's Case (1670) Vaughan 135, 124 ER 1006.
Bradford v. Pickles [1895] AC 587.
Brown v Maryland (1827) 25 US 419.
Coffin v Coffin (1808) 4 Ma 1.
Commonwealth v Knapp (1830) 10 Pick 477.
Commonwealth v Kneeland (1836) 20 Pick 206.
Georgia v Brailsford (1794) 3 US 1.
Lilburne's Case (1649) 4 St Tr 1269.
Mabo v. Queensland [No. 2] (1992) 175 CLR 1.
Marbury v Madison (1803) 5 US 118.
People v Crosswell (1804) 3 Johnson's Cases 337.
Pierce v State (1843) 13 NH 536.
Queensbury Industrial Society v. Pickles (1865) LR 1 Exch 1.
R v Shipley (1784) 21 St Tr 847.
Sparf and Hansen v US (1895) 156 US 51.
State v Rollins (1837) 8 NH 550.
State v Snow (1841) 18 Me 346.
Townsend v State (1828) 2 Blackf 151.
US v Battiste (1835) 2 Sum 240.
US v Morris (1851) 1 Curtis 23.
US v Shine (1832) 1 Baldwin's Rep 510.
US v Wilson and Porter (1832) 1 Baldwin's Rep 78.

BOOKS & ARTICLES ETC

Abramson, J. 1994. *We, the Jury: The Jury System and the Ideal of Democracy*. New York: Basic Books.
Acheson, Dean G. 1919. "Book Review." *Harvard Law Review*, 33: 329–332.
Alborn, Timothy L. 1998. *Conceiving Companies: Joint-stock Politics in Victorian England*. London and New York: Routledge.
Aldous, R. 2007. *The Lion and the Unicorn: Gladstone v Disraeli*. London: Pimlico.
Allen, Gregory. 1977. "The New Police: London and Dublin—The Birth of the Dublin Metropolitan Police." *The Police Journal*, 50 (4): 304–317.
Alschuler, A. and Deiss, A. 1994. "A Brief History of the Criminal Jury in the United States." *University of Chicago Law Review*, 61: 867–928.
Anderson, David and Killingray, David. (eds.). 1991. *Policing the Empire: Government, Authority and Control, 1830–1940*. Manchester: Manchester University Press.
Anon. 1838. *The Australian Aborigines Protection Society*. Sydney: James Spilsbury.

Anon. (ed.). 2007. *Vocal Score of Utopia Limited or The Flowers of Progress. By W.S. Gilbert and Arthur Sullivan*. Authentic Chappell edition. Harlow: Faber Music.

Anson, Sir William R. 1935. *The Law and Custom of the Constitution*. 4th edn. Oxford: Clarendon.

Aristotle. 2002. *The Nicomachean Ethics*. Translated by Christopher Rowe. Oxford: Oxford University Press.

Arnold, M. 1986. *Matthew Arnold: A Critical Edition of the Major Works*. Oxford: Oxford University Press.

Arnstein, W. 2003. *Queen Victoria*. Basingstoke: Palgrave.

Arneil, Barbara. 1996. *John Locke and America: The Defence of English Colonialism*. Oxford: Oxford University Press.

Atkin, Lord. 1932. "Law as an Educational Subject." *Journal of the Society of Public Teachers of Law*, 27–31.

Atkin, Ronald. 1973. *Maintain the Right: The Early History of the North West Mounted Police, 1873–1900*. London: Macmillan.

Atkinson, D. 1996. *The Suffragettes in Pictures*. Stroud: Sutton Publishing Limited.

Austin, John. 2002. *Lectures on Jurisprudence, or The Philosophy of Positive Law*. 2 vols. Edited by R. Campbell. 4th edn. London: John Murray. Reprint, Bristol: Thoemmes Press, 2002.

Ayre, Leslie. 1986. *The Gilbert and Sullivan Companion*. London: W.H. Allen.

Bagehot, W. 2001. *The English Constitution*. Cambridge: Cambridge University Press.

Baily, Leslie. 1952. *The Gilbert and Sullivan Book*. London: Cassell.

Baker, J. 2007. *An Introduction to English Legal History*. Oxford: Oxford University Press.

Balot, Ryan. 2014. *Courage in the Democratic Polis: Ideology and Critique in Classical Athens*. Oxford: Oxford University Press.

Banner, Stuart. 2007. *Possessing the Pacific: Land, Settlers and Indigenous People from Australia to Alaska*. Cambridge, MA: Harvard University Press.

Barrett Browning, Elizabeth. 1844. *Poems*. London: Edward Moxon.

Barrett Browning, Elizabeth. 2010. "The Cry of the Children." In S. Marjorie and T. Beverly (eds.), *The Works of Elizabeth Barrett Browning*. Vol. 1. London: Pickering & Chatto.

Battersby, M. 2012. "Victorian Mugshots Reveal Nineteenth Century Interest in Criminal Anthropology." *The Independent online*, Wednesday June 27, 2012. www.independent.co.uk/life-style/history/victorian-mugshots-reveal-nineteenth-century-interest-in-criminal-anthropology-7892823.html (last accessed August 2015).

Baudelaire, Charles. [1846] 1992. *Critique D'Art*. Paris: Gallimard Education.

Baylis, G. 2009. "Metropolitan Surveillance and Rural Opacity: Secret Photography in Nineteenth Century Ireland." *History of Photography*, 33 (1): 26–38.

Baylis, G. 2014. "A Few Too Many Photographs? Indexing Digital Histories." *History of Photography*, 38(1): 3–20.

Bentham, Jeremy. [1776] 2008. *A Fragment on Government*. In J.H. Burns and H.L.A. Hart (eds.), *A Comment on the Commentaries and a Fragment on Government*. Oxford: Clarendon Press.

Bentham, Jeremy. 1825. "The Rationale of Reward." Classical Utilitarianism website: http://www.laits.utexas.edu/poltheory/bentham/rr/rr.b03.c01.html (accessed November 9, 2015).

Bentham, Jeremy. [1830] 1978. "Security and Equality of Property." In C.B. Macpherson (ed.), *Property: Mainstream and Critical Positions*. Oxford: Basil Blackwell, 41–58.

Bentham, Jeremy. [1928] 1977. *A Comment on the Commentaries*. In J.H. Burns and H.L.A. Hart (eds.), *A Comment on the Commentaries and a Fragment on Government*. London: Athlone Press.

Bentley, M. 1996. *Politics without Democracy 1815-1914*. London: Fontana.
Bentley, M. 2001. *Lord Salisbury's World: Conservative Environments in Late-Victorian Britain*. Cambridge: Cambridge University Press.
Ben-Yishai, Ayelet. 2013. *Common Precedents: The Presentness of the Past in Victorian Fiction*. Oxford: Oxford University Press.
Bergerat, Émile. 1878. "Revue artistique: Exposition des oeuvres d'Honoré Daumier." *Journal official*, 26 April.
Best, G. 1979. *Mid-Victorian Britain 1851–75*. London: Fontana.
Biber, K. 2011. "Wanted: The Outlaw in American Visual Culture; Capturing the Criminal Image: From Mug Shot to Surveillance Society; Pictures from a Drawer: Prison and the Art of Portraiture." *History of Photography*, 35 (4): 439–441.
Biber, K. 2013. "The Cultural Afterlife of Criminal Evidence." *British Journal of Criminology*, 53: 1033–1049.
Binet, Hélène, Allibone, Jill, and Evans, David. 1996. *The Inns of Court*. London: Black Dog.
Blackstone, William. 1979 [1765]. *Commentaries on the Laws of England*. Chicago: University of Chicago Press.
Blake, William. [1789] 2008. "The Chimney Sweeper." *Songs of Innocence*. In David V. Erdman (ed.), *The Complete Poetry & Prose of William Blake*. Berkeley: University of California Press.
Blake, William. [1794] 2008. "The Chimney Sweeper." *Songs of Experience*. In David V. Erdman (ed.), *The Complete Poetry & Prose of William Blake*. Berkeley: University of California Press.
Bodichon, Barbara Leigh Smith. 1854. "A Brief Summary, in Plain English, of the Most Important Laws Concerning Women: Together with a Few Observations Thereon." Reprinted in Tim Dolin, *Mistress of the House: Women of Property in the Victorian Novel*. London: Routledge, 123–133.
Borowitz, Albert I. 1973. "Gilbert and Sullivan on Corporate Law." *American Bar Association Journal*, 59: 1276.
Borowitz, Albert I. 1982. "Gilbert and Sullivan on Corporation Law: *Utopia, Limited* and the Panama Canal Frauds." In *A Gallery of Sinister Perspectives*. Kent, OH: Kent State University Press.
Boyce, R. 2000. "Post-Panopticism." *Economy and Society*, 29 (2): 285–307.
Boyer, A. 1997. "Sir Edward Coke, Ciceronianus: Classical Rhetoric and the Common Law Tradition." *International Journal for the Semiotics of Law*, 10 (3): 36.
Bradley, Ian. (ed.). 1996. *The Complete Annotated Gilbert and Sullivan*. Oxford: Oxford University Press.
Brantlinger, Patrick. 1998. *The Reading Lesson: The Threat of Mass Literacy in Nineteenth-Century British Fiction*. Bloomington: Indiana University Press.
Briggs, A. 1959. *The Age of Improvement*. London: Longmans.
Brogden, Mike. 1987. "The Emergence of the Police—The Colonial Dimension." *British Journal of Criminology*, 27 (1): 4–14.
Brontë, Anne. [1847] 1993. *The Tenant of Wildfell Hall*. Oxford: Oxford University Press.
Brontë, Emily. [1847] 2009. *Wuthering Heights*. Oxford: Oxford University Press.
Brown, R. 1989. *Knowledge is Power: The Diffusion of Information in Early America, 1700–1865*. Oxford: Oxford University Press.
Browning, Elizabeth Barrett. 1843. "The Cry of the Children." *Blackwood's Edinburgh Magazine*, August, 260–262.
Browning, Elizabeth Barrett. [1854] 1993. *Aurora Leigh*. Oxford: Oxford University Press.

Browning, Elizabeth Barrett. [1856] 2010. *Aurora Leigh*. In Sandra Donaldson (ed.), *The Works of Elizabeth Barrett Browning*. Vol. 3. London: Pickering & Chatto.

Browning, Elizabeth Barrett. 2010. "The Cry of the Children." In Marjorie Stone and Beverly Taylor (eds.), *The Works of Elizabeth Barrett Browning*. Vol. 1. London: Pickering & Chatto.

Brownlee, David Bruce. 1984. *The Law Courts: The Architecture of George Edmund Street*. London: MIT Press.

Budd, P., and Budd, D., with Deborah Lister. 2010. *Tested: How Twelve Wrongly Imprisoned Men Held onto Hope*. Dallas: Brown Books.

Buller, Francis. 1768. *An Introduction to the Law Relative to Trials at Nisi Prius, by a Learned Judge*. Dublin: Elizabeth Watts.

Byrnes, Thomas. 1866. *Professional Criminals of America*. Reproduced 2000. London: The Lyons Press.

Cain, Julien. 1959. "Introduction" to *Daumier Les Gens de Justice*. New York: Tudor Publishing Co.

Cannon, J. 1973. *Parliamentary Reform 1640–1832*. Cambridge: Cambridge University Press.

Carey, J. 1989. "A Cultural Approach to Communication." In J. Carey (ed.), *Communication as Culture: Essays on Media and Society*. Boston, MA: Unwin Hyman.

Carey, J. 1997. "The Press, Public Opinion, and Public Discourse: On the Edge of the Postmodern." In E. Munson and C. Warren (eds.), *James Carey: A Critical Reader*. Minneapolis: University of Minnesota Press.

Carlyle, T. [1839] 1971. "Chartism." In Alan Shelston (ed.), *Thomas Carlyle: Selected Writings*. Harmondsworth: Penguin.

Carlyle, T. [1850] 1898. "Jesuitism." In *The Works of Thomas Carlyle*. Vol. 20. London: Chapman and Hall.

Carlyle, T. 1986. *Selected Writings*. Harmondsworth: Penguin.

Carnegie, Andrew. 1889. "Wealth." *North American Review*, 148 (391): 653–665.

Challinor, William. 1849. *A Solicitor, the Court of Chancery: Its Inherent Defects*. London: Stevens and Norton.

Chase, Anthony. 1986. "Toward a Legal Theory of Popular Culture." *Wisconsin Law Review*: 527–569.

Certeau, M. de. 1984. *The Practice of Everyday Life*. Berkeley: University of California Press.

Children's Employment Commission. First Report of the Commissioners. Mines. 1842. London: William Clowes and Sons.

Children's Employment Commission. Second Report of the Commissioners. Trade and Manufactures.1842. London: William Clowes and Sons.

Cobbe, Frances Power. [1868] 1995. "Criminals, Idiots, Women and Minors." In Susan Hamilton (ed.), *Criminals, Idiots, Women and Minors: Nineteenth-Century Writings by Women on Women*. Peterborough: Broadview Press, 108–132.

Coke, E. 1629. *The First Part of the Institutes of the Lawes of England*. London.

Coleridge, S. 1977. *Biographia Literaria*. London: Dent.

Collens, Rupert. 1990. *25 Legal Luminaries from* Vanity Fair. London and elsewhere: Lambourn.

Collini, Stefan. 1991. *Public Moralists: Political Thought and Intellectual Life in Britain, 1850–1930*. Oxford: Clarendon Press.

Collins, Philip. 1962. *Dickens and Crime*. Cambridge: Cambridge University Press.

Colón, Susan. 2012. *Victorian Parables*. London: Continuum.

Conkling, A. 1842. *A Treatise on the Organization and Jurisdiction of the Supreme, Circuit and District Courts of the United States*. New York: Gould, Banks & Co.

Conrad, C. 1998. *Jury Nullification: The Evolution of a Doctrine*. Durham, NC: Carolina Academic Press.

Cornwallis, Caroline. [1857] 1983. "The Capabilities and Disabilities of Women." *Westminster Review* 67 (January 1857): 42–72. In Susan Groag Bell and Karen M. Offen (eds.), *Women, the Family and Freedom*. Stanford, CA: Stanford University Press, I, 310–313.

Cotton, William T. 2003. "Five-fold Crisis in *Utopia*: A Foreshadow of Major Modern Utopian Narrative Strategies." *Utopian Studies*, 14 (2): 41.

Cowan, D. 2004. "Legal Consciousness: Some Observations." *Modern Law Review*, 67: 928–958.

Craig, D. 1983. "The Crowd in Dickens." In R. Giddings (ed.), *The Changing World of Charles Dickens*. New York: Barnes and Noble.

Craig, Randall. 2009. *The Narratives of Caroline Norton*. New York: Palgrave Macmillan.

Craik, Jennifer. 2005. *Uniforms Exposed*. Oxford: Berg.

Crone, Rosalind. 2012. *Violent Victorians: Popular Entertainment in Nineteenth-Century London*. Manchester: Manchester University Press.

Crosby, K. 2012. "*Bushell's Case* and the Juror's Soul." *Journal of Legal History*, 33: 251–290.

Crosby, K. 2016. "Before the Criminal Justice and Courts Act 2015: Juror Punishment in Nineteenth- and Twentieth-Century England." *Legal Studies*, 36: 179–208.

Daily News, 1858 Friday 2nd July, Issue 3785, p. 7.

Davenport-Hines, Richard. 2014. Untitled Book Review. *Guardian Review*, December 20, 2014, 8.

Dawson, Michael. 1997. "'That Nice Red Coat Goes to My Head like Champagne': Gender, Antimodernism and the Mountie Image." *Journal of Canadian Studies*, 32 (3): 119–139.

Day, David. 1997. *Claiming a Continent: A New History of Australia*. Sydney: Angus and Robertson.

Dean, A. 2015. "The CMHR and the Ongoing Crisis of Murdered or Missing Indigenous Women: Do Museums Have a Responsibility to Care?" *Review of Education, Pedagogy, and Cultural Studies*, 37 (2–3): 147–165.

Dicey, A. [1905] 1926. *Lectures on the Relation Between Law and Public Opinion in England During the Nineteenth Century*. London: Macmillan.

Dicey, A. 2012 [1914]. *Lectures on the Relation between Law and Public Opinion in England*. Liberty Fund.

Dicey, Albert Venn. 1959 [1908]. *Introduction to the Study of the Law of the Constitution*. London: Macmillan.

Dickens, Charles. 1843. *A Christmas Carol*. London: Chapman & Hall.

Dickens, Charles. [1848] 1997. *David Copperfield*. Oxford: Oxford University Press.

Dickens, Charles. 1985 [1852–1853]. *Bleak House*. Harmondsworth: Penguin.

Dickens, Charles. [1854] 1985. *Hard Times*. Harmondsworth: Penguin.

Dickens, Charles. [1861] 2008. *Great Expectations*. Oxford: Oxford University Press.

Dickens, Charles. 1880. *The Letters of Charles Dickens, Vol. II, 1857–1870*. London: Chapman and Hall.

Dickens, Charles. 2000. *A Tale of Two Cities*. London: Penguin.

Dillon, Steve. 2001. "Barrett Browning's Poetic Vocation: Crying, Singing, Breathing." *Victorian Poetry*, 39 (4): 509–532.

Disraeli, Benjamin. [1845] 2008. *Sybil; or the Two Nations*. Oxford: Oxford University Press.

Dodsworth, F.M. 2008. "The Idea of Police in Eighteenth-Century England: Discipline, Reformation, Superintendance." *Journal of the History of Ideas*, 69 (4): 583–604.

Dodsworth, F.M. 2012. "Men on a Mission: Masculinity, Violence and the Self-Presentation of Policemen in England, c. 1870–1914." In David G. Barrie, and Susan Broomhall (eds.), *A History of Police and Masculinities*. Abingdon: Routledge, 123–140.

Dolin, Kieran. 1999. *Fiction and the Law: Legal Discourse in Victorian and Modernist Literature* Cambridge: Cambridge University Press.
Dolin, Kieran. 2007. *A Critical Introduction to Law and Literature*. Cambridge: Cambridge University Press.
Dolin, Tim. 1997. *Mistress of the House: Women of Property in the Victorian Novel*. Aldershot: Ashgate.
Donahue, Charles, Jr. 1980. "The Future of the Concept of Property Predicted from Its Past." In J. Roland Pennock and John W. Chapman (eds.), *Property*. [Nomos XXII]. New York: New York University Press, 28–68.
Doyle, P. 2007. *City of Shadows*. Sydney: Historic House.
Dunhill, Thomas F. 1929. *Sullivan's Comic Operas: A Critical Appreciation*. London: Edward Arnold.
Eagleton, Terry. 2015. "Utopias, Past and Present." *Guardian Review*, October 17, 2015, 4.
Edge, S. 2004. "Photographic History and the Visual Appearance of an Irish Nationalist Discourse 1840–1870." *Victorian Literature and Culture*, 32 (1): 17–39.
Edwards, S. 1990. "The Machine's Dialogue." *Oxford Art Journal*, 13 (1): 63–76.
Edwards, S. 2006. *Photography, A Very Short Introduction*. Oxford: Oxford University Press.
Eighteenth-Century Collections Online. Available at www.quod.lib.umich.edu/ecco.
Eliot, George. [1859] 1994. *Adam Bede*. Harmondsworth: Penguin.
Eliot, George. [1860] 1996. *The Mill on the Floss*. Oxford: Oxford University Press.
Eliot, George. [1866] 1987. *Felix Holt*. Harmondsworth: Penguin.
Eliot, George. 1985. *The Mill on the Floss*. Harmondsworth: Penguin.
Euripides. [c.431 BCE] 2006. *Medea*. Translated by Michael Collier and Georgia Machemer. Oxford: Oxford University Press.
Evans, Julie. 2005. *Edward Eyre, Race and Colonial Governance*. Dunedin: University of Otago Press.
Evans, R. 2000. *In Defence of History*. London: Granta.
Exhibition Catalogue. 1999–2000. *Daumier, 1808–1879*. Ottawa: National Gallery of Canada; Paris: Galeries nationales du Grand Palais; Washington: The Phillips Collection.
Eyre, Edward John. [1845] 1964. *Journals of Expeditions of Discovery into Central Australia, and Overland from Adelaide to King George Sound, in the Years 1840–1*. Adelaide: Libraries Board of South Australia.
Ferguson, N. 2003. *Empire: How Britain Made the Modern World*. London: Penguin.
Ferguson, Trish. 2013. *Thomas Hardy's Legal Fictions*. Edinburgh: Edinburgh University Press.
Fildes, L. 1873. "The Bashful Model." *The Graphic*, November 8, 1873, pp. 441.
Finn, J. 2009. *Capturing the Criminal Image*. Minneapolis: University of Minnesota Press.
Firth, C. 1938. *A Commentary on Macaulay's History of England*. London: Macmillan.
Fischler, Alan. 1991. *Modified Rapture: Comedy in W.S. Gilbert's Savoy Operas*. Charlottesville and London: University Press of Virginia.
Foucault, Michel. [1967] 2001. *Madness and Civilization: A History of Insanity in the Age of Reason*. London: Routledge.
Foucault, Michel. [1975] 1991. *Discipline and Punish: The Birth of the Prison*. London: Penguin.
Foucault, M. 1980. "Two Lectures." Reproduced in C. Gordon (ed.), *Michel Foucault: Power/Knowledge*. London:Harvester Wheatsheaf.
Foucault, M. 1988. *Power/Knowledge: Selected Interviews and Other Writings, 1972–1977*. New York: Random House.
Foucault, M. 1991. *Discipline and Punish: The Birth of the Prison*. London: Penguin Books.

Fradin, Joseph I. 1966. "Will and Society in Bleak House." *PMLA (Publication of the Modern Language Association of America)*, 81 (1): 95–109.

Frank, Cathrine O. 2010. *Law, Literature and the Transmission of Culture in England, 1837–1925*. Farnham: Ashgate.

Frankel, Oz. 2006. *States of Inquiry: Social Investigations and Print Culture in Nineteenth-Century Britain and the United States*. Baltimore: Johns Hopkins University Press.

French, Derek, Mayson, Stephen W., and Ryan, Christopher L. 2011. *Company Law*. Oxford: Oxford University Press.

Fritz, C.G. 1997. "Alternative Visions of American Constitutionalism: Popular Sovereignty and the Early American Constitutional Debate." *Hastings Constitutional Law Quarterly*, 24: 287.

Frye, L. 1997. "'Great Burke', Thomas Carlyle, and the French Revolution." In L. Crafton (ed.), *The French Revolution Debate in English Literature and Culture*. London: Greenwood Press.

Galsworthy, John. [1906–1920] 1978. *In Chancery*. In *The Forsyte Saga*. London: Penguin, 371-652.

Galton, F. 1879. "Composite Portraits, Made by Combining Those of Many Different Persons Into a Single Resultant Figure." *The Journal of the Anthropological Institute of Great Britain and Ireland*, 8: 132–144.

Gammage, Bill. 2011. *The Biggest Estate on Earth: How the Aborigines Made Australia*. Sydney: Allen & Unwin.

Gardiner, J. 2002. *The Victorians: An Age in Retrospect*. London: Hambledon.

Gaskell, Elizabeth. [1848] 1991. *Mary Barton*. Oxford: Oxford University Press.

Gentleman's Magazine. 1732. London. "Marriages." (January) II. 13. 588. Excerpted in Geoffrey Tillotson et al. (eds.). 1969. *Eighteenth-Century English Literature*. Toronto: Harcourt, Brace, Jovanovich.

Gerhart, Peter M. 2010. *Tort Law and Social Morality*. Cambridge: Cambridge University Press.

Getty Center, (Los Angeles). 1998. *The Art of the Daguerreotype* (April 14 to July 12, 1998).

Gibson, Richard Hughes. 2015. *Forgiveness in Victorian Literature*. London: Bloomsbury.

Gilmour, R. 1993. *The Victorian Period: The Intellectual and Cultural Context of English Literature 1830-1890*. London: Longman.

Goodman, Andrew. 1983. *Gilbert and Sullivan at Law*. Rutherford and elsewhere: FairleighDickinson University Press.

Goodman, Andrew and Hardcastle, Robert. 1988. *Gilbert and Sullivan's London*. Tunbridge Wells: Spellmount.

Gordon, Andrew. 2015. *The Rules of the Game: Jutland and British Naval Command*. London: Penguin.

Green, T.A. 2015. "The Jury and Criminal Responsibility in Anglo-American History." *Criminal Law and Philosophy*, 9: 423–442.

Gribble, Jennifer. 2004. "Why the Good Samaritan was a Bad Economist." *Literature and Theology*, 18 (4): 427–441.

Grotius, Hugo. [1603] 2006. *Natural Law Paper: Commentary on the Law of Prize and Boot* Indianapolis, IN: Liberty Fund.

Haggerty, K. 2006. "Tear Down the Walls." In D. Lyon (ed.), *Theorizing Surveillance*. London: Routledge.

Hagins, Z. 2013. "Fashioning the 'Born Criminal' on the Beat: Juridical Photography and the Police municipale in Fin-de-Siècle Paris." *Modern & Contemporary France*, 21 (3): 281–296.

Haight, Gordon S. (ed.). 1954–1978. *The George Eliot Letters*. 9 vols. New Haven, CT: Yale University Press.

Hale, J.P. 1842. *Trial by Jury: Remarks on the Attempt by Chief Justice Parker to Usurp the Prerogative of the Jury in Criminal Cases*. Exeter, NH: Grant's Office.

Hampshire Advertiser. (1861). "Yankee Balderdash," Saturday August 24, Issue 1982, p. 2.

Hansard, *Falcarragh Evictions*, HC Deb February 12, 1891, vol. 350, cc 487–8.

Harrington, M.P. 1999. "The Law-Finding Function of the American Jury." *Wisconsin Law Review*: 377–440.

Harvey, John. 1970. *Victorian Novelists and their Illustrators*. London: Sidgwick & Jackson.

Hawkins, Richard. 1991. "The 'Irish Model' and the Empire: A Case for Reassessment." In David Anderson and David Killingray (eds.), *Policing the Empire: Government, Authority and Control, 1830–1940*. Manchester: Manchester University Press, 18–32.

Heffer, S. 1996. *Moral Desperado: A Life of Thomas Carlyle*. London: Phoenix.

Heffer, S. 2013. *High Minds: The Victorians and the Making of Modern Britain*. London: Random House.

Henry, Peaches. 2011. "The Sentimental Artistry of Barrett Browning's 'The Cry of the Children'." *Victorian Poetry*, 49 (4): 535–556.

Hibbert, C. 1997. *Wellington: A Personal History*. London: Harper Collins.

Hibbert, C. 2001. *Queen Victoria: A Personal History*. London: Harper Collins.

Hibbert, C. 2004. *Disraeli: A Personal History*. London: Harper Collins.

Himmelfarb, G. 2007. *The Spirit of the Age: Victorian Essays*. New Haven, CT: Yale University Press.

Hobsbawm, Eric. 1994. *The Age of Empire: 1875–1914*. London: Abacus.

Hollingsworth, Keith. 1963. *The Newgate Novel, 1830–47: Bulwer, Ainsworth, Dickens and Thackeray*. Detroit: Wayne State University Press.

Holme, Charles. (ed.). 1904. *Daumier & Gavarni: The Studio (Special Number)*. London, Paris and New York: Offices of "The Studio."

Hong, Grace Kyungwon. 2007. "Property." In Bruce Burgett and Glenn Hendler (eds.), *Keywords for American Cultural Studies*. New York: New York University Press, 180–183.

Horne, R.H. 1843. "Children Employment Commission." In Douglas Jerrold (ed.), *The Illuminated Magazine*. Vol. 1. London: William Stevens.

Horrell, Sara and Humphries, Jane. 1999. "Child Labour and British Industrialization." In Michael Lavalette (ed.), *A Thing of the Past? Child Labour in Britain in the Nineteenth and Twentieth Centuries*. New York: St. Martin's Press.

Howe, M.D. 1939. "Juries as Judges of Criminal Law." *Harvard Law Review*, 52: 582–616.

Hudson, Ronald and Kelley, Philip (eds.). 1989. *The Brownings' Correspondence*. Vol. 7. Winfield, KN: Wedgestone Press.

Hume, David. [1748] 1994. "Of the Original Contract." In Stuart D. Warner and Donald W. Livingston (eds.), *Political Writings*. Indianapolis, IN: Hackett Publishing.

Humphries, Jane. 2010. *Childhood and Child Labour in the British Industrial Revolution*. Cambridge: Cambridge University Press.

Hunt, Dixon John. 1971. "Dickens and the Traditions of Graphic Satire." In John Dixon Hunt (ed.), *Encounters: Essays on Literature and the Visual Arts*. London: Studio Vista, 124–155.

Hutcheon, W. (ed.). 1913. *Whigs and Whiggism: Political Writings by Benjamin Disraeli*. London: John Murray.

Ignatieff, Michael. 1978. *A Just Measure of Pain: The Penitentiary in the Industrial Revolution 1750–1850*. New York: Pantheon.

Jackson, P. 1994. *The Last of the Whigs: A Political Biography of Lord Hartington*. Cranbury, NJ: Associated Presses.

Jacobs, Arthur. 1984. *Arthur Sullivan: A Victorian Musician*. Oxford: Oxford University Press.

James, Henry. [1907] 2011. "Preface" to *Roderick Hudson*. In Henry James (ed.), *The Art of the Novel*. Chicago: University of Chicago Press.

Jefferson, T. 1853. *The Writings of Thomas Jefferson*. Washington, DC: Taylor & Maury.

Jeffries, Charles. 1952. *The Colonial Police*. London: Max Parrish.

June-Frieson, K. 2007. "Arresting Faces." *Smithsonian Magazine*, January, pp. 60–63.

Karlin, Daniel. (ed.). 1990. *Robert Browning and Elizabeth Barrett: The Courtship Correspondence*. Oxford: Oxford University Press.

Kennedy, R. 2006. "Grifters and Goons, Framed and (Matted)." *New York Times*, September 15.

Kingsley, Henry. [1865] 1970. *The Recollections of Geoffrey Hamlyn*. Melbourne: Lloyd O'Neil.

Kincaid, James R. 1971. *Dickens and the Rhetoric of Laughter*. Oxford: Clarendon Press.

Kirby, Lynne. 1997. *Parallel Tracks: The Railroad and the Birth of Modern Cinema*. Exeter, NH: University of Exeter Press.

Kirby, Peter. 1999. "Child Labour and the Mines Act of 1842." In *A Thing of the Past? Child Labour in Britain in the Nineteenth and Twentieth Centuries*. New York: St. Martin's Press.

Kirby, Peter. 2013. "Victorian Social Investigation and the Children's Employment Commission, 1840–42." In *Childhood and Child Labour in Industrial England*. Farnham, Surrey: Ashgate Publishing.

Knepper, P., and Norris, C. 2009. "Fingerprint and Photograph Surveillance Technologies in the Manufacture of Suspect Social Identities." In Paul Knepper, Jonathan Doak and Joanna Shapland (eds.), *Urban Crime Prevention, Surveillance and Restorative Justice*. Florida: Taylor and Francis, 77–100.

Kramer, L.D. 2004. *The People Themselves: Popular Constitutionalism and Judicial Review*. Oxford: Oxford University Press.

Kramer, L.D. 2006. "'The Interest of the Man': James Madison, Popular Constitutionalism and the Theory of Deliberative Democracy." *Valparaiso University Law Review*, 41: 697–754.

Kuhn, W. 2006. *The Politics of Pleasure: A Portrait of Benjamin Disraeli*. London: Simon & Schuster.

Lacey, Nicola. 2008. *Women, Crime, and Character: From Moll Flanders to Tess of the D'Urbervilles*. Oxford: Oxford University Press.

Landow, George P. 1968. "Ruskin and Baudelaire on Art and Artist." *University of Toronto Quarterly*, 37: 295–308.

Landow, George P. 2015. *Aesthetic and Critical Theory of John Ruskin*. Princeton, NJ: Princeton University Press.

Langbein, J.H. 1993. "Chancellor Kent and the History of Legal Literature." *Columbia Law Review*, 93: 547–594.

Lashmar, P. 2013. "How to Humiliate and Shame: A Reporter's Guide to the Power of the Mugshot." *Social Semiotics*, 24 (1): 56–87.

Laughton, Bruce. 1996. *Honoré Daumier*. New Haven, CT: Yale University Press.

Law, Jules. 1992. "Chiastic Exchange in *The Mill on the Floss*." In Linda M. Shires (ed.), *Rewriting the Victorians: Theory History and the Politics of Gender*. London: Routledge, 52–69.

Lawrence, Elwood P. 1971. "'The Happy Land': W.S. Gilbert as Political Satirist." *Victorian Studies*, 15 (2): 161.

Leavis, Q.D. 1970. "The Dickens Illustrations: Their Function." In F.R. Leavis and Q.D. Leavis (eds.), *Dickens the Novelist*. London: Chatto & Windus, 332–371.

Le Foyer, Jean. 1958. *Daumier au Palais de Justice*. Paris: La Colmbe.
Leigh, Mike. 2009. "*Topsy-Turvy*: A Personal Journey." In David Eden and Meinhard Saremba (eds.), *The Cambridge Companion to Gilbert and Sullivan*. Cambridge: Cambridge University Press.
Levine, Philippa. 1994. "'Walking the Streets in a Way No Decent Woman Should': Women Police in World War I." *The Journal of Modern History*, 66 (1): 34–78.
Levitas, Ruth. 2011 [1990]. *The Concept of Utopia*. Oxford: Peter Lang.
Levitas, Ruth. 2013. *Utopia as Method: The Imaginary Reconstitution of Society*. Basingstoke: Palgrave Macmillan.
Locke, John. [1689] 1978. "Of Property." In C.B. Macpherson (ed.), *Property: Mainstream and Critical Positions*. Oxford: Blackwell.
Locke, John. [1689] 1988. *The Second Treatise of Government*. In Peter Laslett (ed.), *Two Treatises of Government*. Cambridge: Cambridge University Press.
Lockwood, Frank. 1894. *The Law and Lawyers of Pickwick. A Lecture*. London: The Roxburghe Press.
Lombroso, Cesare. 2006. *Criminal Man, According to the Classification of Cesare Lombroso*. Durham, ND: Duke University Press.
Longford, E. 1998. *Victoria RI*. London: Weidenfeld & Nicolson.
Loughlin, Martin. 2003. *The Idea of Public Law*. Oxford: Oxford University Press.
Loughlin, Martin. 2010. *Foundations of Public Law*. Oxford: Oxford University Press.
Loughlin, Martin. 2013. *The British Constitution: A Very Short Introduction*. Oxford: Oxford University Press.
Lunney, Mark, and Oliphant, Ken. 2010. *Tort Law: Texts and Materials*. 4th edn. Oxford: Oxford University Press.
Luxon, John. 1983. *Lewis and Lewis: The Life and Times of a Victorian Solicitor*. London: Collins.
Lyman, J.L. 1964. "The Metropolitan Police Act of 1829." *Journal of Criminal Law & Criminology & Police Science*, 55: 141–154.
Lynch, Deidre. 1998. *The Economy of Character: Novels, Market Culture, and the Business of Inner Meaning*. Chicago: University of Chicago Press.
Macaulay, T. 1986. *The History of England*. London: Penguin.
McCormack, Matthew. 2012. "A Species of Civil Soldier: Masculinity, Policing and the Military in 1780s England." In David G. Barrie and Susan Broomhall (eds.), *A History of Police and Masculinities*. Abingdon: Routledge, 55–71.
McDermid, V. 2015. *Forensics: The Anatomy of Crime*. London: Welcome Collection.
Macfarlane, Alan. 1986. "Socio-Economic Revolution in England and the Origin of the Modern World." In Roy Porter and Mikulás Teich (eds.), *Revolution in History*. Cambridge: Cambridge University Press, 145–166.
MacKay, Carol Hanbery. (ed.). 1989. *Dramatic Dickens*. Basingstoke: Palgrave Macmillan.
McKenzie, Gordon. 1941. "Dickens and Daumier." *Studies in the Comic*. Berkeley: University of California Press, 8 (2): 273–298.
MacLeod, R.C. 1976. *The NWMP and Law Enforcement 1873–1905*. Toronto: University of Toronto Press.
McMullan, John. 1998. "The Arresting Eye: Discourse, Surveillance and Disciplinary Administration in Early English Police Thinking." *Social and Legal Studies*, 7 (1): 97–128.
Macpherson, C.B. (ed.). 1978. *Property: Mainstream and Critical Positions*. Oxford: Blackwell.
Mac Suibhne, B., and Martin A. 2005. "Fenians in the Frame: Photographing Irish Political Prisoners 1865–68." *Field Day Review*, 1: 101–120.

Maine, Henry Sumner. [1861] 1906. *Ancient Law: Its Connection with the Early History of Society and its Relation to Modern Ideas*. London: John Murray.
Maine, Henry Sumner. 2012. *Ancient Law*. Cambridge: Cambridge University Press.
Maitland, Frederic William. 1908. *The Constitutional History of England: A Course of Lectures*. Cambridge: Cambridge University Press.
Maitland, F.W. 1911. "Why the History of English Law is Not Written." In H.A.L. Fisher (ed.), *The Collected Papers of Frederic William Maitland: Downing Professor of the Laws of England*. Cambridge: Cambridge University Press.
Malthus, Thomas. 1798. *An Essay on the Principle of Population, as It Affects the Future Improvement of Society*. London: Johnson.
Mander, Raymond and Mitchenson, Joe. 1975. *The Theatres of London*. Rev. edn. London: Times Mirror.
Mandler, P. 1990. *Aristocratic Government in the Age of Reform: Whigs and Liberals 1830–1852*. Oxford: Oxford University Press.
Marsh, A. 1999. "Leah King-Smith and the Nineteenth-century Archive." *History of Photography*, 23 (2): 114–117.
Marten, Harry. 1974. "The Visual Imagination of Dickens and Hogarth: Structure and Scene." *Studies in the Novel*, 6: 145–164.
Marten, Harry. 1976. "Exaggerated Characters: A Study of the Work of Dickens and Hogarth." *Centennial Review*, 20: 290–308.
Marx, Karl and Friedrich Engels. [1848] 1978. *The Communist Manifesto*. In Robert C. Tucker (ed.), *The Marx-Engels Reader*. New York: Norton, 473–500.
Maurer, Sara L. 2012. *The Dispossessed State: Narratives of Ownership in Nineteenth-Century Britain and Ireland*. Baltimore: Johns Hopkins University Press.
May, E.T. 1861. *The Constitutional History of England since George III*. London: Longman.
Meier, T. and Wolfensberger, R. 1998. "Police Photography of Swiss Itinerants 1852–3." *History of Photography*, 22 (3): 278–281.
Michaelson, M. 2006. *Least Wanted: A Century of American Mugshots*. New York: Steidl Kasher.
Mill, John Stuart. [1848] 1978. "Of Property." In C.B. Macpherson (ed.), *Property: Mainstream and Critical Positions*. Oxford: Blackwell.
Mill, John Stuart. [1869] 1983. *The Subjection of Women*. London: Prometheus.
Mill, John Stuart. [1861] 2002. *Utilitarianism*. 2nd edn. Edited by George Sher. Indianapolis, IN: Hackett Publishing.
Miller, J. Hillis. 2001. "Moments of Decision in *Bleak House*." In John O. Jordan (ed.), *The Cambridge Companion to Charles Dickens*. Cambridge: Cambridge University Press, 49–63.
Mitchell, L. 1997. *Lord Melbourne 1779–1848*. Oxford: Oxford University Press.
Mladek, Klaus. 2007. *Police Forces: A Cultural History of an Institution*. New York: Palgrave Macmillan.
Mnookin, J. 1998. "The Image of Truth: Photographic Evidence and the Power of Analogy." *Yale Journal of Law & the Humanities*, 10: 1.
Monkkonen, Eric H. 1982. "From Cop History to Social History: The Significance of the Police in American History." *Journal of Social History*, 15: 575–591.
Monkkonen, Eric H. 1992. "History of Urban Police." *Crime and Justice*, 15: 547–580.
Morgan, Lewis Henry. 2005. "The Historical Place of Property." In Sally Falk Moore (ed.), *Law and Anthropology: A Reader*. Malden, MA: Blackwell, 26–27.
Morrow, John. 2007. *Thomas Carlyle*. London: A & C Black.
Mulcahy, Linda. 2011. *Legal Architecture: Justice, Due Process and the Place of Law*. Abingdon: Routledge.

Mulcahy, Linda. 2015. "Docile Suffragettes? Resistance to Police Photography and the Possibility of Object–Subject Transformation." *Feminist Legal Studies*, 23(1): 79–99.

National Archives. 1873. *Home Office and Prison Commission Records Series One: Wandsworth*, PCOM 2/290-103.

National Archives. 1897. *Home Office Registered Papers: Prisons and Prisoners—Photographing Untried Prisoners, 1897* reference HO 144/514/X67509.

Nelson, W.E. 2010. "The Lawfinding Power of Colonial American Juries." *Ohio State Law Journal*, 71: 1003–1029.

Newmyer, R.K. 1985. *Supreme Court Justice Joseph Story: Statesman of the Old Republic*. Chapel Hill, NC: University of North Carolina Press.

Newsome, D. 1998. *The Victorian World Picture*. London: Fontana.

Nichols, Chelsea. "Suspicious Looking: 19th Century Mug Shots in the Collection of the New Zealand Police Museum." *New Zealand Police Museum* online exhibition. March 2010. http://sites.google.com/site/newzealandpolicemuseum/home/online-exhibitions/mug-shots/.

Nietzsche, Friedrich. [1888] 2008. *The Twilight of the Idols*. Translated by R.J. Hollingdale. Oxford: Oxford University Press.

Norton, Caroline. 1855. *A Letter to the Queen on Lord Chancellor Cranworth's Marriage and Divorce Bill*. London: Longman.

Nussbaum, Martha. 1990. *Love's Knowledge: Essays on Philosophy and Literature*. New York: Oxford University Press.

Oakeshott, Michael. 1975. "The Character of a Modern European State." In *On Human Conduct*. Oxford: Oxford University Press.

Onslow, Arthur. 1789. *An Institute of the Law Relative to Trials at Nisi Prius, Originally Published in the year 1760*. London: Whieldon & Parker.

Orth, John V. 2014. "Brent Crude Market and a Comic Opera [Letter]." *Financial Times*, August 25, 2014, 8.

Palmer, Stanley H. 1988. *Police and Protest in England and Ireland 1780–1850*. Cambridge: Cambridge University Press.

Parker, J. 1842. *Reports of the Cases, the State vs Samuel Small, & the State vs Andrew Pierce, Jr & a Tried in the County of Stafford, January Term, 1842*. Concord, NH: Asa McFarland.

Parry, J. 1993. *The Rise and Fall of Liberal Government in Victorian Britain*. New Haven, CT: Yale University Press.

Pavlich, G. 2009. "The Emergence of Habitual Criminals in 19th Century Britain: Implications for Criminology." *Journal of Theoretical and Philosophical Criminology*, 2 (1): 1–62.

Petch, Simon. 1997. "Law, Equity, and Conscience in Victorian England." *Victorian Literature and Culture*, 25 (1): 123–139.

Petch, Simon. 2007. "Law, Literature and Victorian Studies." *Victorian Literature and Culture*, 35: 361–384.

Phillips, S., Haworth-Booth M., and Squires, C. 1997. *Police Pictures—The Photograph as Evidence*. San Francisco: Chronicle Books.

Plumb, J. 1963. *Men and Places*. London: Cresset.

Plumer, W., Jr. 1857. *The Life of William Plumer*. Boston, MA: Phillips, Samson & Co.

Pocock, J. 1957. *The Ancient Constitution and the Feudal Law*. Cambridge: Cambridge University Press.

Pollock, Frederick. [1887] 1895. *Law of Torts*. 4th edn. London: Macmillan.

Pound, R. 1938. *The Formative Era of American Law*. New York: Little, Brown.

Psomiades, Kathy Alexis. 1999. "Heterosexual Exchange and Other Victorian Fictions: *The Eustace Diamonds* and Victorian Anthropology." *Novel: A Forum on Fiction*, 33: 93–118.

Purdy, Jedediah. 2010. *The Meaning of Property*. New Haven, CT: Yale University Press.

Rafter, N.H. (ed.). 2009. *The Origins of Criminology: A Reader*. Abingdon: Routledge.

Rahe, Paul. 2009. *Soft Despotism, Democracy's Drift: Montesquieu, Rousseau, Tocqueville and The Modern Prospect*. New Haven, CT and London: Yale University Press.

Rajchman, John. 1994. "Foucault's Art of Seeing." In Barry Smart (ed.), *Michel Foucault: Critical Assessments*. Vol I. London: Routledge, 224–236.

Rawls, John. 1990. *A Theory of Justice*. Cambridge, MA: Harvard University Press.

Read, D. 1987. *Peel and the Victorians*. Oxford: Blackwell.

Readman, Paul. 2008. *Land and Nation in England: Patriotism, National Identity, and the Politics of Land, 1880–1914*. Woodbridge: Boydell Press.

Reid, J.P. 1986. *Constitutional History of the American Revolution: The Authority of Rights*. Madison, WI: University of Wisconsin Press.

Reiner, Robert. 1985. *The Politics of the Police*. New York: St. Martins Press.

Reitz, Caroline. 2000. "Bad Cop/Good Cop: Godwin, Mill and the Imperial Origins of the English Detective." *Novel: A Forum on Fiction*, 33 (2): 175–185.

Reynolds, Elaine A. 1998. *Before the Bobbies: The Night Watch and Police Reform in Metropolitan London, 1720–1830*. Basingstoke: Macmillan.

Ricks, Christopher. 1972. *Tennyson*. London: Macmillan.

Ricoeur, Paul. 2000. *The Just*. Translated by David Pellauer. Chicago: University of Chicago Press.

Rizzo, L. 2013. "Visual Aperture: Bureaucratic Systems of Identification, Photography and Personhood in Colonial Southern Africa." *History of Photography*, 37 (3): 263–282.

Robson, Ann M. and Robson, John M. 1994. *Sexual Equality: Writings by John Stuart Mill, Harriet Taylor Mill and Helen Taylor*. Toronto: University of Toronto Press.

Roche, Daniel. 1994. "The Discipline of Appearances: The Prestige of Uniform." In *The Culture of Clothing: Dress and Fashion in the "Ancien Regime."* Cambridge: Cambridge University Press.

Rodensky, Lisa. 2003. *The Crime in Mind: Criminal Responsibility and the Victorian Novel*. Oxford: Oxford University Press.

Rose, Carol M. 1994. *Property and Persuasion: Essays on the History, Theory and Rhetoric of Ownership*. Boulder, CO: Westview Press.

Rose, Carol M. 2006. "Introduction: Property and Language, or, the Ghost of the Fifth Panel." *Yale Journal of Law and the Humanities*, 18 [Supplement]: 1–28.

Royle, E. 2000. *Revolutionary Britannia? Reflections on the Threat of Revolution in Britain 1789–1848*. Manchester: Manchester University Press.

Ruskin, J. [1843] 1903. *Modern Painters*. In *The Works of John Ruskin*. Vol. 2. London: George Allen.

Ruskin, J. 1949 [1885–1889]. *Praeterita*. Oxford: Oxford University Press.

Ruskin, J. 2004. *Selected Writings*. Oxford University Press.

Ryfe, D.M. 2006. "News, Culture and Public Life." *Journalism Studies*, 7: 60–77.

Schechter, Roger E. 1996. "Changing Law Schools to Make Less Nasty Lawyers." *Georgetown Journal of Legal Ethics*, 10: 367–394.

Schramm, Jan-Melissa. 2000. *Testimony and Advocacy in Victorian Law, Literature, and Theology*. Cambridge: Cambridge University Press.

Schramm, Jan-Melissa. 2004. "'The Anatomy of a Barrister's Tongue': Rhetoric, Satire, and the Victorian Bar in England." *Victorian Literature and Culture*: 285–303.

Schramm, Jan-Melissa. 2012a. *Atonement and Self-Sacrifice in Nineteenth-Century Narrative*. Cambridge: Cambridge University Press.

Schramm, Jan-Melissa. 2012b. "Dickens and the National Interest: On the Representation of Parties in Bleak House." *Law and the Humanities*, 6 (2): 219–244.

Schweber, H. 1999. "The 'Science' of Legal Science: The Model of the Natural Sciences in Nineteenth Century American Legal Education." *Law and History Review*, 17: 421–466.
Scientific American. 1904. "The Bertillon Identification System," December 17th reproduced in Michaelson, M., *Least Wanted: A Century of American Mugshots*, New York: Steidl Kasher.
Searle, G.R. 2004. *A New England? Peace and War 1886–1918*. Oxford: Clarendon.
Sekula, A. 1986. "The Body and the Archive." *October*, 39: 3–64.
Seed, Patricia. 1995. *Ceremonies of Possession in Europe's Conquest of the New World*. Cambridge: Cambridge University Press.
Shaffer, Thomas L. 1978. "A Lesson from Trollope for Counselors at Law." *Washington & Lee Law Review*, 35: 727–752.
Shanley, Mary Lyndon. 1989. *Feminism, Marriage, and Law in Victorian England*. Princeton, NJ: Princeton University Press.
Shaw, Bernard. 1934. *Music in London, 1890–1894*. London: Constable.
Sheehan, C.A. 2004. "Madison v Hamilton: The Battle over Republicanism and the Role of Public Opinion." *American Political Science Review*, 98: 405–424.
Shelfer, L.F. 2013. "Special Juries in the Supreme Court." *Yale Law Journal*, 123: 208–252.
Shpayer-Makov, Haia. 2002. *The Making of a Policeman: A Social History of a Labour Force in Metropolitan London, 1829-1914*. Aldershot: Ashgate.
Shpayer-Makov, Haia. 2011. *The Ascent of the Detective: Police Sleuths in Victorian and Edwardian England*. Oxford: Oxford University Press.
Shpayer-Makov, Haia. 2012. "Shedding the Uniform and Acquiring a New Masculine Image: The Case of the Late Victorian and Edwardian English Police Detective." In David G. Barrie and Susan Broomhall (eds.), *A History of Police and Masculinities*. Abingdon: Routledge, 141–162.
Silbey, S., and Ewing, P. 1998. *The Common Place of Law: Stories of Everyday Life*. Chicago: The University of Chicago Press.
Simpson, Brian. 1995. *Victorian Law and the Industrial Spirit*. London: Selden Society.
Sinclair, Georgina. 2008. "The 'Irish' Policeman and the Empire: Influencing the Policing of the British Empire—Commonwealth." *Irish Historical Studies*, 142: 173–187.
Smith, Adam. [1759] 2005. *The Theory of Moral Sentiments*. Edited by Knud Haakonssen. Cambridge: Cambridge University Press.
Smith, Grahame. 2003. *Dickens and the Dream of Cinema*. Manchester: Manchester University Press.
Smith, S. 2000. "'Looking at One's Self through the Eyes of Others': W.E.B. Du Bois's Photographs for the 1900 Paris Exposition." *African American Review*, 34 (4) (Winter): 581–599.
Spurr, David. 1993. *The Rhetoric of Empire: Colonial Discourse in Journalism, Travel Writing, and Imperial Administration*. Durham, NC: Duke University Press.
Stark, K. 2006. "The Accidental Beauty of the System." In Steidl Kasher, Mark Michaelson and Steven Kasher (eds.), *Least Wanted: A century of American Mugshots*. New York: Steidl Kasher.
Stedman, Jane W. 1996. *W.S. Gilbert: A Classic Victorian and his Theatre*. Oxford: Oxford University Press.
Stein, Richard L. 2001. "Dickens and Illustration." In John O. Jordan (ed.), *The Cambridge Companion to Charles Dickens*. Cambridge: Cambridge University Press, 167–188.
Stephen, Leslie. 2010. *George Eliot*. Cambridge: Cambridge University Press.
Stone, Marjorie. 1986. "Cursing As One of the Fine Arts: Elizabeth Barrett Browning's Political Poems." *Dalhousie Review* 66: 155–173.

Stone, Marjorie. 1995. *Elizabeth Barrett Browning*. Houndmills: Macmillan Press.
Stone, Marjorie and Taylor, Beverly. (eds.). 2010. *The Works of Elizabeth Barrett Browning*. London: Pickering & Chatto.
Storey, Graham. 1987. *Charles Dickens: Bleak House*. Cambridge: Cambridge University Press.
Strachey, L. 1971. *Queen Victoria*. London: Penguin.
Styles, John. 1987. "The Emergence of the Police—Explaining Police Reform in Eighteenth and Nineteenth Century England." *British Journal of Criminology*, 27 (1): 15–22.
Sunderland, E. 1920. "Verdicts, General and Special." *Yale Law Journal*, 29: 253–267.
Sutton, Max K. 1975. *W.S. Gilbert*. Boston, MA: Twayne Publishers.
Sydney Gazette. October 18, 1838. Aborigines Protection Society (18 October), 2. http://trove.nla.gov.au/ndp/del/article/2550827 (accessed November 9, 2015).
Tagg, J. 1988. *The Burden of Representation*. Minneapolis: University of Minnesota Press.
Tagg, J. 2009. *The Disciplinary Frame: Photographic Truths and the Capture of Meaning*. Minneapolis: University of Minnesota Press.
Taylor, James. 2006. *Creating Capitalism: Joint-Stock Enterprise in British Politics and Culture 1800–1870*. Woodbridge: Royal Historical Society and Boydell Press.
Tennyson, Alfred. [1866] 1971. "Northern Farmer—New Style." In Robert W. Hill (ed.), *Tennyson's Poetry*. New York: W.W. Norton and Co.
Terrill, Richard J. 1980. "Politics, Reform and the Early-Nineteenth Century Reports on the Committees on the Police of the Metropolis." *Police Journal*, 53: 240–256.
Thompson, E. 1991. *The Making of the English Working Class*. Harmondsworth: Penguin.
Thompson, N. 1996. *Reviewing Sex: Gender and the Reception of Victorian Novels*. London: Macmillan.
Thomson, David. 1950. *England in the Nineteenth Century*. Harmondsworth: Penguin.
Tobias, J. 1972. "Police and Public in the United Kingdom." *Journal of Contemporary History*, 7: 201–219.
Tocqueville, A. de 2003. "Democracy in America." In I. Kramnick (ed.), *Democracy in America and Two Essays on America*. London: Penguin.
Tombs, Robert. 2014. *The English and Their History*. London: Allen Lane.
Trimolet, Louis and Maurisset, Théodore (illustr). 1841. *Physiologie de l'homme de loi par un homme de plume*. Paris: Aubert.
Trollope, A. [1874] 1963. *Harry Heathcote of Gangoil*. Melbourne: Lansdowne Press.
Trollope, A. 1996. *An Autobiography*. London: Penguin.
Tuttle, Carolyn. 1999. *Hard at Work in Factories and Mines*. Boulder, CO: Westview Press.
Twain, Mark. 1897. *Following the Equator: A Journey Around the World*. New York: Harper and Brothers.
Twining, William. 2006 [1990]. "The *Ratio Decidendi* of the Case of the Prodigal Son." In William Twining (ed.), *Rethinking Evidence: Exploratory Essays*. Cambridge: Cambridge University Press.
Tynan, Jane. 2013. *British Army Uniform and the First World War: Men in Khaki*. Basingstoke: Palgrave Macmillan.
Vandevelde, Kenneth J. 1980. "The New Property of the Nineteenth Century." *Buffalo Law Rev*, 23: 325–367.
Vincent, Howard P. 1968. *Daumier and His World*. Evanston: Northwestern University Press.
Walden, Keith. 1982. *Visions of Order: The Canadian Mounties in Symbol and Myth*. Toronto: Butterworths.
Ward, Ian. 2012. *Law and the Brontës*. Houndmills: Palgrave.

Watson, Vera. 1952. *A Queen at Home: An Intimate Account of the Social and Domestic Life of Queen Victoria's Court*. London: W.H. Allen.
Watt, Gary. 2009a. *Equity Stirring: The Story of Justice Beyond Law*. London: Hart Publishing.
Watt, Gary. 2009b. "The Character of Social Connection in Law and Literature: Lessons from Bleak House." *International Journal of Law in Context*, 5(3): 29–46.
Watt, Gary. 2009c. "The Equity of Esther Summerson." *Law and Humanities*, 3 (1): 43–67.
Watt, Gary. 2013. *Dress, Law and Naked Truth: A Cultural Study of Fashion and Form*. London: Bloomsbury.
Watt, P. 2005. "Foreword." In P. Doyle (ed.), *City of Shadows: Sydney Police Photographs 1912–1948*. Sydney: Historic Houses Trust.
Weisberg, Richard. 1992. *Poethics and Other Strategies of Law and Literature*. New York: Columbia University Press.
Welch, M. 2012. "Penal Tourism and the 'Dream of Order': Exhibiting Early Penology in Argentina and Australia." *Punishment & Society*, 14 (5): 584–615.
Werner-Marien, M. 2006. *Photography—A Cultural History*. 2nd edn. London: Laurence King Publishing.
Weston, Helen. 1975. "Prud'hon: Justice and Vengeance." *The Burlington* Magazine, 117 (867): 353–363.
White, James Boyd. 1973. *The Legal Imagination*. Chicago: University of Chicago Press.
Whitman, J.Q. 2008. *The Origins of Reasonable Doubt: Theological Roots of the Criminal Trial*. New Haven, CT: Yale University Press.
Wilde, Oscar. [1891]. *The Soul of Man under Socialism*. In Vyvyan Holland (introd.), *Complete Works of Oscar Wilde*. London: Collins.
Wilf, S. 2000. "The First Republican Revival: Virtue, Judging, and Rhetoric in the Early Republic." *Connecticut Law Review*, 32: 1675–1698.
Williams, Carolyn. 2011. *Gilbert and Sullivan: Gender, Genre, Parody*. New York: Columbia University Press.
Wilson, A. 2002. *The Victorians*. London: Hutchinson.
Wilson, Robin and Lloyd, Frederic. 1984. *Gilbert and Sullivan: The D'Oyly Carte Years*. London: Weidenfeld and Nicolson.
Winter, James. 1993. *London's Teeming Streets 1830–1914*. London: Routledge.
Wittgenstein, Ludwig. 1958. *Philosophical Investigations*. Translated by G.E.M. Anscombe. Oxford: Basil Blackwell.
Wolfe, Patrick. 1994. "Nation and MiscegeNation: Discursive Continuity in the Post-Mabo Era." *Social Analysis*," 36: 93–152.
Wolfson, John. 1976. *Final Curtain: The Last Gilbert and Sullivan Operas*. London: Chappell.
Woloch, Alex. 2010. *The One vs. The Many: The Space of the Protagonist in the Novel*. Chicago: University of Chicago Press.
Wood, John. (trans.). 1953. *Molière, The Miser and Other Plays*. Harmondsworth: Penguin Books Ltd.
Woodward, L. 1962. *The Age of Reform 1815–1870*. Oxford: Oxford University Press.
Worden, B. 2001. *Roundhead Reputations: The English Civil Wars and the Passions of Posterity*. London: Penguin.
Young, E. 2015. "Constitutionalism Outside the Courts." In M. Tushnet, M.Graber and S. Levinson (eds.), *The Oxford Handbook of the US Constitution*. Oxford: Oxford University Press.
Young, T. 1975. "A Look at American Law Reporting in the 19th Century." *Law Library Journal*, 68: 294–306.

INDEX

Aboriginal people 124–7
Acheson, Dean M. 112
administrative law 12, 13, 45, 49
adultery 6
"age of improvement" 2, 4
Age of Reform 91, 147, 159
Ambler, Ann 82
America
   Georgia v Brailsford 96, 98, 109
   indigenous peoples 113, 122
   judge-jury relations 91–2, 94, 95 (*see also Pierce v State*)
   judicial review and popular review 92–5
   licensing requirements 99
   newspapers 94, 95, 102–5
   police 64
   prisons 29, 31
   republican values 95, 104, 105, 110
American Revolution 74
American War of Independence 96
Anderson, David 68
Andrews, Malcolm xiii
anthropology 113
Arbus, Diane 32
Aristotle 134
Armitage, George 80
army uniforms 63, 67, 68, 70, 71
Arnold, Matthew 16, 41, 143
Arnold, Thomas 5
Ashley Cooper, Anthony, 7th Earl of Shaftesbury 75
Atget, Eugene 32
Austin, John 13, 73
Australia 123–7
Ayton, Richard 81

Bagehot, Walter 11, 12–13, 15
Baldwin, Henry 102
Balfour, Arthur 1
Balot, Ryan 144
Banner, Stuart 124
Barrett Browning, Elizabeth 120, 136, 167
   'The Cry of the Children' 74, 75, 80, 82, 83–9

Barrington, Rutland 39
Battersby, M. 166
Baudelaire, Charles 150–1, 152, 163
Baylis, G. 25, 165
Bellamy, Edward 45
Benjamin, Walter 32
Bentham, Jeremy 13, 73, 74–5, 115, 134, 143
Bergerat, Émile 155
Bertillon, Alphonse 22
Biber, K. 31
Blackmore, Enes 40
Blackstone, Sir William 114, 115, 118, 119, 124, 128
Blake, William 83, 84, 85
Bodichon, Barbara 119
Bow Street Runners 55–6
Boyce, R. 24, 166
Boyd, Hugh Stuart 83
Braddon, Mary Elizabeth 6, 7
Bramwell, George, 1st Baron 128
Briggs, Asa 2, 13
Bright, John 8
British Empire 1, 122, 123. See also colonies
Brogden, Mike 66
Brontë, Anne 3, 6
   The Tenant of Wildfell Hall 119
Brontë, Charlotte 3, 6
   Jane Eyre 136, 143
Brontë, Emily 6
   Wuthering Heights 3, 119
Brougham, Henry 164
Brown, John 56
Browne, Hablôt Knight ("Phiz") 150, 157, 162
Browning, Robert 120, 137
Budd, P. and D. 29
Buller, Francis 129
Burke, Edmund 7
Butler, Josephine 7
Byrnes, Thomas 24, 26, 28

Cain, Julien 155
Caldecott, Randolph 116

INDEX

Canada
    Mounted Police 70–1
    Vancouver Police Department 62
capitalism 48, 52, 111, 112, 113
Carey, James 92, 94
Carlyle, Thomas 2, 6, 7–8, 11, 16, 73, 112, 132, 134, 167
Carnegie, Andrew 112
censorship 46, 168
Certeau, M. de 24, 29
Chadwick, Edwin 12
Chamberlain, Joseph 12
Chancery 137, 139, 142, 143, 149, 156, 158, 161, 164
Chartism 5, 7, 8, 112, 132
child labor 74, 75–90
chimney sweeps 84–5
Churchill, Winston 1, 9
Church of England 15, 16
coalmines 75–83, 85, 87, 89
Cobbe, Frances Power 119
Cockburn, Henry Thomas 7
codification 13
Coke, Edward 93, 95, 105
Coleridge, Samuel Taylor 7
collectivism 13, 143
Collier, Michael 168
Collins, Wilkie 66
Colón, Susan 131
colonies
    indigenous peoples 112, 113, 122, 124–7
    policing 61, 64, 66–9, 70, 71
    property 112, 122–8
Colquhoun, Patrick 56
common law 13, 41, 108, 111, 112, 123
Communism 113
company law 36, 41, 42, 44–5, 49, 50, 51, 53
Conan Doyle, Sir Arthur 66
constitutional law 45, 49, 53
constitutional reform 9, 10, 36–7
    Utopia, Limited 35–53
Cooper, Anthony Ashley, 7th Earl of Shaftesbury 75
Cornwallis, Caroline 119
corruption 50, 51
Corry, Montagu 9
Cotton, William 44
Court of Chancery 137, 139, 142, 143, 149, 156, 158, 161, 164
coverture 118, 119
Craik, Jennifer 63
Crimean War 63

crime fiction 138
criminal justice
    fingerprints 21, 23
    mugshots (*see* mugshots)
    police (*see* police)
    surveillance techniques 23
    utilitarianism 56
criminology 22, 23
Cruikshank, George 169
cultural history xii–xiii
cultural superiority 122

Daguerre, Louis 19, 20
Dallas, E. S. 6
Daniell, William 81
Darwin, Charles 16
Daumier, Honoré 147, 149–50
    attitude to lawyers 157–8
    Baudelaire's appreciation of 150–2
    binary stereotypes 149
    experience of the law 155, 156–7
    "Grand escalier du Palais de Justice" 152, 153, 159
    Les Gens de Justice 152, 154, 155, 158–9, 160, 161, 162, 163
    possible influence on Dickens 159–62
    rhetorical power 152
Davenport-Hines, Richard 43
Delteil, Loÿs Henri 168
"democratic despotism" 46, 49
democratic excess 94
Denny, W. H. 38, 40
Derby, Edward Smith-Stanley, 14th Earl of 11
detectives 65–6
Dicey, Albert Venn 13, 14, 37, 49, 143
Dickens, Charles 6, 16, 56, 119, 138, 145
    attitude to lawyers 157–8
    Barnaby Rudge 8
    binary stereotypes 149–50, 151
    Bleak House 13, 65, 131, 136–7, 139–43, 149–50, 152, 155–8, 159–61
    caricatures 148, 151
    David Copperfield 125
    Dombey and Son 13
    early life 147–8
    Francophile 160
    Great Expectations 3, 125, 131
    Hard Times 131, 134, 135
    illustrations by Phiz 150, 157, 161
    knowledge of the law 155–6
    Little Dorrit 131
    love of new technology 163

Martin Chuzzlewit 151
  Nicholas Nickleby 2, 81
  Oliver Twist 2, 13, 131
  Our Mutual Friend 131
  Pickwick Papers 2, 149, 154, 156, 160
  possible influence of Daumier 159–62
  radical sympathies 132
  reforming legacy of art 143, 164
  Tale of Two Cities 8, 131, 149
Dickens, Henry Fielding 156, 157
Dillon, Steve 168
"disciplinary society" 56, 57
Disraeli, Benjamin, 1st Earl of Beaconsfield 7, 9, 10, 11, 15, 113, 132
divorce 7, 14
"docile bodies" 20, 23, 28, 56
Dodsworth, Frank 56, 58
Donahue, Charles 114
Donnelly, John Jr. xii
Dore, Gustave 132
Doyle, Peter 29, 166
D'Oyly Carte, Richard 35
Dublin Metropolitan Police 58
Duchatel, Count Charles Tanneguy 20
Dudley, John 93
Dunhill, Thomas F. 53
Durnheim, Carl 32
duty of care 129–30. *See also* neighborly duty
Dyson, William 82

education 5, 12
Edwards, S. 22, 24, 26
Elgar, Edward 1, 3
Eliot, George 6, 13, 135, 137, 138, 143
  Adam Bede 138
  agency and the ethical value of intention 138, 139
  Daniel Deronda 138
  ethical value of artistic work 144
  Felix Holt 131, 138, 139, 144
  Middlemarch 3, 138
  Mill on the Floss 115–16, 117, 134
Elizabeth II, Queen of England 15
enclosures 114
Engels, Friedrich 113
Enlightenment 122
equity 41, 137, 142
Erskine, Thomas 98, 101, 102, 104, 107
Euripides 83, 84
Evangelical revival 143
Ewing, P. 29, 32–3
Eyre, Edward 124–5

factories 77
female novelists 6, 7
feminine ideal 6–7
feminism 65, 118
Fenian uprising 25
Fielding, Henry 55
Fildes, Sir Samuel Luke 24, 25
fingerprints 21, 23
Finn, J. 24, 26
First World War 65
Fischler, Alan 36, 37, 46, 47, 48
Fisher, Alice 31
Flaubert, Gustave 6
Forster, John 12
Foucault, Michel 20, 23, 24, 56–8
franchise 10, 11, 12, 36–7, 45, 136
Frantz, Henri 151
French Revolution 7, 8, 75

Galsworthy, John 111, 112, 122
Gardiner, J. 9
Gaskell, Elizabeth 6, 132, 136, 137, 138
Geoffrey-Dechaume, Adolphe-Victor 148
George III, King of England 1
George IV, King of England 1
Gerard, James 64
Gerhart, Peter 135, 145
Gilbert, Thomas 56
Gilbert, W. S. 35–7, 42–3, 45–8, 53
Gladstone, William Ewart 1, 5, 7, 36
Glorious Revolution 9
Good Samaritan, parable of 130–4
Gordon riots 8
Great Exhibition (1851) 3–4
Grey, Charles, 2nd Earl 10
Gribble, Jennifer 131
Grotius, Hugo 86

Hale, John P. 97, 100–1, 104, 105, 109, 110
Hamilton, Alexander 93, 98
Hanoverian kings 1
Hardy, Thomas 119
Harper, Margaret 79
Harrington, M. P. 94, 98
Harvey, John 151, 159, 162
Hayek, Friedrich 41
Heffer, Simon 3
Henry, Peaches 168
Himmelfarb, Gertrude 2
Hipps, Margaret 81
Hobbes, Thomas 86
Hogarth, George 157

INDEX

Hohfeld, Wesley Newcomb 114
Home Rule 36, 37, 53
Hong, Grace Kyungwon 114
Horne, Richard Hengist 80, 81, 83, 87, 88, 167
Horner, Leonard 75
Horrell, Sara 76
House of Commons 37
House of Lords 37
Hume, David 74
Humphries, Jane 76
Hunt, John Dixon 161
Huxley, Thomas Henry 16

Ignatieff, Michael 58
impartiality 144, 145
imperial expansion. *See* British Empire; colonies
India 67, 68, 69
indigenous peoples 112, 113, 122, 124–7
individualism 112, 143
industrial capitalism 111, 113
Industrial Revolution 4–5, 58, 59
inequality 112
Ireland
    experiments in modern policing 58, 59, 64, 66–69
    famine and immigration 132
    Home Rule 36, 37, 53
    Republicans 25, 29

James, Henry 9, 136
Jay, John 96, 98, 99, 109
Jefferson, Thomas 91
Jeffries, Charles 6
Jenkins, Roy 1
John, King of England xi
Jowett, Benjamin 134
judicial directions 96
judicial review 92–5
juratores non respondent 96
jury lawfinding 91
    legal certainty and 98, 108
    prior to 1842 95–98
    shifts to judge-centric view of adjudication 91–2, 94, 95, 109–10 (*see also Pierce v State*)

Kent, James 98
Killingray, David 68
Kingsley, Charles 7
Kingsley, Henry 126–7

Kirby, Peter 78, 82, 85
Kramer, L. D. 93, 94

Lagerfeld, Karl 31
laissez-faire economics 112, 135
Lamb, William, 2nd Viscount Melbourne 5, 10
landscape art 122, 128
Lashmar, P. 21, 166
Lavery, Michael 28, 29
Law, Jules 116
law enforcement. *See* police
law reports 93
legal certainty 98, 108
legal positivism 41, 45, 46, 73, 74, 75, 83, 86, 89, 115
legal profession
    admission of women 147
    America 105
    caricatures 148, 151, 154, 156–7, 160–2, 164
    legal clerks 156
    reform 147, 164
    theatricality 154, 155
legal reform 13–14
legislation 12, 41, 73, 145
le Hay, John 38, 40
Leigh, Mike 36
Levitas, Ruth 45
Lewis, Sarah 6
Lilburne, John 101
Lindley, Matthew 80
Linton, Elizabeth Lynn 6
literacy 5
Lloyd, Frederic 167
Locke, Hew xi
Locke, John 74, 86, 115, 118, 122, 124
Lockwood, Frank 155, 156, 157
Lombroso, Cesare 22
London Metropolitan Police 61–2, 63, 64
Loughlin, Martin 45
Luddites 58

Macaire, Robert 162
Macaulay, Thomas Babington 3, 9, 10, 113
MacDonald, Sir John A. 70
Macfarlane, Alan 112
Machemer, Georgia 168
MacKay, Carol Hanbery 168
McKenzie, Gordon 148, 154
McMullan, John 57
McNeil, Margaret 78
Macpherson, C. B. 111, 113–14

MacSuibhne, B. 29
Madison, James 93
"magic lanterns" 163
Magna Carta xi, xii, 7, 9
Maine, Sir Henry Sumner 111, 124, 130
Maitland, F. W. 49
Malraux, André 122
Malthus, Thomas 137
Manesta, Evelyn 25, 26
Mansel, Dean 6
Mansfield, William Murray, 1st Earl of 93, 102, 103, 106
marriage 118, 120–1
Marsh, A. 29
Martin, A. 29
Marx, Karl 113
masculine ideal 58, 63, 65, 70
mass violence 58
Maurice, F. D. 134
Maurisset, Théodore 154
May, Erskine 10
Mayne, Richard 62
Meier, T. 24, 32
Melbourne, William Lamb, 2nd Viscount 5, 10
Meredith, George 119
Metropolitan Police 62, 63, 64, 65
militarism 67–9, 70, 71
military uniforms 63, 67, 68, 70, 71
Mill, John Stuart 2, 5, 7, 14, 75, 115, 120–1, 122, 134
  The Subjection of Women 119, 120, 121
Millais, John Everett 127
Miller, George James 133
Miller, J. Hillis 157
mining industry 75–83, 85, 87, 89
Mnookin, J. 166
modernity 113, 122, 150
Moffat, Agnes 78
Molière, Jean-Baptiste Poquelin 154
monarchy 15
  political capacity 36, 42
morality 73
moral law 137
moral panic 57
More, Sir Thomas 42, 43, 44, 45
Morgan, Lewis Henry 113, 114
Morris, Philip Richard 133
Morris, William 45
Morrow, John 167
mugshots 20
  aesthetic qualities 31–2
  dominant narratives of capture and containment 21–3
  earliest examples 165
  evidence of resistance 25–9, 166
  poses 165
  possibility of resistance 23–5
  rediscovery 30–2, 33
Murray, William, 1st Earl of Mansfield 93, 102, 103, 106

Napier, Sir Charles James 67
Napoleonic wars 63, 68, 71
Native Americans 113, 122
natural law 73, 74, 75, 83, 84, 86, 87
neighborly duty 129, 130
  Christian understanding 130–4, 137, 143
  Good Samaritan 130–4
  limitations of sympathy 142–6
  novels 131–2, 134–7, 146
  parodies of 139–42
  tort law 129, 135–40, 145
Newman, John Henry 6, 16
newspapers 5, 94, 95, 102–5
Nietzsche, Friedrich 143
Night Watch 55, 59–61
Norton, Caroline 119
novels 6
  crime genre 138
  neighborly duty 131–2, 134–7, 143, 145
Nussbaum, Martha 143

Oakeshott, Michael 41
O'Connor, Feargus 7
Oliphant, Margaret 131

Palmer, Stanley 66, 67
Palmerston, Henry John Temple, 3rd Viscount 4, 11
Pankhurst, Christabel 14
Parker, David 168
Patmore, Coventry 6
Peel, Sir Robert 5, 10, 59, 61, 64, 67, 68, 71
Peterloo Massacre 58
Phillips, S. 26
"Phiz" 150, 157, 161
photography 19–20. *See also* mugshots
Pierce v State 91–5, 110
  arguments at trial 99–102
  journalistic arguments between trial and appeal 102–5
  judgments on appeal 105–9
Pocock, J. 108
police
  America 64
  Bow Street Runners 55–6

Canada 62, 70–1
codes of behavior 64
colonial dimension 61, 64, 66–9, 70, 71
concerns about individual liberty 59, 61
consensual law enforcement 58, 63
crowds at a police funeral 57
detectives 65–6
"disciplinary society" 56, 57
female officers 65
helmets 64–5
Ireland 59, 61, 64, 66–9
London Metropolitan Police 62, 63, 64, 65
militarism 67–9, 70, 71
Night Watch 55, 59–61
photography (*see* mugshots)
physical masculinity 58, 63, 65, 70
reform 59–62
Sir Robert Peel 59, 61, 64, 67, 68, 71
surveillance 58, 71
uniforms 55, 58, 60, 62–6, 68, 70, 71
visibility 58, 59, 60, 64, 71
Pollock, Frederick 130
"polyphonic testimony" 20
Poor Law 12
positive law 41, 45, 46, 73, 74, 75, 83, 86, 89, 115
power dynamics 20, 23, 24, 28, 57
Price, Richard 74
prisons 165, 166
America 29, 31
Holloway 25, 29
private law 137
progress 122
property
claims of ownership 111–12
colonialism 112, 122–8
"commanding view" 122, 126
cultural studies of 113
definitions of 113–14
"dephysicalization" 114, 128
"index of identity" 118, 128
industrial capitalism 111, 112, 113
land 114
"possessive instinct" 111, 120, 122
rights, interests, and relations 114–17
riparian rights 116–17
squatters 125, 126
women's rights 112, 118–21
Protestantism 112
Prout, Skinner 128
Prud'hon, Pierre-Paul 158, 163
Psomiades, Kathy Alexis 120
public law 45

racial attitudes 69, 70
Radicalism 8, 12, 58, 113, 131
Rahe, Paul 45
railway 4–5
Rawls, John 145
"reading revolution" 5–6
realism 138
reform 2, 3, 9–14, 37, 143
Age of Reform 91, 147, 159
child labor 64, 75–90
constitutional reform 9, 10, 36–7
judge-jury relations 91–2, 94, 95, 109–10
(*see also Pierce v State*)
law enforcement 58, 59–62
legal profession 147, 163
women's rights 119
Reform Acts 9, 10, 11
Reform League 9
Reid, Helen 78
Reitz, Caroline 68
religion 15–16, 112
Evangelical revival 143
neighbourly duty 130–4, 137, 143
revolution 2, 3, 75
Chartism 5, 7, 8, 112, 132
constitutional 9
industrial 4–5, 58, 59
reading 5–6
sexual 6
Reynolds, George 162
Ricoeur, Paul 145
Riis, Jacob 32
riparian rights 116–17
Rizzo, L. 166
Roche, Daniel 62
Roman law 130
Romantic poets 83
Rose, Carol M. 111, 115, 118, 119, 124, 125
Rowan, Charles 62
Royal Irish Constabulary 61, 64, 67, 68
rule of law 94, 107
Ruskin, John 6–7, 12, 73, 112, 151, 167
Russell, John, 1st Earl 9, 11
Ryfe, D. M. 94

satire 42, 43–4, 53, 139–42, 145, 152, 161, 164, 167
binary stereotypes 149–50
Saunders, Robert John 75
Savoy Operas 35, 36
Schweber, H. 95, 105
scientific progress 122
Sekula, A. 20, 24

self-interest 135
sensationalism 6
sexual revolution 6
Seymour, Robert 154
Shaftesbury, Anthony Ashley Cooper, 7th Earl of 12, 75
Shanley, Mary Lyndon 121
Shaw, George Bernard 36, 45
Shelley, Mary 143
Shelley, Percy Bysshe 83
Shpayer-Makov, Haia 58, 63, 65
Sidney, Algernon 74
Silbey, S. 29, 32–3
Simpkin, John 80
Simpson, Brian 117
Sinclair, Georgina 66
Smiles, Samuel 113
Smith, Adam 134
Smith, Thomas Southwood 75
Smith, W. H. 13
social contract 73, 74, 75, 86, 87
Socialism 11, 13, 45, 53, 113
socio-legal studies 32
sociology 113
Spencer, Herbert 13
Spurr, David 122, 123, 126
squatters 125, 126
Statute of Westminster 96, 105
Stedman, Jane 47
Stephen, James Fitzjames 13
Stephens, Leslie 144
Stephenson, George 5
Story, Joseph 98, 101, 102, 109, 110
Styles, John 66
suffrage 10, 11, 12, 36–7, 45, 136
suffragettes 14, 23, 25, 29, 33, 69
Sullivan, Sir Arthur 35
Sutton, Max 53
Swinburne, Sir John 68
sympathy 143–6

Tagg, J. 23, 24, 25, 166
Talbot, Fox 19
Taylor, Harriet 120–1
"technologies of power" 20
technology 4–5, 163
Temple, Henry John, 3rd Viscount Palmerston 4, 11
Tennyson, Alfred, Lord Tennyson 5, 117, 128, 137
testamentary freedom 114–15
Thackeray, William Makepeace 13, 138, 161

Thompson, Elise 79
Thornbury, Walter 56
Tocqueville, Alexis de 45, 95
Tönnies, Ferdinand 41
Tooke, Thomas 75
tort law 129, 135, 136–7, 138–9, 140, 145
Tractarianism 131
trades unions 13
Trevelyan, G. M. 9
trial juries. *See* jury lawfinding
Trimolet, Louis 154
Trollope, Anthony 13, 16, 125, 126, 127, 138, 164
Tuttle, Carolyn 76
Twain, Mark 125
Twining, William 131, 146
Tyrell, James 74

uniforms 55, 58, 60, 62–6, 67, 68, 70, 71
utilitarianism 56, 73, 74–5, 82–3, 89, 115, 134, 143, 167
Utopia, Limited 35–53

Vandevelde, Kennet J. 114
Van Gogh, Vincent 147, 148, 168
Victoria, Queen of England 7, 9, 14
　funeral 1, 2
　mourning 14–15
　political capacity 36
Victorian epoch 1–3
Vincent, Howard 149, 150, 152
Voltaire, François-Marie Arouet 163

Walden, Keith 70
Warhol, Andy 166–7
Watts, P. 30
Webb, Beatrice and Sidney 45
Weber, Max 41
Weisberg, Richard 74
Welch, M. 166
Wellington, Arthur Wellesley, 1st Duke of 2, 10
"Whiggish" accounts 1, 3, 7, 9, 10
Wilde, Oscar 5, 113, 143
Wilding, Emily 14
Wilf, S. 95, 110
William IV, King of England 1, 10
Williams, Caleb 31
Williams, Raymond 3
wills 114–15
Wilmot, E. E. 59
Windeyer, Richard 124

INDEX

Winter, James 63
Wittgenstein, Ludwig 121
Wolfensberger, R. 24, 32
Woloch, Alex 144
womanly ideal 6–7
women police officers 65
women's rights 14
    admission to the legal profession 147
    property 112, 118–21

women workers 78–82
women writers 6, 7
Wood, Ellen 6, 7
Wood, John 154
Wordsworth, William 5
working hours 77

Yonge, Charlotte 131